Robert Frost's
Poetry of Rural Life

ALSO BY GEORGE MONTEIRO

*Elizabeth Bishop in Brazil and After:
A Poetic Career Transformed* (McFarland, 2012)

Robert Frost's Poetry of Rural Life

George Monteiro

McFarland & Company, Inc., Publishers
Jefferson, North Carolina

LIBRARY OF CONGRESS CATALOGUING-IN-PUBLICATION DATA

Monteiro, George.
 Robert Frost's poetry of rural life / George Monteiro.
   p.   cm.
 Includes bibliographical references and index.

 ISBN 978-0-7864-9789-8 (softcover : acid free paper) ∞
 ISBN 978-1-4766-1945-3 (ebook)

 1. Frost, Robert, 1874–1963—Criticism and interpretation.
 2. Country life in literature.   3. Farm life in literature.
 I. Title.

 PS3511.R94Z794 2015
 811'.52—dc23   2015001225

BRITISH LIBRARY CATALOGUING DATA ARE AVAILABLE

© 2015 George Monteiro. All rights reserved

No part of this book may be reproduced or transmitted in any form or by any means, electronic or mechanical, including photocopying or recording, or by any information storage and retrieval system, without permission in writing from the publisher.

Cover image iStock/Thinkstock

Printed in the United States of America

McFarland & Company, Inc., Publishers
  Box 611, Jefferson, North Carolina 28640
    www.mcfarlandpub.com

For Brenda

Acknowledgments

The editors of the journals and presses mentioned below have kindly consented to my use of previously published material in this book: *American Quarterly, Arthur Miller Journal, College Literature, Iowa Review, New England Quarterly, Robert Frost Review, South Carolina Review,* the University Press of Mississippi, and Winthrop University Studies.

Table of Contents

Acknowledgments vi
Introduction 1

1. The Poetry of Agriculture 5
2. All Legends Are Local 34
3. The Poet's Facts 41
4. His Metaphysical Sonnet 49
5. An Occupation Gone 55
6. Adam's Curse 62
7. The Passing Glimpse 67
8. Solitary Griefs 76
9. An Art of the Possible 83
10. His Best Bid for Fame 99
11. Crowe Ransom 117
12. Axe and Helve 122
13. A Single Peel 127
14. Poem / Play 132
15. Nothing Gold Can Stay 141

Chapter Notes 153
Bibliography 169
Index 178

Introduction

He views objects from the greatest height, and his reflections acquire a sublimity in proportion to their profundity, as in deep wells of water we see the sparkling of the highest fixed stars. The chain of thought reaches to the centre, and ascends the brightest heaven of invention. Reason in him works like an instinct: and his slightest suggestions carry the force of conviction. His opinions are judicial. His induction of particulars is alike wonderful for learning and vivacity, for curiosity and dignity, and an all-pervading intellect binds the whole together in a graceful and pleasing form. His style is equally sharp and sweet, flowing and pithy, condensed and expansive, expressing volumes in a sentence, or amplifying a single thought into pages of rich, glowing, and delightful eloquence.[1]

There are readers who would accept these sentences as a fairly accurate description of Robert Frost's poetic virtues and strengths. Actually, however, they were written in the nineteenth century by William Hazlitt in praise of the Elizabethan Sir Francis Bacon. It is hardly doubtful that that Frost would have objected to the company. Bacon was someone one could rely upon, even if he did not write poems. After all, it was Francis Bacon who, in *The Advancement of Learning* (1605), defined the ideal of contemplative inquiry by referring to the work of a poet: "surely if the purpose be in good earnest not to write at leisure that which men may read at leisure, but really to instruct and suborn action and active life, these Georgics of the mind, concerning the husbandry and tillage thereof, are no less worthy than the heroical descriptions of Virtue, Duty, and Felicity" (Book II, xx, 3). "Georgics of the mind of the poet" would be a good way of describing what the New England poet-farmer had in mind for himself as poet-thinker.

It was during his few short months as a student at Dartmouth College in the early 1890s, recalled a friend, "that something in the *Georgics* of Vergil showed him the way, confirmed him in his poetic purpose. Whatever it was, he saw clearly what poetry meant—not what one thinks, but the way one feels about what one thinks."[2] The same friend also is the source for Frost's observation about his own "puttering" around his farm in Vermont. "I go over into the Green Mountains on my farm and putter around every late spring and early summer," Frost is quoted as saying. "Puttering on my farm's my refuge. Wise old Vergil says in one of his Georgics, 'Praise large farms, stick to small ones.' Twenty acres are just about enough."[3] And when Frost looked back on his work, it has been noted, this bemused "throwback to Chaucer and Virgil" asked himself a question that revealed much about how he himself saw his achievement: "'Doesnt [sic] the wonder grow that I have never written anything or as you say never published anything except about New England farms?'"[4]

Ezra Pound, who had so much to do with the discovery and promotion of Frost's first books of poetry, reviewing them in early issues of *Poetry*, Harriet Munroe's new journal in 1913 and 1914, entitled his review of *North of Boston* the "Modern Georgics."[5] Grateful at the time though he may have been at the time, later in life Frost tended to brush aside the significance of Pound's early push on his behalf. In the course of setting the record straight, he told Mertins that "these two reviews made up the sum total of the making of me by him.... They mainly consisted of Ezra's opinions about poetry, not much about the books under review. He called, if I remember, my *North of Boston* things 'Modern Georgics.' They weren't 'Georgics.' They *were* modern, though; so he was half-right."[6] "Georgics," or not, Pound did say, "he is quite consciously and definitely putting New England rural life into verse.... I know more of farm life than I did before I had read his poems. That means I know more of 'Life.'"[7]

But Pound's linking of Frost's poetry in *North of Boston* with Vergil's "Georgics" has been only sporadically pursued in Frost scholarship. The reason for this relative neglect, it has been argued, is that "the severity of much of Frost's poetry confounds the expectations raised by pastoral, and the assumption that Frost belongs to this tradition predisposes the reader to overlook the importance of georgic themes—centering on work and the earth—in Frost's vision." Continuing on in this vein, the writer suggests that "Frost's vision of nature is not so much bleak as unflinching; and this attitude is consistent with the georgic perspective, in which nature is not an idealized stage-set but the context of a struggle for subsistence, a struggle at least to stand still 'in the rush of everything to waste.'"[8]

To Vergil as an influential Roman source can be added Catullus, a poet Frost was fond of bringing into his talk-readings when he recited the poem "Take Something Like a Star," first published in 1943.[9] "Choose something like a star / To stay our minds on and be staid." That something need not be a star; it could just as well be a poem, Frost's lines suggest, and such a poem could be a poem by Catullus or, as I imagine he thought himself, it could be a poem by Frost himself. Neither arbitrary nor casual, those moments of exchange constitute what Ezra Pound, addressing Walt Whitman, called for: "commerce between us." Only Frost expanded and democratized the desire for commerce with all his readers, including the poets, and he did this, largely, by writing poetry that is, above all, accessible to the common and uncommon reader alike.

This sense of a communal poetic spirit and its potential for practical use is the rock on which Frost built his edifice of words, placing a high value on the give-and-take exchange of words, opinions, advice. He made certain, first of all, that his poems—consider them to be his delayed response to things said, sometimes centuries ago, he suggested—were, without condescension, accessible to all those who would listen or read. How else—if they were not accessible—could his poems make a place for themselves in their memory, a place where lines and images would resonate? Thus he had no use for what he called the "secrets" of the modernist poems fashionable in his time. If he insisted that his poems were written for glory, first, and, secondarily, for use, his life shows that "glory" and "use" are two roads not "just as fair" but for all intents and purposes the same, perhaps inevitable, road. He relished in the fact that the practical was not inimical to the aesthetic or, to put it another way, that "use" should follow from form. The "pleasantest use" of one of his poems, he said, was "seeing a fragment of it quoted in an editorial, we'll say, in a New York paper. That's a very great triumph. Somebody I don't know quoted me—part of me, a line or two. That's being put to use."[10] He was barely joking when he said that he would not have minded being a U.S. senator. How he must have envied the Irish poet William Butler Yeats his public license to speak out as a member of the Irish Senate.

The fifteen chapters of *Robert Frost's Poetry of Rural Life* consider Frost's work in the context of vernacular New England poetry published in modestly popular agricultural and homestead journals, his use of sources ranging from poems by Derry, New Hampshire's Lucinda T. Carleton, his friend Ridgely Torrence and the fin de siècle poet Lionel Johnson, to the Book of Genesis, along with an examination of Frost's peculiar mistakes regarding certain facts of "nature" and his examination of the ancient argument from design. Chapters looking at Frost's poet-farmer's set of political interests and national concerns and at the many and the varied uses to which Frost's poem "Stopping by Woods on a Snowy Evening" has been put since its initial publication over nine decades ago are followed by chapters that consider the influence of Frost's "georgic" poems on specific works by the poets John Crowe Ransom, Robert Francis, and Richard Wilbur, and the playwright Arthur Miller. The last chapter speculates on how Baseball (writ large) decided the Pete Rose gambling case and how Frost, given his clear-cut views on how to play his beloved game, might have settled it far differently.

1

The Poetry of Agriculture

The phrase "The Homestead Idea Man" stands alone in Robert Frost's *Notebooks*.[1] It does not appear to be related to anything that comes before it or after it. What the poet intended by the words he set down remains mysterious even to the editor of his notebooks, one surmises, for the entry is not annotated. While no sure solution to this riddle occurs to me, it is nevertheless possible to entertain the notion that this mention of "Homestead" refers to the *New-England Homestead*, a widely-circulated trade journal in Frost's time, one that flourished during his farming years in Derry, New Hampshire, and long afterwards.

"There doesn't seem to be much chance for you as a writer if you are going to engage in farm work." Such was Wallace Stevens' best advice to a young novelist who had just outlined his plan to take up farming as a way to support his literary career. That the insurance-executive poet felt comfortable enough in his own skin to offer such avuncular wisdom, more than thirty years after Robert Frost's literary reputation had established him as, among other things, a farmer-poet, urges one to ask a related question. Just what did Stevens think of Frost's poetry? Was his advice to the young writer a case of deciding that what had worked for Frost could not be expected to work for him? In any case, the grand example of the always didactic *Georgics* notwithstanding, the notion that it is possible to take seriously something called the "Poetry of Agriculture" would have held, to say the least, little or no appeal for Stevens.[2]

"Poetry of Agriculture"—the phrase as well as the notion—derives from the pages of the *Homestead*, circulated weekly among the region's suburban and rural populations.[3] As employed in that journal, the phrase refers not specifically to poetry about the specifics of agriculture, used metaphorically or not, but the pursuit and practice of agriculture itself as a kind of poetry. Without recourse to the expressed notion as such, Robert

Frost nevertheless wrote a myriad of poems that explored and fulfilled the very idea that there might be such a thing—a "poetry of agriculture."[4] No American poet cultivated the materials for such poetry as assiduously or more fruitfully than Frost, but, as the poetry and essays in the *Homestead* demonstrate he was not the only one taking up such themes or, in many cases, the first to do so. It needs to be said, however, that there is no *Homestead* poet adduced in this chapter whose productions approach those of Frost in merit by any standard. There are no inglorious geniuses whose work has been lost to time past or gem-like poems that in themselves call for resuscitation or rehabilitation. In short, there is no challenge to Frost's preeminence here. There are only markers and materials in a landscape shared and somewhat surprisingly reflected in some of the greatest American poems of the twentieth century.

"It is not a fact that farmers are more ignorant than town people. They have more occasion to use their mother wit." So wrote a physician-contributor to the *Homestead* in 1896.[5] Frost's poetry (see "The Ax-Helve," for example, or, even, "Mending Wall") shows by his example that he could not have been more in agreement. Moreover, in his late and last volume of poetry, *In the Clearing* (1962), as good as applying the notion to himself, he famously cautions his readers—rural, urban and otherwise—"It takes all sorts of in and outdoor schooling / To get adapted to my kind of fooling" (478).[6] The statement could have served to answer the *Homestead* poet who shortly after Frost set out to learn farming in Derry, published "Unwritten Poetry," groused about poets who write down things that are only too well-known to "other folks" but who have never themselves learned the ways of farming.

> If I could give my thoughts a tongue
> I'd tell some marvelous things
> 'Bout beauty in the abstract
> And virtue without wings.
> But no! some nice, soft-handed chap
> That can write things down, you know,
> That other folks have thought and said
> Though he's never learned to hoe,—
> Will write all down in jinglin' shape,
> Poem style and beautiful prose,
> The things I've thought of time and again,
> And that everybody knows.[7]

The characterization of the would-be farmer-poet as a "nice, soft-handed chap that can write things down, you know, that other folks have thought and said though he's never learned to hoe," would have made Frost wince, realizing, of course, that there were those who would so characterize him and perforce dismiss his poetry. Only toward the end of his life, perhaps, was Frost fully comfortable with the risk he had taken long before, becoming a farmer-poet to claim a farmer's credentials: "I've written a lot of farm poetry—country poetry,—mainly because I lived in the country, knew and loved the country and farm life," he explained. "I know all about rakes and hoes."[8]

So naturally had Frost taken on the farmer's mantle, it seems, almost as if it were a birthright, that it still surprises an occasional reader to learn that Robert Lee Frost was "an elective New Englander," an "outsider" who was born in San Francisco and spent ten years in San Francisco before first laying eyes on a New England scene; and even then the New England he encountered was neither pastoral nor rural but the mill-city environment of Lawrence, Massachusetts.[9] It is somewhat ironic, then, that New England's archetypal poet had to make himself into a rural New Englander before he could write the poetry that made him famous. If John C. Kemp argued this point thirty or so years ago, it is Dana Gioia who isolates it as the inexplicable counter-intuitive truth about Frost's life.[10] That "the first woodlands he [Frost] visited were not the birch forests he would eventually immortalize in verse but the Pacific live oaks, madrones, and giant redwoods of the Napa Valley," was the "central paradox that deeply shaped the mature poet's imaginative identity."[11]

Leaving behind the mill-city of Lawrence shortly after graduating from high school and embarking on marriage, Frost began his years of movement northward. Following his doctor's orders "to find work out of doors, preferably on a farm," in the spring of 1899, Frost rented half a house in Methuen, Massachusetts, close to the New Hampshire border, and set about raising chickens.[12] In the fall of 1900, with the financial aid of his grandfather, Frost moved on, to a farm in Derry, New Hampshire, living there a dozen years until, in November 1911, he sold out and moved north to take a teacher's job in Plymouth, New Hampshire. Two years later he moved his family to England. But it was his long sojourn in Derry—"the farm was an idyllic retreat"—that had the most determinant effect on his poetry, he insisted: "Its small and relatively new house was conveniently connected to shed and barn. Orchards, gardens, and hayfields surrounded the modest set of buildings, with a woodlot and two good pastures nearby. The former owner had worked for years in a fruit nursery…. Its apple trees included in their varieties Gravensteins, Northern Spies, and Baldwins. There were smaller groves of peach, pear, and quince."[13] Yet Frost had been ambivalent about leaving the Derry farm for good. He had not made a great success at farming; yet the experience had enriched his life emotionally and spiritually. Something of what he thought the Derry experience would mean to him in the future is revealed in a poem he did not publish in his lifetime. He called it "On the Sale of My Farm." Although he confesses that he has been a failure at farming and is happy enough to pass his farm on to a "stranger," he leaves with a well-meant warning that someday he may return. He will do so with the understanding that his return "shall be no trespassing" if he were to "come again some spring / In the grey disguise of years, / Seeking ache of memory here" (519).[14]

Frost's stay in Plymouth had been short, not more than a year, and his decision to uproot his family still again, may have been prompted by the consideration that his removal to England might prove to be permanent. But it was not to be, and the Frost family's stay in England lasted just over two years. What he did accomplish, of course, was getting two books of poetry published, events that started him squarely on the road to acceptance as an established poet. The books he had placed—*A Boy's Will* (1913) and *North of Boston* (1914)—appeared before Frost and his family sailed from Liverpool in February 1915. With increasing concern over the war that had broken out in August 1914, the Frost family had left England, returning home to settle on another farm in New Hampshire.

Arguably, Frost never became a successful or self-fulfilled New England farmer. "It is not fair to farmers to make me out a very good or laborious farmer," he admitted. "I have known hard times, but no special shovel-slavery."[15] Yet he had tried. As a highly literate being who took seriously the idea that farming could provide him with a living, Frost—it is safe to assume—had some acquaintance with specialized journals devoted to the various aspects of rural life. In fact, during his years in Derry Frost published his "farm-poultry" sketches in the specialized trade journals, *Farm-Poultry* and *The Eastern Poultryman*. It cannot be documented beyond the shadow of a doubt, but it does seem plausible that besides the poultry journals he also read other publications aimed at an audience of farmers and other non-city folk. One such journal was the long-lasting, commercially successful *New-England Homestead*.[16]

Started in April 1867, in Northampton, Massachusetts, but relocated to Springfield the next year, the *Homestead* pretty much fulfilled the functions of the typical trade newspaper, as those functions were viewed in Frost's time.

> The trade newspaper ... should emphasize ideas, feelings, and interests that are not immediately connected to the style of life and work that a particu-

lar species of reader has as a profession. Together with the sections that contain specialized information and commentary relative to professional interests, newspapers should include items that transmit a general notion of activities and concerns from other spheres of society, from which nobody could remain absolutely isolated without the deterioration of his culture and professional effectuality.[17]

At the turn of the twentieth century, selling at five cents a copy—a dollar for a year's subscription—the *Homestead* had nearly 38,000 subscribers throughout the New England states.[18] Less narrowly specialized than the poultry journals to which Frost contributed, it was aimed at the typical farm-family. Its pages, at times headed as "Poetry of Agriculture," are filled with essays and poems on the subjects and themes that Frost would later make his own.[19] That the farmer's existence, full of difficulties and hard work, is nevertheless the stuff of poetry is the message delivered in the poem "Pleasures on the Farm" (1894).[20]

> Oh! Too numerous to mention when we stop to count them all
> Are the pleasures in the country on the farm, from fall to fall.
> To be sure, a minor sadness sometimes stirs this life of ours;
> For we know, for we have seen it, that there's sunshine after showers.
> And whate'er our occupation, in the shop, or on the farm,
> We can find the "silver lining"; and so, now, what's the harm
> In this our little life here, to catch these brighter gleams
> And hold them ere they vanish like sweet forgotten dreams?

The preservation of some of those "dreams" is a lesson reiterated by a different *Homestead* poet whose poem concludes with these lines.

> Fairest of flowers, that rare fringed gentian,—
> A bit of heaven's blue among the green!
> It is so frail, it dies so quickly,
> I will not gather it, but let it stay,—
> To bear, perchance, a heavenly message
> Of peace and love, to those who pass that way.[21]

It is the *Homestead* poet's expression of forbearance that might strike a familiar note, for it anticipates the generous gesture attributed to the farmer in "The Tuft of Flowers" (1906) when he spares the flowers standing beside a brook (but with no ulterior motive, as Frost has it): "The mower in the dew had loved them thus [the tuft of flowers], / By leaving them to flourish, not for us, / Nor yet to draw one thought of ours to him, / But from sheer morning gladness at the brim" (31).

By way of suggesting the richness of that material, I shall point to representative examples of those poems and essays that caught my attention when I looked into the *Homestead* for those years, mainly, during which Frost farmed in Derry, New Hampshire. And while most of the "farm" poetry in the *Homestead* blandished the positive moments and frugal rewards of life on the farm, those very examples, in the aggregate, will give us a sense of the range of concerns and attitudes prevailing in the poetry, mainly, but also the prose, offered to rural New England households. It might even be argued that Frost, whose poetry was more thoughtfully realistic and far less sentimental than that of the poets whose verse appeared in the *Homestead*, built lines and stanzas of his own poems on hints encountered in the verse that was featured in virtually every issue of that popular publication. One such hint, for example, that he may have taken was the poetic use of the word "hiss" in conjunction with the ocean. In "December," published in the *Homestead* in 1906, the poet writes, "Snowflakes in the soughing pine, / Hissing in old ocean's brine."[22] In "I Will Sing You One-O" (1923), Frost writes, "The snow fell deep / With the hiss of spray" (201). Of course, for most of the examples presented below, as for this one, there is no attempt to establish lines of direct influence. It is possible, however, that such materials (along with much else) would undergo a "controlled seething" before emerging as part of other works.[23] To claim more than that in cases of resemblance is to ignore Frost's cautionary note to himself: "the logic must be flowed not pieced out."[24]

Most of the "belletristic" writing published in the *Homestead* was up-beat—well-meaning, sentimental, and optimistic in its outlook. There was much poetry about mothers, children, the seasons, flowers and birds, God and Providence. There were poems about farm work, farmers and, occasionally, their wives. It could also be remarkably direct and succinct, as in these untitled and unsigned lines in the ready-made form of the syllogism: "Grass makes stock. / Stock makes manure. / Manure makes stock."[25] There were lists, too, of advice and wisdom, admonitions in aphoristic form. Some of these could serve as texts (contrary or corroborative) to familiar Frost poems. The *Homestead*'s bromide, "Every day's work should show a profit," for instance, is countered by Frost in "Mowing"—"The fact is the sweetest dream that labor knows"; while the magazine's "The surest way to throttle correct thinking is to echo other people's thoughts" is exemplified by the speaker's neighbor, in Frost's "Mending Wall," who "will not go behind his father's saying" and repeats and reiterates. "Good fences make good neighbors."[26]

A different message is derived from "the fence" in the *Homestead*'s "Keep Up Your Fences."

> Don' let no hole git ir your mortal fence,
> But keep it jest above temptation's nose,

> For if one little peccadillo goes
> Ter t'other side, a score will follow hence.²⁷

But "Cost and Waste of Fences," a *Homestead* article published in 1900, states categorically: "Fences are dead capital; they pay no interest and are a constant drain of the pocket. As Mr. Greely said, 'We poison our land with fences. They are a shelter for weeds as well as a vast and useless expense.'"²⁸ Later in the same year, in "Discard Useless Farm Fences," someone else decided once and for all that "the stone wall was, is and always will be a nuisance and an abomination."²⁹ Yet, not so fast, as Frost might have said, for there are those who do believe that "good fences make good neighbors"—to go back to the proverbial expression that fits right in with the litany published in the *Homestead* in 1906: "Good farmers make good farms; / Good farms make good crops; / Good crops make good stock; / Good stock make good prices; / Good prices make good farmers; / Dispute it ye who dare."³⁰

Frost's motives were never materialistic but heuristic and aesthetic. "Set Toil to a Tune" (1901), the title of a *Homestead* poem, could have served Frost as a mantra.

> Set your toil to a tune, yea, a happy tune,
> And sing as you hoe, my laddie;
> Set your toil to a tune as sweet as the June,
> And sing as you sew, my lassie.
> For toil is pleasure
> When set to measure
> Of mystical rhythms and rune,
> And commonplace toil
> On fabric or soil
> Can be set to a thousand tunes.³¹

"I have never said to myself: go to, I will write farm poetry," Frost insisted, but in "Mowing" and myriad other farm and country poems he does seem to have taken it upon himself to set farm work to as many tunes as he could compose.³²

The farmer's work also had the advantage of bringing him closer to nature and her redemptive power. That such work restores personal—psychological and spiritual—equanimity is the message of the *Homestead* poem "Pokin' 'Round."

> Pokin' 'round in ferns and mosses,
> Like a hop-toad or a snail,
> Kinder seems ter lighten crosses
> Where my heart would elsewise fail.³³

Or take the bird-lore expressed so confidently in the *Homestead*: "In the realm of birds, the lark is the optimist, the crow is the pessimist. Why be a crow?"[34] Frost's oblique answer to such generalizations can be seen in "Dust of Snow," in which the poet recognizes that it is the way a crow has dusted snow on him that has changed his mood: "And saved some part / Of a day I had rued" (205). Among other things, Frost's poem can be seen as neatly illustrative of the bit of sentiment and wisdom that appeared in the pages of the *Homestead*: "Worse than wasted is the day on which the only thoughts we think are those we don't want to think."[35]

One would be hard put to claim that it was such "farm poetry" that Paul Rosenfeld, speaking for many in 1921, had in mind when, acknowledging "the earthiness, the salt and homeliness of Robert Frost's poetry," he insisted that he would have to look elsewhere for that "something of majesty and power that the New Hampshire singer has not."[36] Others thought otherwise, arguing Frost's case, as did Allen W. Porterfield. In "only thirty-four words," he wrote, "Dust of Snow" tells "how a crow shook the dust of snow from a tree on a passerby, and thus made him see that the whitest can come from the blackest.... The moral drive of Mr. Frost's poem is tremendous." Moreover—and here he takes on the criticism implied in Rosenfeld's nominative phrase, "the New Hampshire singer"— Frost does so in "a farm poem":

> Crows do not fly into cities and perch on the flagpoles of skyscrapers nor do they light on the ugly overhead wires of Main Street. Nor are they noted as habitués of the wild, à la Jack London, fly over it though they may in migration. They hang around and hover over the farm where the sustenance for which they have developed an appetite may be had for the swooping down.

Such poems, he insists, "can be written without intimate knowledge of farm ways" or individual farmers, who are "generally caricatured." What he is interested in, rather, is the whole of the farm and "all that goes with it." "And for the right treatment of a theme of such grand and varied proportions, the lyric and the drama are inadequate; only the epic will suffice."[37]

"My Good Samaritan" can be hardly said to display the epic quality that Porterfield calls for, but the poem, which appeared in the *Homestead* in 1901, can be singled out for its suggestive anticipation of Frost's use of the common expression "rue the day" in "Dust of Snow" with its social message.

> Some time in future years,
> When the cruel hand of time

1. The Poetry of Agriculture

> And the winter's angry blast
>   Have laid
>   The bird-nest
>   Low;
> When my weary feet have wandered,
> And these various chatty notes
> Are "vexations" of the past,
>   They bored you so;
> When the rugged wild declivity
> We have never trod in vain
> Shall blossom as the rose,
> And God has healed my pain,—
> He will never let you rue the day
> When you lifted up a blighted
>   Woman
>   On her
>   Way.[38]

If it is unlikely that Frost would have taken to much of the belletristic writing featured in the *Homestead*, he nevertheless may have seen possibilities for poems expressive of the farmer's point of view—his attitude toward work, his crops, and nature herself. There were possibilities for poetry in agriculture, even if Frost's ventures in that regard turned out to be quite different, if not radically so in origin, from those attempted in the pages of the *Homestead*. It is possible, even, that he would have found truth in the position expressed in an essay titled "The Farmer as a Thinker": "The farmer is the man whose environment is conducive to thought. He is near to nature's heart, and nature makes the man of mind to think. For it is by communion with nature that God has prepared great leaders for their work. Separated from their fellow men, they heard the voice of nature and the voice of God, and they have gone forth to be the leaders of the race."[39]

Leaders of the race, perhaps, but not, it seems, poets—at least not many poets. For, while the *Homestead* celebrated James Whitcomb Riley as "a poet of the farm,"[40] it also published "Unwritten Poetry," lines set against what it considered generally to be pretentious poetry, lines that bear repeating:

> If I could give my thoughts a tongue
> I'd tell some marvelous things
> 'Bout beauty in the abstract
> And virtue without wings.
> But no! some nice, soft-handed chap
> That can write things down, you know,
> That other folks have thought and said
> Though he's never learned to hoe,—

> Will write all down in jinglin' shape,
> Poem style and beautiful prose,
> The things I've thought of time and again,
> And that everybody knows.
> But little deeds of kindness,
> And the best longings of the soul,
> Will count for more, sometime,
> Then the longest poet's roll.[41]

Surely not a member by his own lights of the "nice, soft-handed" tribe of poets, Frost the farmer had certainly "learned to hoe." Settled in to farm at Derry, he was also ready to write up a storm. Yet even in the *Homestead* there were poems cautioning against the blind and thus inhumane pursuit of what one poet targeted as "An Immortal Song."

> A poet labored patiently and long
> On (as he trusted) an immortal song.
> His little girl disturbed him with her play,
> And angrily he sent the child away.
> The poem was completed and forgot,—
> E'en by the poet's friends remembered not.
> But the harsh words the tender-hearted maid
> Bore in her breast till she in dust was laid![42]

Still the risks that attended an earnest dedication to the writing of poetry were risks that Frost was willing to take, for he took to heart as his true occupation the need to set his work to poetry.

"I have never said to myself: go to, I will write farm poetry," Frost insisted.[43] But in "Mowing" and elsewhere it does look as if he took it upon himself to set the farmer's various tasks (and experiences) to tune as well as he could. This determination resulted in an impressive array of forthright farm and country poems in the Frost canon. Most of those poems, if not all of them, can be placed in categories such as "The Pasture," "Spring," "Birches," "Old Age," "The Hired Man," "Tramps," "The Housewife," "Birdsong," "The Single Flower," "Snow Tracks," "Instinct," "The Apple Harvest," "Leaves," "Butterflies," "The Homestead," and "The Road." Poems in these categories, as is the case with poems previously discussed or at least mentioned, share subjects and themes with individual poems published in the *Homestead*. The caveat in the discussion is that there is no need to argue in any particular case that a specific poem or bit of prose in the *Homestead* is a direct source for any single example of Frost's own "poetry of agriculture." After all, it should be noted that during his time in Derry the poet-farmer had much direct experience to draw upon for his verse. But the existence of farm poems such as those featured in virtually every issue of the *Homestead*, of which those adduced below are exemplary, tend to support the overall idea that there exists something that might be called a "poetry of agriculture," a notion that should have been as appealing to Frost as it was to those many now long forgotten, well-meaning, and earnest versifiers who for generations graced the pages of the *Homestead* with their homely goods and wares.

First published in *North of Boston*, "The Pasture" was Frost's choice as a signature poem for later selective and collective volumes. It begins: "I'm going out to clean the pasture spring; / I'll only stop to rake the leaves away / (And wait to watch the water clear, I may)" (3). He won't be gone long, he promises, before issuing an invitation: "You come too." All he is going to do is "fetch the little calf" that totters when its mother "licks it with her tongue."

A dozen years before Frost published "The Pasture," the *Homestead* published "April Rain," an elegiac account of a lover's invitation to walk out in the rain. Note that the lovers talk of "poetic" subjects, while Frost's speaker turns to more practical farm matters, a young calf and its mother.

> I heard my lover calling,
> Ere yet the day could be.
> "Arise! Arise!" He softly said,
> "And come and walk with me."
> He sang without my window
> An exquisite refrain.
> I rose and went with gladness
> To meet the April rain.
> All in the early twilight,
> Ere yet the day could be,
> We talked of love and beauty,
> And joy and poetry.
> His steps were set to music
> Along the April lands,
> And yet his tender touches
> Were on my face and hands.
> He vanished through a golden door,
> Beside a woodland dim,
> And every weed a jewel wore
> In memory of him.[44]

This poem, like Frost's "Pasture," owes a debt to Christopher Marlowe's famous lyric. The next year, at the end of June, "In the Pasture" appeared in the *Homestead*.

> Grass and flowers and humming bees,
> And soft winds sighing amid the trees;

> The songs of birds and the cricket's fife.
> The secret joy of the brooklet's life;
> The stars to watch through the quiet night
> Till the dawn grows red with the break of light—
> Such is the life of the pasture folk,
> Free of care and ambition's yoke.[45]

The emphasis in the last line of "In the Pasture" is on "pasture folk"—bees, birds, crickets—who are "free of care." But Frost's emphasis is on farm folk. That pastures require timely human "care" is one way to state Frost's theme in the poem he placed at the beginning of collective and selective editions of his poetry.

As to be expected, the *Homestead* brightened up its pages with poems announcing the advent of Spring with all its promise. Here is an excerpt (lines 16–25) from "The Springtime Miracle," published in 1902.

> To-morrow, springtime from the mold
> The hidden world will rise;
> The meadows turn to green and gold,
> The great woods all their flags unfold,
> And sunshine fills the skies;
> When every little seed shall hear
> The resurrection call.
> What hath the mortal, then, to fear?
> One human soul is yet more dear
> Than all the flowers are![46]

Less celebratory of the common spring miracle is Frost's "Nothing Gold Can Stay," which turns on an observation similar to the notice in the *Homestead* poem that "meadows turn to green and gold." "Nature's first green is gold," Frost begins his poem, and concludes it with a note of Ecclesiastes-like wisdom: "So Eden sank to grief, / So dawn goes down to day. / Nothing gold can stay" (206). Notably, Frost's poem gains its effect omitting words common to poesy— "spring" and "springtime," for example—which appear right on cue in the *Homestead* poem.

A prose piece published in the *Homestead* in 1902 anticipates Frost's image of "swinging" birches in his celebrated poem "Birches." The author of "The White Birches" writes: "No two trees stood in the same degree of straightness, but all looked sociable, even though their whiteness and the snow gave them a cold look. The top of one birch was bent to the ground, as though some child had been swinging on it, as I used to swing when a child. I wondered why it had not sprung back into an upright position. Perhaps it was in love with the snow, for it looked as though kissing it."[47] Only too obvious are the lines from the poem originally called "Swinging

1. The Poetry of Agriculture

Birches"—"When I see birches bend to left and right," he writes, " I like to think some boy's been swinging them," though experience soon takes over: "But swinging doesn't bend them down to stay / As ice-storms do" (117).

To be considered as well in this discussion of "Birches" is "God's Healing Breezes," a poem published in the *Homestead* in 1902, on the world-is-too-much-with-us theme customarily associated with Wordsworth but which Frost labels "considerations."

> When your life seems fraught with sorrow,
> When your mind by care's oppressed,
> When you dread each coming morrow,
> Take your woes to Nature's breast.
> She will find for you new pleasures,
> Softly whisper words of cheer;
> She will show you untold treasures,
> Make existence sweet each year.
> When you find toil's burden pressing
> Deeper furrows on your brow;
> When for you youth has no blessing,
> Fortune ne'er her smiles bestow;—
> Then away to woods and pastures,
> Where God's healing breezes blow,
> Where you dream on Hope's bright borders,
> And forget your pain and woe.[48]

In "Birches" Frost, although anticipated by the *Homestead* poet, makes the theme his own. When he is "weary of considerations, / And life is too much like a pathless wood," Frost writes, he would "like to get away from earth awhile / And then come back to it and begin over." After all, "Earth's the right place for love" (118).

Unlike the *Homestead* poem, "Birches" does not hector its audience or directly advocate any particular action or response. In this dramatic lyric Frost talks about himself, explaining rather than exhorting. His poem tells us how life has gone with him, the speaker. It does not generalize about Nature's healing or redemptive powers. Indeed it talks about the rhythm of getting away from earth for a moment but, and always, returning. What Frost has done is dramatize his consideration of considerations, finding the language—words, images, and metaphors—to do so as he goes.

As for Frost's lines—"Earth's the right place for love: / I don't know where it's likely to go better" (118), consider their wordy anticipation in "Pretty Good Place," published in the *Homestead* in 1903: "Treats a feller purty well, this ol' world of ours! There's a smile fer every tear an' sigh; / There's a rainbow peekin' through every cloud that lowers, / Tellin' of the sunshine by an' by. / Likely place, this here, to dwell— / Treats a feller purty well!"[49] Frost's spin in "Birches" on the matter of "this ol' world of ours" goes: "Earth's the right place for love: / I don't know where it's likely to go better" (118).

The theme of "old age," which was one of Frost's preoccupations, is broached in "The Lonesome Old Man," which appeared in the *Homestead* in 1901. Here are the first and the final stanzas of this forty-line poem:

> It seems as if I always happen to meet
> The lonesome old man, as he walks through the street.
> He stoops o'er his cane, and he studies the ground,
> And all the day long he is plodding around.
> He looks up to greet me with nod and with smile,
> And yet his dim eyes look so sad all the while!
> And thus he replies, as the sunshine we scan
> "Nice day but so quiet!" Poor, lonesome old man!
> .... Sometime, when I look for him coming along,
> I'll wonder, and wait, and fear something is wrong.
> I'll see the last figure he drew with his cane—
> A tremulous square in the dust of the lane.
> And then we will go, all our neighborhood clan,
> To visit at last with the lonesome old man.
> But silent we'll stand o'er a casket of clay—
> The angels of God will have led him away![50]

In 1916, Frost published "An Old Man's Winter Night," an unsentimental poem on the "lonesome old man" theme he shared with the *Homestead* poet. Unlike his predecessor, who describes his subject as "lonesome," Frost, making dramatic the state of "loneliness" rather than naming it, concludes: "One aged man—one man—can't keep a house, / A farm, a countryside, or if he can, / It's thus he does it of a winter night" (106).

The *Homestead* printed several poems on the not unrelated theme of the hired man, a subject that Frost, with only a poem or two, would make his own, treating it both incisively and sympathetically. "The Code" (1914) and "The Death of the Hired Man" (1915) were both written during Frost's tenure as a farmer in Derry. Yet by the time Frost wrote his poems about the "hired man," he was no longer a sure fixture on New England farms. His imminent demise had been signaled twenty years earlier by a contributor to the *Atlantic Monthly*,[51] even as the *Homestead* continued to celebrate, in "The Hired Man," a type rapidly fading out New England's farming economy.

> In clumping boots and jumpers blue
> He wades through early frost and dew,
> The first to hear the birds' low talk,

> The first to time Dame Nature's clock.
> His arms are strong, his heart is warm;
> He loves the touch of sun or storm.
> His life is spent with fresh delight,
> And earns him peace—and appetite.
> No care assails him. He can go
> Through life as peaceful waters flow.
> His path—ah! Happiest son of God!—
> Through fields of grass to Land of Nod.[52]

This poem—despite the understated wry note at the end—was followed in the *Homestead*, a year later, by "Our Hired Man," a poem about one Haggerty, seen as both a figure of humor and a trickster who successfully gets the younger workers around him to do his work for him. The poem is told in the admiring voice of one of Haggerty's young "dupes," a son of the farmer he serves as "hired man."

> He'd tell us fellers the things he'd done,
> An' brag of his strength an' skill
> A-pitchin' an hoein' an' choppin' an' mowin'
> An' everythin' else, until
> We both agreed he wuz drawin' it mild
> When he 'lowed in his offhand way,
> He could "turn off work like a haythen Turk
> An' kape it up all day!"
> But somehow, when Haggerty went to mow,
> You could usually figger he
> Wuz either a-whettin', or else he wuz settin'
> A-talkin' to Joe an' me.
> An' whenever he did get started in,
> His scythe wouldn't work as it should,
> So he'd send us for water, an' reckon he'd orter
> Grind the pesky ol' thing till it would.
> So me and Joe'd lay to an' turn
> Till our backs wuz nearly broke,
> While Haggerty'd tell us what husky young fellers
> We wuz, as he'd stand an' smoke.
> An' he'd tell us how healthy it wuz for us
> A-pluggin' away like this,
> An' he'd smile an' say he guessed some day
> Our muscles w'd equal his![53]

Just as, in "The Death of the Hired Man," Frost presents Silas not in his own voice but entirely through the words of others, so, too, does the *Homestead* poet present the hired man through the words of another person. The poems—the *Homestead*'s and Frost's—differ markedly, of course, in the character of the hired man each has chosen to portray. Haggerty, in the *Homestead* poem, plays something of a "confidence game" to get the younger boys to do his work for him. In Frost's far more sympathetic portrait, Silas is a skillful worker who would be a teacher to the young college boy. It is notable that unlike the *Homestead* poet, Frost does not resort to transcribing the dialect of his speakers; he is not interested in local color or humor at the expense of any of the figures in "The Death of the Hired Man," an elegy on an occupation, a way of life, and the solitude and loneliness of an old man come home to die.[54]

The seeming ubiquity of "tramps" at certain times of the year bothered *Homestead* writers as it did Frost. Frost's poetry on this theme indicates that he was ever suspicious that the tramp who came to his door asking for food or looking for work might steal from him or, worse, burn down his barn. Such fears were not alien to the pages of the *Homestead*. Here is a joke about tramps, inserted as filler, at Christmastime 1900: "*Mrs. Youngwife* (to appealing tramp): Here, my poor man, are some of my homemade biscuits. You will find the saw and ax in the woodshed. *Tramp* (examining the biscuits): Holy Moses, mum! Are they as bad as that?"[55] The words "appealing tramp" mean, of course, that "the tramp is making an appeal." Yet there is also, ambiguously, a hint that the tramp's looks might appeal to the *young* woman with the eponymous name. Is this the fear of the farmer who often is well off in the fields or even the barn when the tramp appears at his door? Is there a veiled sexual content is the choice of the word "appealing"? Is there, perhaps, such a veiled sexual content in "Two Tramps in Mud Time" (1934)? Is the speaker's fear that the tramp will take away the one he loves and possesses? Is this part of the import of the reference to "two eyes make one"? Obviously, "Two Tramps in Mud Time" is the Frost poem one would think of first in this regard, but consider "Love and a Question," written during the poet's early years at the Derry farm and published in *A Boy's Will*. To the door comes a "Stranger" who speaks to the "bridegroom fair," asking for "shelter for the night." The bridegroom is suspicious and fearful of a stranger at the door, one who somehow seems to pose a threat to the young couple in their "bridal house" (17–18). Of course, the fear of violence at the hands of the tramp—he might set fire to the barn or, worse, do harm to the woman of the house. "I used to be afraid of them [tramps], and I am yet; pack peddlers, too," wrote one young man to the *Homestead* in 1900.[56] Two weeks earlier the journal had published a cautionary anecdote.

> One day mamma went to town and left me and my sister at home. I had washed the dishes and was going to take the water round to the other kitchen and sent my sister in to the other house to see what time it was, for

> I wanted to take some water to the field for the men. When I got to the kitchen there sat an old tramp eating some cake and sweet bread. I dropped my pan of water and ran into the house and told my sister that an old tramp was out in the kitchen and we should go to Marllatt's, our neighbor across the road, and some of them would make him go away. She would not come, she thought I was fooling. She came when I started out. Gertrude came over but the tramp would not go, so she got her mother to come and she sent him a flying. But don't you believe I was crying all the while. He still had some cake.[57]

Also to be considered in this context is Frost's "The Smile," published as part of "The Hill Wife," in which the young wife speaks fearfully and suspiciously of the tramp and his mysterious smile. Did he smile that way because "the wretch knew" that they were poor? Or was it that he smiled that way because he had allowed them to give him bread instead of seizing it himself? Or was he mocking them because they were wed or were very young? "I wonder," she concludes, "how far down the road he's got. / He's watching from the woods as like as not" (123).

The life of the busy, contented and dedicated housewife is a common theme in the *Homestead*'s pages. "Her Heart's Domain," a poem published in 1904, is typical.

> Deep in their shady nooks,
> Screened from the sun,
> Musical hidden brooks
> Ripple and run.
> So, in her quiet way,
> Many a life
> Turns from the garish day—
> Mother and wife.
> Home is her heart's domain;
> Love is her need.
> Not to have lived in vain—
> This is her creed.[58]

In Frost's poetry there are no such paeans to the joys and comforts of housewifery. But it should be acknowledged that the *Homestead* also published, occasionally, poems that question such rather breezily expressed views. Take, for example, "Without and Within," which appeared in 1903.

> Some houses are so fine and grand,
> The windows look so rich and fair,
> The passerby might say offhand,
> "There's surely peace and plenty there!"
> And yet within the mansion great
> There may be bitter spite and gall;

> There may be hate that soon or late
> Will bring its inmates to the wall.
> The tenement of human clay—
> In which a soul is pent—
> May look so well, the people say,
> "He looks the picture of content!"
> And yet within that smooth abode,
> The outward seeming calm below,
> Of grief there may be such a load
> As only souls in sorrow know.[59]

As evidence that this view of the housewife is more in accordance with Frost's, consider the five-verse sequence "The Hill Wife" (1916), which culminates in "The Impulse" in an omniscient voice's "truth" about the young wife's dark and obscure "within" that leads her to disappear once and for all, for "It was too lonely for her there, / And too wild." After she disappeared, he looked "Everywhere," but never found her. "Sudden and swift and light as that / The ties gave," and he "learned of finalities / Besides the grave" (124). To some readers, "The Hill Wife" will also recall E. A. Robinson's "Eros Turanos," but in their pointing to the mysteries "within" the house, it is undeniable that both Robinson and Frost have as one of their predecessors this *Homestead* poet.

As for the hard-work of "housekeeping," it is notable that behind Frost's "A Servant to Servants," a monologue presenting the "servant" woman's case from her own perspective—"I can't express my feelings any more / Than I can raise my voice" (65)—are several *Homestead* poems. Typical of them is "The Housekeeper's View," published in 1905.

> Did you speak of work, ol' man?
> Why, what you be'n doin',
> That you talk so weary-like—
> What set you to stewin'?
> Farmin' is discouragin',
> But so's an empty larder;
> Feedin' cattle's pretty hard
> But feedin' men is harder.
> Tough work plowin' in the fields
> Where it's nice an' breezy—
> How'd you like the sweepin' then?
> S'pose you think that's easy!
> Washin' harness dirty work?
> P'raps dishwashin's cleaner!
> Yes, don't doubt milkin's mean,
> Only—churnin's meaner.
> Takes forever mendin' walls—

> Mendin' clothes takes longer;
> Farm needs someone strong, you say—
> House needs someone stronger,
> I don't know? Oh, yes, I do!
> I quite grasp your meanin';
> You think farmin's hard, ol' man—
> Ever tried house cleanin'?[60]

At the National Poetry Festival, held at the Library of Congress, October 22–24, 1962, just three months before his death, the evening session on October 23 was given over to Frost. Among the many interesting things he emphasized in addressing his audience of poets and critics was his oft-repeated distinction between "grievance" and "grief"—"poetry is about grief and politics is about grievance."[61] In "Phoebe," a poem in the *Homestead* in 1904, Frost could have found an emblematic use of the phoebe as a grieving creature, a use that he would later emulate in one of most often quoted poems. Here is "Phoebe," the *Homestead* poem.

> O mother, see that little bird
> Up in the tree alone!
> She calls "Phoebe. Phoebe. Phoebe!"
> Why doesn't Phoebe come?
> O where is Phoebe that she fails
> To hear her mother call?
> Or does she hear and never heed
> Or answer back at all?
> Dear mother, when you speak my name
> I'll answer your first word,
> And never let you call and grieve
> Like that poor mother bird.[62]

At the end of "The Need of Being Versed in Country Things" (1920), Frost introduces the phoebe to define by contrast the human grief that follows a destructive homestead fire. "For them there was really nothing sad," he writes, "But though they rejoiced in the nest they kept, / One had to be versed in country things / Not to believe the phoebes wept" (223). Like Walt Whitman's "Out of the Cradle Endlessly Rocking," the *Homestead* poem also locates its theme of loss and grief in a bird. But that its grieving bird is a phoebe links it to the phoebes in Frost that might appear to weep to those who do not know the hard reality in "country things."

The poem "The Perfect Whole" announces its optimism in its title. It appeared in the *Homestead* in 1904, three months before the phoebe poem.

> A little bird, within a tangled wood,
> Sang sweetly to the forest solitude;

> From matin hour to vesper time it sang—
> Until the leafy woodland spaces rang
> With such a chorus of ecstatic glee
> That all the world seemed pulsing harmony.
> "Why," croaked a tree toad on a neighboring limb,
> "Do you pour out such glad, perpetual hymn?
> "You are so small, in this vast universe
> No song of yours could either bless or curse."
> "If I am small," trilled back the little bird,
> "I then must sing the more that I be heard."
> One walking through the wood paused, listening;
> "How good to hear that happy creature sing!
> "And if it has a part in God's great plan,
> Much more must I—who bear the name of man."⁶³

The "perfect whole" notion of this poem stands in contrast to the much "diminished thing" harshly enunciated in "The Oven Bird" (1916) by Frost's "mid-summer" and "mid-wood bird" that "knows in singing not to sing" (116).

In 1903 the *Homestead* published "The Flower in Her Hand," a sentimental allegory in which, with easy certitude, a simple flower is made to stand for love.

> She carried in her hand a little flower,
> And everywhere she went
> A subtle fragrance seemed to steal like that
> Of precious ointment spent.
> She carried in her hand a little flower,
> And when her footsteps came,
> From its pure whiteness selfishness and pride
> Shrank back for very shame.
> She carried in her hand a little flower,
> And like a flame it lit
> Up darkened homes and made sad faces smile—
> Love was the name of it.⁶⁴

"Love," not coincidentally, I think, is also the name given to the otherwise unnamed flower in Frost's "The Subverted Flower" (1942), but in Frost it is a love convoluted by physicality, lust and brutality. "She drew back; he was calm," the poem begins, "'It is this that had the power.' / And he lashed his open palm / With the tender-headed flower." His predatory smile turns up the "corners of his lips" and cracks "his ragged muzzle." The poem then works its menacing way to this conclusion: "A girl could only see / That a flower had marred a man," but what she could not see was that the flower might be something "other than base and fetid"; that "what the

1. The Poetry of Agriculture 25

flower began / Her own too meager heart / Had terribly completed." She had looked and seen, as the poet judges, "the worst" (308–09).⁶⁵

"Snow tracks," less a theme than a motive, makes its appearance in the *Homestead* in "Footprints on the Snow," a poem published in 1906.

> All along down the roadway
> Where e're my feet may go,
> I see them on before me,
> Wee footprints on the snow.
> Where will those small feet wander?
> Will they go straight and true
> When they shall choose their pathway,
> As one day they must do?
> And so I ask, dear Father,
> As on through life they go,
> Thou keep from downward pathway,
> The footprints on the snow!⁶⁶

An untitled poem about chopping down a maple tree in the woods in winter, written "right off the reel" (Frost's words) for a documentary being done at Amherst College in 1962,⁶⁷ concludes: "And in the afterglow / I link a line of shadowy tracks / Across the tinted snow" (478).

The single quatrain of "Tell-Tale-Tracks," published in the *Homestead* in 1902, reads: "In a clear and frosty morning, when the snow is soft and white, / Ere the sun has wiped the dainty footprints out, / You can see the tracks of squirrels who went calling through the night / On their neighbors in the forest round about."⁶⁸ Three months later, the *Homestead* published "Stories in the Snow."

> Here the fox went stepping swiftly,
> And his feet fell straight in line;
> He went up the snowy hillside,
> Passed into the grove of pine.
> Next the rabbit's hieroglyphics
> Plainly printed on the snow;
> Next the red squirrel's tiny pawprints
> Tell us where he chanced to go.
> Then the snowbird's dainty pathway,
> Then the partridge's clumsy track
> Shows where he tried to go forward,
> But was frightened and came back.⁶⁹

Anticipated in both poems is the imagery—messages in the snow—of the conclusion of Frost's "Closed for Good" (1948). "And so on into winter / Till even I have ceased / To come as a foot printer," he writes, and "only some slight beast / So mousy or so foxy / Shall print there as my proxy" (429).[70]

When Frost first published "The White-Tailed Hornet" (1936), the poem featured a thematic subtitle: "Doubts About an Instinct." After observing that the white-tailed hornet's mistake in taking a nail-head for a fly, doing it not once but twice, followed by another mistake, taking a huckleberry for a fly, the poet questions: "Won't this whole instinct matter bear revision? / Won't almost any theory bear revision?" (254). These questions bring into doubt the notion of the infallibility of instinct that is assumed in "Some Insect Guests on Familiar Plants," an article published in the *Homestead* in 1904, which opens with an epigraph from *The Bee*, a long poem by Dr. John Evans (1786–1864), a Welsh surgeon: "—Instinct her simple guide / A heaven taught insect baffles all your pride. / Not all your marshall'd orbs, that ride so high, / Proclaim more loud a present deity, / Than the nice symmetry of these small cells, / Where on each angle genuine science dwells."[71]

The way that insect instinct and the philosophical-religious note of design inheres in the lesson the spider teaches when it re-builds its web after it has been destroyed is adumbrated in "Perseverance Conquers Ill," a poem published in the *Homestead* in 1895: "Another web, more firmly done, / Was stretched across the pane: / Each silken mesh securely hung, / Each guy renewed again."[72] If this poem stops short of explicitly naming the purpose of the spider's web—art as handmaiden to survival—Frost's sonnet "In White" (1912)—the precursor of the more profound "Design" (1922)—with its tableau of death delivered to a white moth by a white spider on a white heal-all, does not. Yet Frost's little drama of domesticity and horror is challenged by the more elaborately detailed drama enacted in "Dinner for Two" (1907), a *Homestead* poem illustrated with decorative drawings of cobwebs, spiders, flies, hornets and moths, and featuring the anthropomorphized voices of two spiders, Madam Epeira and Lady Lycosa. Reminiscent of Fontaine's parable of the grasshopper and the ant, Margaret Wentworth Leighton's "Dinner for Two" relates how the efficient spider, Epeira, gathers her prey: "'Oh, a grey moth! /And a grasshopper too, / With such a fine feast / How well I shall do!' / She wound them and bound them, / So snug and so tight, / And hoisted them slowly / Up, up to the height / Of her pretty sky parlor, / So snug and so green. / 'I've the daintiest feast now / That ever was seen.'" "Make your web and stop wandering about," Epeira counsels Lycosa, and "you won't have to make a supper of your young."[73] Of course the Leighton poem does aspire to the metaphysical meaning Frost finds in his own natural tableau of design and death.

As for the Frost's spider's modus operandi in getting its food, consider its resemblance to the following prose description of the spider's way with its prey, published in the *Homestead* in 1901: "This exquisite net is a snare laid to catch flies, mosquitoes and gnats. Just look at a fly in a spider's web and see how tightly its wings are tied down so they cannot flutter, its feet bound so that it cannot walk—silken manacles from which there is no escape. These insects are the spider's food; an easy way to get it, you will say."[74]

In "After Apple-Picking" (1914) the poet meditates on his experience as an apple-grower and apple-picker. The situation explored in the poem needs no erudite explanation. Yet it may be useful to see it also in the context of the ways the *Homestead* covered one of the New England farmer's most important crops. Frost's poem begins: "My long two-pointed ladder's sticking through a tree / Toward heaven still, / And there's a barrel that I didn't fill." And beside that barrel, "there may be two or three / Apples I didn't pick upon some bough. / But I am done with apple-picking now" (70). The overly tired poet now turns to weary and troubled sleep. He is "drowsing off," he writes, but "cannot rub the strangeness" from his sight that he "got from looking through a pane of glass" he "skimmed" that morning from a "drinking trough" and "held against the world of hoary grass." In his dream "magnified apples appear and disappear, / Stem end and blossom end," with "every fleck of russet showing clear" (70).

In New England the business of growing, harvesting and selling apples had long been a matter of major importance to farmers, and thus the *Homestead* was careful to attend to its readers' interest in the matter with frequent reports on what was termed "the apples situation" or "the apple outlook." Published in 1895, "Under the Apple Trees" is a paean to the apple, a thing of quotidian use and mythological import. But the hard work it takes to plant and care for apple orchards or the labor-intensive apple-picking goes unmentioned.

> Bend down your branches, Apple Tree.
> See, here are a couple of hands outspread;
> Good friends tried and tested are we,—
> Do drop me an apple ripe and red,
> While I rest me here on this gnarled old stump—
> An ancient ancestral tree no doubt;—
> Thank you, old giant! There fell one plump!
> Sound and mellow within and without.
> How do you do it? I wish I knew!
> For you take a clod of common earth,
> Mold it and quicken it thro' and thro,'

> Till, rounded and grown to a goodly girth,
> Stuffed with sunshine from skin to core,
> Drunken with sunshine, and brimmed with heat,
> With the colors of dawn it is painted o'er
> And turns out—this luscious apple I eat.
> Talk of the fabled fruit of old
> In the sacred deeps of the western sky!
> Hesper's apples were gleaming gold,
> Mine are red of the deepest dye;
> No dragon guards my loaded trees,
> The birds and I in our feast rejoice;
> Hesper's for beauty, if you please,
> But when one is hungry, mine for choice.[75]

Note the proverbially Yankee touch as the poem swerves in each stanza from the mythological golden apple to the edible red apple of the everyday New England orchard.

Over the years the *Homestead* featured photographs of apple orchards at harvest time, showing ladders poking prominently through the tops of trees and filled and half-filled baskets of apples next to the ladders—eminently suitable to illustrate the poem Frost would later write, but with this great difference: the ladder in Frost's poem coaxes the reader to read it symbolically, for it pokes its way "toward heaven," toward the suggestion, that is, there is something symbolic about its placement.[76] The *Homestead* photographs seem to imply that while apple-picking has its great rewards, it should not be forgotten that those rewards come at the price of strenuous and protracted labor. Argued in "The Curse" (1906), however, is the idea that it is the labor required to bring in the "luscious fruit" (including "luscious apple" of the *Homestead* poem just quoted) that is itself the real benefit.

> God said, "Let thorns and briars spring up,
> For man has sinned. Let labor be a curse."
> But God's great heart of love could not content
> Itself with justice done. His mercy yearned
> O'er wretched man, so helpless in his fall.
> The briars, God made bloom and bear
> Sweet, fragrant flowers and luscious fruit,
> And labor, man's great primal curse, He made
> A blessing great, as he who labors with his hands has found.
> So great, that he who labors, finds
> Rich health, sweet peaceful rest, and grand content.
> And as each day, he tills the fertile soil,
> He feels, in every fiber of his being, God is good![77]

What links such *Homestead* poems to Frost's "After Apple Picking" is the notion that human labor—a curse—is to be accepted in resignation, for

1. The Poetry of Agriculture

"he who labors, finds / Rich health, sweet peaceful rest, and grand content," a bit of Scripture welcomed in "The Curse" but questioned in the apple-harvesting poet-speaker's troubled "long sleep" referenced in "After Apple-Picking." Typical of the customary *Homestead* poem on this theme is "The Sleep of the Laboring Man," which begins by quoting Ecclesiastes.

> The sleep of the laboring man is sweet!
> When the trudge of the day is o'er
> God measures to him the repose that's meet
> To rank with the toil before.
> The stars filter down from ethereal sheen,
> Through the shadowy watches of night,
> A shimmer of hopes that abide between
> His margins of daily light.
> The sleep of the laboring man is sweet!
> When the brain of the tradesman wakes,
> When the pulses of merriment throb and beat,
> No stir on his slumber breaks;
> The woof of his dream is the subtle blend
> The whisper of wind, the voice of a friend,
> And call of the night-bird near,
> Of the sounds which he last gave ear—[78]

Of Frost's many autumnal poems, consider only "A Leaf Treader" (1935), in which the poet reports that he is "autumn-tired" from having treaded on leaves all day: "All summer long they were overhead, more lifted up than I. / To come to their final place in earth they had to pass me by. / All summer long I thought I heard them threatening under their breath." And when, in the fall, they came, "it seemed with a will to carry me with them to death." They "tapped at my eyelids and touched my lips with an invitation to grief. / But it was no reason I had to go because they had to go. / Now up my knee to keep on top of another year of snow" (270–71). The poem "Gathering Autumn Leaves" appeared in the *Homestead* in 1902. It ventures that even the denuded tree rewards those who gather fallen leaves, for the loss of leaves permits stars to shine through bare branches.[79] Frost takes up the same "gathering leaves" theme in a number of poems, before and after he published "A Leaf Treader" (1935): "In Hardwood Groves" (1925) ("The same leaves over and over again!"), "November" (1938) (entitled "In Praise of Waste" in manuscript), and "Gathering Leaves" (1923), which reads: "Spades take up leaves / No better than spoons." He raises mountains of leaves till he fills "the whole shed" with leaves that have no value to the farmer. Still, "a crop is a crop, / And who's to say where / The harvest shall stop?" (216–17). In this case, it stops with a poem.

Frost published a fair number of poems about butterflies, beginning with "My Butterfly" (1894), some years before he moved to the farm in Derry, and continuing with "Range-Finding" (1916), "Fragmentary Blue" (1920), and "Pod of the Milkweed" (1954). "Pod of the Milkweed" is anticipated in the *Homestead*, most notably by "The Roadside Party" (1901):

> There's a party by the roadside.
> The guests come faster and faster!
> The butterflies in golden gauze
> Are visiting Purple Aster.
> Oh, charming is her parlor,
> Her housekeeping the neatest;
> She bows and bows to her lovely friends
> With manners quite the sweetest.
> Though busy at her housework,
> Mistress Ant feels slightest;
> Chipmunk is scolding overhead
> Because he's not invited.
> Still to the roadside party
> The guests come faster and faster,—
> Butterflies in golden gauze.
> Visiting Purple Aster.[80]

Published as Frost's Christmas greeting for 1954 and later included as *In the Clearing*'s first poem, "Pod of the Milkweed," like the *Homestead* poem just quoted, entertains the idea that nature knows how to throw a party, complete with invitations and, of course, much drink. Yet while the *Homestead* poet praises natural orderliness and social formality, Frost's poem celebrates nature's perceived saturnalia, calling "all butterflies of every race / From source unknown but from no special place." The "distilled honey" of the milkweed is so sweet that it inebriates the butterflies until "they knock the dyestuff off each other's wings," raising in "their intemperance a cloud / Of mingled butterfly and flower dust / That hangs perceptibly above the scene" (425). Think, too, in this context, of the nature of nature's intemperance exemplified in Frost's "Blue-Butterfly Day," first published in the *New Republic* and collected in *New Hampshire* in 1923. These butterflies, "flowers that fly and all but sing," "now from having ridden out desire" lie "closed over in the wind and cling / Where wheels have freshly sliced the April mire" (208).

Almost always treated sentimentally, the subject of the old family homestead was something of a *Homestead* staple. At the turn of the century, for example, there appeared several such poems, which, taken together, convey a set of human attitudes and a display of natural images reminiscent of those characteristic of Frost. Not to Frost's liking, however,

1. The Poetry of Agriculture

is "The Old Homestead," which offers a saccharine view of a return to a place once lived in. That someone is living there is not stated in so many words, but it is implied by imagery that suggests that house, flowers, and fruit-bearing trees are still in good order.

> Beside the gate the lilacs sweet
> Are bright with gleaming May-rain pearls,
> And soft against my wandering feet
> The grass of tender green uncurls.
> Bright tulips near the doorway bloom,
> And crocuses peep from the mold;
> Sweet hyacinths lend their perfume,
> And jonquils the sun's yellow hold.
> The bees are humming sweet and low,
> The happy insects drone and hum,
> Bird voices softly come and go,
> From swaying pear, and peach, and plum.
> The garden pathway wanders through
> The peaceful shade of trees until
> Beneath the elm it falls into
> A little, bubbling, laughing rill.
> The dusty road begins to wind,
> I leave the peaceful, homely scene.
> It gently melts from sight behind
> A grove of cedars' billowy green.[81]

The next year the *Homestead* published a poem offering a different and far more plaintive vision of "the old home." "The Deserted Homestead" is more in line with Frost's way of looking at things.

> The children all have gone away, to south and west and on the sea,
> And through the bleak and empty house the birds and squirrels wander free,
> The meadows now are dreary fields, the orchard is a sprouting wood,
> And there is but a heap of ruins where once the rambling old barn stood.
> The paths are overgrown with weeds, the garden but a waste of green,
> While here and there a faithful sword of blazing hollyhock is seen,
> And on the hill beyond the brook, with but a granite slab and name—
> The old folks lying side by side, their faces hidden from the shame.[82]

This poem, in theme and situational imagery, anticipates Frost's more stringent, less sentimental poems about deserted homesteads, such as "The Black Cottage" (1914) and "Directive" (1946).

"The Road to Anywhere" was published in the *Homestead* two weeks before Christmas, in 1908. Here is the poem, in part.

> Across the newly furrowed fields
> And meadows brown and bare,

> My aimless feet mark out a path
> That leads to anywhere.
> It wanders by the old rail fence
> With tangled vines o'ergrown
> Hiding the drifts of withered leaves
> By last year's breezes blown....
> In wav'ring, shimm'ring, slanting lines
> The mellow sunshine falls
> To where, within the woods' dark edge,
> A wild bird softly calls.
> A wind steals softly thro' the vines
> And somehow soothes my pain,
> Sweeping the shadows from my heart,
> The cobwebs from my brain.
> Again I am a barefoot child
> And know no greater care
> Than just to follow, as I will
> The road to anywhere.[83]

In 1897 the *Homestead* reprinted the Scottish poet George MacDonald's "Which Road Would You Take?" MacDonald's work, in fact, had been a great favorite with Frost's mother, and his poems were among those she read aloud to her young son.[84] "Which Road Would You Take?" anticipates, closely at times, both "Directive" and "The Road Not Taken."

> If you could go back to the fork of the road,
> Back the long miles you have carried your load,
> Back to the place where you had to decide
> By this way or that through your life to abide;
> Back to the sorrow, back to the care;
> Back to the place where the future was fair;
> If you were there now a decision to make,
> O, pilgrim of sorrow, which road would you take?
> Then after you'd traveled the other long track,
> Suppose that again to the fork you went back,
> After you found that the promises fair
> Were but a delusion that led to a snare;
> That the road you first traveled with sighs and unrest,
> Tho' dreary and rough, was most graciously blest
> With balm for each bruise and a charm for each ache,
> O, pilgrim of sorrow, what road would you take?[85]

While it may be said that MacDonald belabors his metaphor of "the fork of the road," spelling out its import in fulsome fashion and comes to a rather doleful conclusion, it is significant that Frost recalls in intentionally overly dramatic fashion a situation which starts out, seemingly, with indecision but ends up, if one reads the poet's tone aright, with a somewhat consoling shrug of the shoulders. Faced with the need to make a choice—some choice—the speaker chooses one road over the other and does so for a reason that harbors a condition—one road wanted wear but as for the poet's passing there, they were both worn about the same. As most of Frost's readers have determined, this consideration of what goes into making a decision leads to a greater metaphorical emphasis on the meaning and import of making choices. Yet Frost himself affirmed that his poem—aimed at a friend whose habitual procrastination before they set out on their morning's walk as to which route to take—was really about the fact that whatever the choice it did not much matter, for choosing any one of the possibilities would have amounted to pretty much the same thing in the end.[86] That Frost wished to make his poem work as a teasing remonstrance to a poet friend—even if the friend did not get the gentle joke (as apparently he did not)—serves as one way to differentiate it from MacDonald's more straightforward and more mundane poem on paths and roads. Yet, as Frost himself came to recognize, he had failed to convey his intentions in the poem, for readers—beginning, in a university forum, with the learned president of the Massachusetts college that first hired him—took as pure truth what he had intended to be taken as sententious (and thus hollow) wisdom.

2

All Legends Are Local

In mid-career, in an effort to universalize his early poetry, T. S. Eliot stripped away the place names that tied individual poems to his personal experience. Titles of early versions of the poems later collected as "Preludes," for example, refer to such Boston places as Dorchester and Roxbury. Eliot's naming impulse may be a sign of the naturalistic vision still evident in the opening lines of the early poems "The Love Song of J. Alfred Prufrock" and "Sweeney among the Nightingales."[1] Just as he disavowed naturalism, Eliot also later renounced the dazzling modernism on display in "The Wasteland." In the late poems collected as "The Four Quartets," while still attempting to achieve an overarching universality of spirit, Eliot returned to the facts of biography and heredity and forcefully named his poems after sites saturated with personal meaning—Burnt Norton, Little Giddings, and East Coker. In "Directive," which can be read as a response to the major currents of Eliot's poetry as epitomized in "The Wasteland" and in "The Four Quartets," Robert Frost adopts the original telltale trait of literary modernism, the suppression of place names, to establish the geographical and geological universality of his "directive."

In avoiding names, Frost also conveniently, if not intentionally, obscured the particular origins for his poem. If the "exact setting for 'Directive' doesn't really matter," it is nevertheless certain, as Jay Parini notes, that Frost "had in the back of his mind the farm at Derry and the brook nearby, Hyla Brook, where his children played." "There is also an abandoned farm much like the one in 'Directive' not far behind the Homer Noble farm," continues Parini, though "abandoned farms, even whole villages, are commonplace in northern New England." "As a hiker, Frost came across them regularly," commented Reginald L. Cook. "It would be a mistake to try to locate this farm anywhere in particular. It is typical, even universal, in its complexion and details."[2] Perhaps; but the story does not end there.

Parini also reminds us that "Directive" (1946) was anticipated by "Ghost House" (1906), given second place in *A Boy's Will*. There, too, the poet arrives in a "deserted landscape."[3] "'Ghost House,'" writes Jeffrey S. Cramer, "may have been inspired by an old cellar hole with a tall chimney standing in it, all that remained of a house which had burned down years earlier, near the Derry farm, halfway between Klein's Hill and the house of their [the Frosts'] neighbor, Napoleon Guay.... The house, which had burned down in 1867, had belonged to Marshall Merriam, who owned almost all of the land which became the Frost farm."[4] A latter-day note to Lesley Frost's journals, which she kept as a child while living on the Derry farm, informs us that "while Mr. Merriam was attending Fast Day services in the Congregational Church at East Derry, in 1867, his house caught fire and burned down. The cellar hole, still easily located, gradually became surrounded by lilac bushes and double-petal red-rose bushes, some of which Robert Frost transplanted to his own gardens at the front of his farmhouse in 1907."[5] But in "Ghost House" the poet refers to "the purple-stemmed wild raspberries" (15) that grow in the cellar; he does not mention roses or lilacs. Decades later, however, the last cellar hole of "Directive" (there were "forty cellar holes" in this "town that is no more a town") is described as "belilaced" (341–42).

This trace of "lilacs" points to a probable literary source for "Directive" if one follows the path to the now lost town, of which the speaker informs us "there's a story in a book about it." One possible candidate for such a book is *Rhymes and Legends of the Nutfields*, a chapbook by Lucinda T. Carlton, printed in 1919 in Manchester, New Hampshire. The poems focus on Derryfield and its inhabitants, past and sometimes present. The well-meaning if pedestrian "rhymes" in this modestly unassuming collection bear titles intriguing to anyone interested in Frost's life and work, titles such as "The Pinkertons" (about Major John and Deacon James Pinkerton, who founded Pinkerton Academy, which later employed Frost as a teacher), "The Legend of Westrunning Brook," "The Land of Canada," and "The Old Cellars."

Lucinda Carlton's "The Legend of Westrunning Brook" opens with references to the vestigial evidences of human life, something that Frost makes so much of, especially in "Directive."

O yes, it is a little stream, this westward-running brook
And who among us all has been upon her banks to look
For trace of ancient cellar wall or old and unused well
That had they voices soon would speak of the Pioneers to tell.

Then might we hear how once this stream that in the sunlight shines
Lay hidden 'neath the lacy limbs of hemlocks and of pines,
How chestnut, butternut and beech, the oak and walnut tree
Spread a green mantle o'er the stream that now runs clear and free.

And how one day when spring was new and birds were caroling their lays
Strange men from far across the sea came searching through her woodland ways,
Nor bending bough, nor budding limb, nor graceful willow's tasseled stem,
Nor leaves of interlacing vines could keep her sweet, sweet song from them.

"This is the spot, the stream runs west into the winding Gaentake
That through fair meadows, verdure drest, her way to Dracut town doth make;
These streams mark a plain path to friends,
Give thanks—'tis here your searching ends."
....
They built their cabins on this little stream
Whose waters today in the sunlight gleam
And here they lived and daily sought
The love of God and freedom of thought.[6]

Omitting Carlton's exposition of the legends of West-running Brook, Frost chooses instead to focus on the stream as the dramatic setting for a conversation between a wife and her husband. She asks: "'Fred, where is north?'" He answers: "'North? North is there, my love. / The brook runs west.'" So, she decides, "'West-running Brook then call it.'" And the poet adds: "(West-running Brook men call it to this day.)" That the drama begins with the naming of the brook fulfills Frost's own prediction, made a few years earlier to a student-poet who had published a poem titled "Joe Wright's Brook," that when he got around to building a poem around the naming of a river or stream he would make something quite different out of it.[7] In "West-Running Brook," true to his word, Frost followed up the act of naming with the protagonists' far more meaningful speculations about sources and the origins of life. The husband speaks: "'Speaking of contraries, see how the brook / In that white wave runs counter to itself.'" "It is from that in water we were from," he adds. "Long, long before we were from any creature. / Here we, impatient of the steps, / Get back to the beginning of beginnings, / The stream of everything that runs away." For it is "this backward motion toward the source, / Against the stream, that most we see ourselves in, / The tribute of the current to the source." And it is "from this in nature we are from. / It is most us" (236–38).

In "The Old Cellars," Lucinda Carlton re-imagines "the ancient cellar wall or old and unused well" from the opening lines of "The Legend of Westrunning Brook," and she proceeds to elaborate on those images:

2. All Legends Are Local

> All over the town I see them, guarded by the lilac bush and rose,
> Peacefully resting upon the plains or where a radiance glows
> Earliest upon the hill-tops when comes the morning light,
> And lovingly lingers longest ere the stars come out at night.
>
> Oft in a fond, fond fancy, I wander, again and again,
> Over these plains and hill-tops, through vale and grassy glen,
> 'Twixt many an old lane's stony sides, by lake and stream let small,
> And listen to the voices that then so clearly call.

There, before "the cellar walls," the poet has a vision of "sturdy children" playing.

> Then wander to some wayside spot where grow old lilac bushes,
> Or where the stiff, sweet mullein stalk, its way 'twixt gray stones pushes,
> Some spot where only wild flowers list the morning song of thrushes,
> Or where some cellar's faintest trace is lost 'neath clover blushes,
> And rest and think of early times and those that now are near,
> And thank God that in distant days a brave race settled here.[8]

The majority of Carlton's chapbook is devoted to poems, including this one that she subsumes under "History." "O Friends," she implores, "seek not in distant lands for fair Romance's soul, / Our little town's a romance—a romance as a whole."

In "Directive" Frost is less interested in the facts and expository details of pure history than in the lines and force of myth. While Carlton's "The Old Cellars" revels in naming and recalling through history, no less than in celebrating, the settlers and their no-longer town (Derryfield), Frost is engaged in universalizing and making meaningful the experience of those who would be saved by journeying backwards through time.

Perhaps I would go too far if I were to suggest that "Directive" was inspired by "The Old Cellars," but it is intriguing to note that Frost borrows some of its details. There is, first of all, "the lilac bush" (Frost's "belilaced cellar hole"), joined by "an old lane's stony sides" and "the old, old clay pit" lay (the road that "should have been a quarry—/ Great monolithic knees the former town/ Long since gave up pretense of keeping covered"), and "the ledgy hill" ("the ledges show"). Indeed, "Directive" takes to heart the imprecation in "The Old Cellars," "O friends, seek not in distant lands for fair Romance's soul, / Our little town's a romance—a romance as a whole." Obeying that logic, the lyricist observes that in the unnamed Derryfield, knights will be rewarded for their search for the Grail: "Here are your waters and your watering place. / Drink and be whole again beyond confusion." (In a poem entitled "Our Stars of Service," which is about wartime patriotism, Carlton refers to those who seek, "as did the knights of Arthur's day," "to give protection to the weak."[9])

Halfway through "Directive" (1946), the speaker both instructs and dares: "And if you're lost enough to find yourself / By now, pull in your ladder road behind you / And put a sign up CLOSED to all but me." The last line foreshadows the poem "Closed for Good" (1948), the title of which suggests "closed permanently," then perhaps "closed for the good of all," or more likely—considering Jesus' explanation that parables excluded the unworthy from understanding, an account from St. Mark that Frost invokes in "Directive"—"closed for the benefit of someone in particular." Frost's ladder, when pulled up, separates and excludes. In this regard, it brings to mind the ship's side ladder that Herman Melville's Father Mapple pulls up behind him as he ascends his pulpit. As Melville suggests, "there must be some sober reason" for Mapple's action; "it must symbolize something unseen." "Can it be," Ishmael asks, "that by that act of physical isolation, he signifies his spiritual withdrawal for the time, from all outward worldly ties and connexions?"[10] So too does "Directive" emphasize that the journey is a solitary one, an act in which one loses one's self (Thoreau's advice) in order to find one's self.[11]

There are two published versions of "Closed for Good." The shorter version, which omits the original's first and last stanzas, was collected in *In the Clearing* in 1962. The longer one, from the *Complete Poems of Robert Frost 1949*, was revived in Frost's last public readings. (In July 1962, at Breadloaf, he explained, the original first stanza "ought to be back in," and "that's the way that's going to be."[12]) Thus the longer version of "Closed for Good" opens: "Much as I own I owe / The passers of the past / Because their to and fro," and continues, "Has cut this road to last, / I owe them more today / Because they've gone away."[13] When he read the longer version of the poem in 1956, he prefaced his reading with some personal information. "I live on a road closed for good," he stressed. "Behind me, nothing, up the mountains, into Canada, nothing but Canada, I might say."[14] It is this remark that reveals how "Closed for Good" relates to Carlton's poem "The Land of Canada."

> When I was young my grandame told
> Of a land called Canada,
> And then I thought that lovely land
> Lay far and far away.
>
> When I a little older grew
> My father took me there,

2. All Legends Are Local

> And then I thought there was no land
> That with it could compare.
>
> But still the land seemed far away
> To one who yet was young,
> And feared she ne'er again would see
> Those woods where wild birds sung.
>
> But now I know that Canada
> Lay very near at hand,
> As oft lie blessings in our lives
> When we do not understand.

In a footnote to "The Land of Canada," Carlton provides information that clarifies her reference to Canada at the same time as it sheds light on Frost's poem: "The section of Londonderry known as Bartley Hill in District No. 8 was formerly called Canada."[15]

There is good reason, at this point, to summon Emerson, who in the poem "Hamatreya" names the no longer illustrious dead to illustrate the "all is vanity" theme of Ecclesiastes. He calls in vain for Bulkeley, Hunt, Willard, Hosmer, Meriam, and Flint, all farmers who once "possessed" the land that now possesses them.

> Where are these men? Asleep beneath their grounds:
> And strangers, fond as they, their furrows plough.
> Earth laughs in flowers, to see her boastful boys
> Earth-proud, proud of the earth which is not theirs;
> Who steer the plough, but cannot steer their feet
> Clear of the grave.[16]

It is cold comfort, indeed, to know that that "hot owner" who annexed land to his farm, "add[ing] ridge to valley, brook to pond," thinking "that's my park," adds "Death ... to his land, a lump of mold the more." Carlton also names the notable figures of local history, but for nostalgic, patriotic reasons her naming sparkles with brightness and pride. Frost refers to past inhabitants but flatly; they remain unnamed, generic. Neither the chiding preacher of Ecclesiastes nor the public sage of Concord, Frost also rejects Carlton's boosterism. At all costs, contamination must be avoided. "There must be something coming from your mind to protect it from infection. A source cant be contaminated."[17]

What is salutary is that a strong mind will protect against contamination, Frost insists. Unlike the paintings of Andrew Wyeth, and all those others who have featured what has been called the American "vernacular ruin," Frost's "Directive" presents no such scene.[18] The poem does not fulfill its implied promise, to take us back to "a house that is no more a house / Upon a farm that is no more a farm / And in a town that is no more a town." The point is, you can't go there; if you think you can (in your unquenchable appetite for the "vernacular ruin"), you are fooling yourself. Nostalgia longs to make the past meaningful to the present. But nostalgia is poisonous to those who would begin anew, to those who would drink from the source to refresh themselves. *Use the goblet, lose the child.* "All that is human must retrograde if it do not advance," wrote Gibbon. But even so, it will not advance indefinitely, this being the Gospel, according to Robert Frost.

Different in intention and uneven in aesthetic achievement, the poems of Lucinda Carlton, T. S. Eliot, and Robert Frost are similarly concerned with notions of history and its uses. The recourse reluctantly offered in Eliot's "Wasteland" is to shore up fragments against the ruins of history. Carlton less ambitiously commemorates persons, places, and events of a parochial past in danger of being forgotten. Adapting aspects of Eliot's poetry and incorporating elements of Carlton's, Frost issues in "Directive" a guide, to be interpreted figuratively, on how to journey back through history and geology toward spiritual regeneration.

3

The Poet's Facts

Whether or not he "was carried out screaming" from San Francisco at the age of ten, as he claimed when put on the spot by "a very high official in California," the well-known fact is that Robert Frost's early upbringing did not take place in rural New England.[1] He was born in San Francisco and attended his first schools in that wild and loose place, and when, after his father's death, he was brought to New England to live, the New England he was brought to was not that of the farms and woods of New Hampshire or Vermont but that other New England of the mills and tenement houses. It was to Lawrence, Massachusetts, where his education carried him through high school, and where he worked in the city's sprawling factories. As Frost said in a talk at Haverford College in 1937, "I was brought up in a family who had just come to the industrial city of Lawrence, Massachusetts. My grandfather was an overseer in the Pacific Mills. They had just come to the city from Kingston, New Hampshire, up by Exeter."[2] Not until his marriage, in fact, did the poet whose name would in time become synonymous with rural and rustic New England turn to farming as a possible way to earn his living for himself and his family. It is no wonder that as late as 1930 Frost confessed, only half-jokingly, to his "masquerade as a Vermonter."[3]

It cannot be affirmed that Frost chose to be a farmer primarily because he expected farming to provide him with poetic images, metaphors, and subject matter, but he did sometimes act as if his sole interest lay in heeding Emerson's advice in the essay "Resources."

> The first care of a man settling in the country should be to open the face of the earth to himself by a little knowledge of Nature, or a great deal, if he can; of birds, plants, rocks, astronomy; in short, the art of taking a walk. This will draw the sting out of frost, dreariness out of November and March, and the drowsiness out of August.... But the uses of the woods are many, and some of them for the scholar high and peremptory. When his

task requires the wiping out from memory "all trivial fond records / That youth and observation copied there," he must leave the house, the streets and the club, and go to wooded uplands, to the clearing and the old brook. Well for him if he can say with the old minstrel, "I know where to find a new song."[4]

Yet inasmuch as Frost began learning about the fields and the woods rather late in life for such education (and he extolled the virtues of being "versed in country things"), he found himself struggling to catch up.

Not the least of his tasks was to learn about the fauna and flora of northern New England. His friend Carl Burrell taught him about the flowers and birds (as well as the stars), but the poet could not absorb everything all at once, and naturally he made mistakes. He did not know as much about geese as he pretended to know, he got flowers and flowering dates mixed up, and he took a flier on the behavior of spiders and moths and got a detail wrong. Yet this poet loved facts and had an unswerving commitment to getting things down accurately. It is all the more instructive, then, to look at some of these mistakes.

But first, to set the proper tone and to provide some sense of the poet's own ethical and aesthetic stance on the matters of accuracy and facts, let me quote a few of the things Frost said about the poet's way with facts. To the critic Edward Garnett, he explained: "They [the English reviewers] get some fun out of calling me a realist, and a realist I may be if by that they mean one who before all else wants the story to sound as if it were told the way it is because it happened that way. Of course the story must release an idea, but that is a matter of touch and emphasis, the almost incredible freedom of the soul enslaved to the hard facts of experience."[5] In an early interview that makes much of his poem "The Axe-Helve," he says: "But people say to me: 'The facts themselves aren't enough. You've got to do something to them, haven't you? They can't be poetical unless a poet handles them.' To that I have a very simple answer. It's this: anything you do to the facts falsifies them, but anything the facts do to you—yes, even against your will; yes, resist them with all your strength—transforms them into poetry."[6] And finally his friend Sidney Cox quotes Frost as follows: "A poet must lean hard on facts, so hard, sometimes, they hurt."[7]

While farming in Derry, New Hampshire, when he was in his late twenties, Frost tried his hand at writing prose pieces—stories, essays, reports—for some New England poultry journals. In one of his last contributions (there were eleven in all) he got himself into hot water with the farmers who read *Farm Poultry* by engaging in a boast totally based on some wrong information on the roosting habits of geese. "Mr. Hall's geese," he claimed, "roost in the trees even in winter."[8] Frost's authoritative claim called forth expressions of utter disbelief from readers, the first from an old hand, who struck what became the typical Yankee note of these complaints: "Will you kindly inform me through your next issue what kind of geese Mr. Hall has that Mr. R. L. Frost speaks of in your issue of Dec. 15th? According to Mr. Frost these geese roost in the trees even in the winter time. Now I am 45 years old and have been among geese all my life time, and I can never remember seeing a goose in a tree. I thought if I could get a breed of that kind I could dispense with coops."[9] This letter, along with others voicing similar complaints, moved Frost to an answer—a joking answer in which he hoped to get himself out of his predicament. But he compounded his error when he insisted, after admitting that it was hens that roosted in trees, that his friend Hall's geese at least chose to winter outdoors. This time the editor of the journal himself corrected Frost by pointing out that "geese generally remain out of doors by choice practically all the time."[10] But the young poet who within a decade would publish *North of Boston* chose to answer his detractors one last time, not in his own voice this time but in that of his friend John Hall, who was the subject of the original offending piece. Frost at last squirmed out of the difficulty with wit and some charm, but what is notable about the affair is that he would not come right out and admit to his error in the same pages in which he had appeared as a knowledgeable poultry man. It was an early sign that in a pinch about the "truth," when he got his facts wrong, he was not beyond resorting to deviousness. Only after the passing of several years would he admit his mistake in the matter. To his friend John T. Bartlett, he admonished: "You mustn't fake articles any more.... I'll tell you why.... I wrote up one or two poultrymen ... filling in the gaps in my knowledge with dream material. I think I managed fairly well except for the time I spoke of John Hall's geese roosting in the trees. I should have let geese severely alone. It took an artistic letter from John Hall himself (I wrote it for the douce man) to save me from the scandal that started."[11]

The mistake Frost made about the flower he first called the orchis never brought him much if any attention. What he did about his mistake when he discovered it (for himself apparently), however, deserves notice. The poem we now know as "The Quest of the Purple-Fringed" was originally entitled "The Quest of the Orchis."[12] Frost, less versed in country things than he thought, had apparently mistaken the early-blooming gentian for the late-season orchis. He was probably following too closely Emerson's directions in "Woodnotes" about the "seer": who "as if by secret sight he knew / Where, in far fields, the orchis 'grew.'"[13] By 1942—that is, forty years later—when he reprinted the poem in *A Witness Tree*, he had discovered his mistake about the orchis and the gentian and corrected it silently. Rather than admitting his mistake outright, he chose not to correct it by revising his title to read "Gentian" instead of "Orchis" but by substituting the adjective "Purple-Fringed," which is appropriately descriptive both of one kind of orchis and the gentian.

Oddly, Frost's error was not detected by Susan Hayes Ward, the literary editor of *The Independent*, when she aided and abetted the poet in his error by holding up the poem's publication in 1901 until the end of June. She did this to give the "lines … a timely appearance"—as Lawrance Thompson put it—"at exactly the moment in spring when the purple-fringed orchis should be in bloom."[14] The title Frost had given his poem supported her decision, of course, but the text did not. What his editor failed to notice was that the speaker of Frost's poem presents himself as having been in quest of this hard-to-find flower, not in late spring, but in summer; and that having found the flower he has been searching for, he mistakenly identifies it as an orchis. He then, having arisen and "silently wandered home," he reports conclusively: "And I for one / Said that the fall might come and whirl of leaves, / For summer was done."[15] Summer's end is not the time to set out in quest of the purple-fringed orchis, but it is the right time to search out the purple-fringed gentian.

Some of the differences between the orchis and the gentian are spelled out in Mrs. William Starr Dana's *How to Know the Wild Flowers*, Frost's acknowledged guide to the subject in the 1890s.[16] Of the purple-fringed orchis, the poet read in Mrs. Dana's account: "We should search the wet meadows in early June if we wish to be surely in time for the larger of the purple-fringed orchises."[17] Of the fringed gentian, on the other hand, he undoubtedly read:

> In late September, when we have almost ceased to hope for new flowers, we are in luck if we chance upon this [to quote William Cullen Bryant] "—blossom bright with autumn dew," whose "—sweet and quiet eye / Looks through its fringes to the sky. / Blue—blue—as if that sky let fall / A flower from its cerulean wall"; for the gentian is fickle in its habits, and the fact that we have located it one season does not mean that we will find it in the same place the following year; being a biennial, with seeds that are easily washed away, it is apt to change its haunts from time to time.[18]

Frost's unexplained tampering with his poem's title confused Lawrance Thompson. In 1966, attempting to complete Frost's later title, he harked back to the earlier one: "The Quest of the Purple-fringed [Orchis]."[19]

3. The Poet's Facts

But three years later, commenting on his daughter Leslie's liking for the gentian, Thompson suggested that her choice may have been influenced by her father, whose "favorite member of the gentian family inspired one of his early poems entitled 'The Quest of the Purple-fringed [Gentian].'"[20]

A third and last example of Frost's not getting his facts entirely straight occurs in the canonical poem "Design." I would not quarrel with Reginald Cook, whose view typifies that of most readers of the poem, when he assumes that "Design" had its basis in personal observation. "One day Frost found a fat *white* spider on a *white* heal-all (*Prunella vulgaris*) holding up a *white* moth, and speculated inquisitorially," writes Cook.[21] But Frost did more than speculate, for actually the poem offers us a significant example of the poet's inventing a detail in a putatively "observed" incident and getting that detail wrong.

> I found a dimpled spider, fat and white.
> On a white heal-all, holding up a moth
> Like a white piece of rigid satin cloth—
> Assorted characters of death and blight
> Mixed ready to begin the morning right.
> Like the ingredients of a witches' broth—
> A snow-drop spider, a flower like a froth,
> And dead wings carried like a paper kite.
> What had that flower to do with being white,
> The wayside blue and innocent heal-all?
> What brought the kindred spider to that height,
> Then steered the white moth thither in the night?
> What but the design of darkness to appall?—
> If design governs in a thing so small [275].[22]

There is no gainsaying the brilliance of Frost's achievement in this poem. Yet one of its salient observations calls the poem's accuracy into doubt. It does not square with the known entomological facts about spiders. J. Henri Fabre wrote extensively about what he called "the spider's designs."[23] And it was in 1912, coincidentally the year Frost wrote the early version of "Design" ("In White"), that there appeared in English translation a selection of Fabre's essays published as *The Life of the Spider*. Of use in a consideration of Frost's "In White" and "Design" is Fabre's account of the way the Spider handles "an average head of game, a Moth or Fly of some sort" after it has been caught in her web:

> Warned by the shaking of the net, the Epeira [spider] hastens up; she turns round about the quarry; she inspects it at a distance, so as to ascertain the extent of the danger before attacking. The strength of the snareling

will decide the plan of campaign. Let us first suppose the usual case, that of an average head of game, a Moth or Fly of some sort. Facing her prisoner, the Spider contracts her abdomen slightly and touches the insect for a moment with the end of her spinnerets; then, with her front tarsi, she sets her victim spinning....

What is the object of this circular motion? See, the brief contact of the spinnerets has given a starting-point for a thread, which the Spider must now draw from her silk-warehouse and gradually roll around the captive, so as to swathe him in a winding-sheet which will overpower any effort made....

Be it feeble or strong, the game is now neatly trussed, by one of the two methods. The next move never varies. The bound insect is bitten, without any persistency and without any wound that shows. The Spider next retires and allows the bite to act, which it soon does. She then returns.

If the victim be small, a Clothes-moth, for instance, it is consumed on the spot, at the place where it was captured. But, for a prize of some importance, on which she hopes to feast for many an hour, sometimes for many a day, the Spider needs a sequestered dining-room, where there is naught to fear from the stickiness of the network. Before going to it, she first makes her prey turn in the converse direction to that of the original rotation. Her object is to free the nearest spokes, which supplied pivots for the machinery. They are essential factors which it behooves her to keep intact, if need be by sacrificing a few cross-bars.

It is done; the twisted ends are put back into position. The well-trussed game is at last removed from the web and fastened on behind with a thread. The Spider then marches in front and the load is trundled across the web and hoisted to the resting floor, which is both an inspection-post and a dining-hall.[24]

When the details of Frost's poem (either version) are measured against Fabre's standard account of the way a spider does deal with such small game as a moth, we come up against some large discrepancies. The descriptions of the operations whereby the spider spins a tight winding-sheet around its prey before removing it from the web and transporting it to its "dining-hall" impugns the probability (at least) of the image of the Moth in "In White" in which it is "carried like a paper kite."[25] In addition, there is in the spider's rather random, and catch-as-catch-can capture of a moth, no hint of any mystery of the kind projected in Frost's portentous questions suggesting an overall "design" in the conjunction of such all-white things: "snow-drop" spider, "white" flower, and "white" moth.

Of course, when Fabre talks of the "Spider's design" he means to consider only the design(s) inherent in the spider's instinctive operations in building a web and hunting, killing, and eating its prey. Frost, on the other hand, would talk of the "design" not only behind the spider's operations but in the entire spatial and temporal context of the little assassination of moth by spider he would convince the reader he has witnessed. It is doubtful that Fabre, for one, would have believed him. Perhaps Frost could not keep himself from stacking the cards both to enhance the uncanny circumstances of the murderous encounter between arachnid and insect and to strengthen his case against those philosophers and theologians who would sponsor and promote notions of the benevolence of the Creator by evoking the standard argument from design.

By now, even I will ask the question. What does it matter, after all, if the core of the poem is sound and the meaning basically intact, that the poet got a fact wrong, contrived a detail, or invented an observation? It matters because it mattered to Robert Frost. Once he was asked if he ever thought about rewards—for himself, for others. His answer was that the greatest reward was clearly self-esteem, and that, rather than depending upon gaining the approval of society, he knew that he had to take the poet's "responsibility of deciding when the world was wrong."[26] Yet the artist, he continued, "can't help wishing there was some third more disinterested party, such as God, or Time, to give absolute judgment."[27] The artist in him longed for the kind of judgment available to others, say the scientist or the engineer. The advantage in this matter of judgment and "approval" seemed to be all on their side. "The scientist seems to have the advantage of him [the artist] in a court of larger appeal. A planet is perturbed in its orbit. The scientist stakes his reputation on the perturber's being found at a certain point in the sky at a certain time of night. All telescopes are turned that way, and sure enough, there the perturber is as bright as a button. The scientist knows he is good without being told." For the scientist has "a mind and he has instruments, the extensions of mind that fit closely into the nature of the Universe." "It is the same when an engineer has plotted two shafts to meet under the middle of a mountain and make a tunnel. The shafts approach each other; the workmen in one can hear the pickaxes of the workmen in the other. A sudden gleam of pickaxe breaks through. A human face shows in the face of the rock. The engineer is justified of his figures. He knows he has a mind. It has fitted into the nature of the Universe."[28] Partly because he believed it and partly because the occasion for those remarks was the ceremony in which he accepted a gold medal from the Institute of Arts and Letters, Frost does go on to concede that the artist's hope is "that his work will prove to have fitted into the nature of people."[29]

But a part of him was not satisfied with that kind of judgment—it was really no more than "the approval of society"—for his self-esteem required that he be right in the same way that the scientist and engineer could be right. The poet could notice things and get them down accurately. He admired Thoreau for this trait above all. "The most noticing man that ever lived maybe was Thoreau, wasn't he?" Frost asked; "He noticed some things wrong, they like to point out. But he was a very noticing man."[30] We have come a long way in our understanding of Thoreau's genius since Mark Van Doren many years ago decided that the rising impulse in Thoreau to notice and observe and, above all, measure (that is to say, his impulse to be "scientific") diminished him as a poet. Frost would not have tolerated Van Doren's notion for a minute, I suspect. For it was the scientific impulse wedded to the act of artistic creation that impelled Frost to see accuracy in what he said as well as fact in what he observed. Over the decades he became less and less subject to the temptation to "fill the gaps" in his knowledge with "dream material" as he had in his story about geese roosting in trees. If, as he said in "Mowing," "the fact is the sweetest dream that labor knows" (26), the labor was worth the effort it took to get things down accurately. Moreover, they must remain accurate. It was the poet's responsibility to verify his facts. Long after "Birches" was published and certainly long after he could with impunity change anything in that poem, the poet was still checking out his facts. Once, before reciting the poem in public, he confessed tellingly: "I never go down the shoreline [from Boston] to New York without watching the birches to see if they live up to what I say about them in the poem."[31] Reginald Cook, to whom we are indebted for this notation of Frost's speech, goes on to say, "Invariably the listener laughed, but on the double take he realized that Frost, the careful craftsman, was confirming his assertion that birches bend left and right *by verification*. Getting details right was a telling responsibility."[32] But it was even more than just a responsibility to his craft. Seeing those birches bent in the right way, that is to say, in the way the poet of "Birches" said they were bent, was a verification for Frost tantamount to the scientist's verification when he accurately predicts the perturbed planet's appearance at a "certain point in the sky at a certain time of night" and the engineer's confirmation when the workman's "sudden gleam of pickaxe breaks through" to make the tunnel.

Frost could have said, with Emerson, that it is "a forgotten maxim that 'accuracy is essential to beauty,'"[33] adding "and essential to truth, as well." It was the standard to which he held himself, even though, like every other mortal being, he could not always measure up.

4

His Metaphysical Sonnet

Published rather inauspiciously in the same year that saw the appearance of Eliot's "The Wasteland," Robert Frost's sonnet has wonderfully ridden out the long years. Its reputation has so grown that the poem now flourishes fully apace with its lengthy rival as one of the century's most explosive poetic statements on the metaphysics of darkness.[1] Indeed, historically "Design" can be located rightfully somewhere between the visionary expanse of "The Wasteland" and the mind-stretching speculations of Herman Melville's chapter on "The Whiteness of the Whale" in *Moby-Dick*, a book whose "rediscovery" came several years after Frost had independently examined the poetic-philosophical relationship between metaphors of whiteness and the idea of cosmic design. In paradigm, "Design" expresses those perplexing fears spawned and scattered by evidence which indicates that (1) human existence continues without supportive design and ultimate purpose, or (2) human existence is subject to a design of unmitigated natural evil. The details of the poem appear to sustain these complementary readings without choosing between them.

No student of Frost's poetry can afford to ignore the implications of "Design." For one thing, it is one of those rare poems, archetypal of the entire oeuvre of a poet, which in brief compass offers a valuable key to a poet's richness and reach. Although it would be rash to insist that "Design" answers all the important questions about Frost's thought overall, it is equally true that to ignore this key to the truths of the poet's inner being would be most unfortunate.

"Design" is Frost's most carefully shaped investigation of the darker implications of the classical argument from design. The poem did not spring fully formed from a single bout with the Muse. The manuscript evidence bespeaks the contrary. In 1912, apparently to get the poem on record as well as to try it on a sympathetic reader, Frost forwarded an early version to an old friend, calling it a sonnet for his "'Moth and Butterfly' book."[2] Although he did not choose to publish that early version, the manuscript copy preserved in the Susan Hayes Ward papers enables us to trace Frost's philosophical-aesthetic development as he reworked his poem and rethought his ideas over a period of ten years.

Frost's extant manuscript version bears a title, "In White," which though it indicates the poem's principal image and motif, does not have the thematic resonance of the simpler and more title, "Design."[3] A more explicit title for the final version of the poem, but a far less effective one, it strikes me, would combine the two. "Design in White," a melded title, arty and somewhat arch, would compromise Frost's theme. Rather, concerned with any and all designs which would foster poetic and philosophic resonance, Frost revised his poem in the direction of line-by-line concision and toward making each image appropriate and every word totally functional.

The 1912 manuscript version ("In White"), collected only after the poet's death, reads in its entirety:

A dented spider like a snow drop white	(1)
On a white Heal-all, holding up a moth	(2)
Like a white piece of lifeless satin cloth—	(3)
Saw ever curious eye so strange a sight?—	(4)
Portent in little, assorted death and blight	(5)
Like the ingredients of a witches' broth?—	(6)
The beady spider, the flower like a froth,	(7)
And the moth carried like a paper kite.	(8)
What had that flower to do with being white,	(9)
The blue prunella every child's delight.	(10)
What brought the kindred spider to that height?	(11)
(Make we no thesis of the miller's plight.)	(12)
What but design of darkness and of night?	(13)
Design, design! Do I use the word aright?[4]	(14)

This early version of the poem is to be compared with the final version published first in an early miscellany, and later gathered in *A Further Range* (1936), Frost's sixth volume.

I found a dimpled spider, fat and white,	(1)
On a white heal-all, holding up a moth	(2)
Like a white piece of rigid satin cloth—	(3)
Assorted characters of death and blight	(4)
Mixed ready to begin the morning right,	(5)
Like the ingredients of a witches' broth—	(6)
A snow-drop spider, a flower like a froth,	(7)
And dead wings carried like a paper kite.	(8)

4. His Metaphysical Sonnet 51

> What had that flower to do with being white, (9)
> The wayside blue and innocent heal-all? (10)
> What brought the kindred spider to that height, (11)
> Then steered the white moth thither in the night? (12)
> What but design of darkness to appall?— (13)
> If design govern in a thing so small [275].[5] (14)

Frost's revisions turn the poem to narrative and away from naked lyric, thereby enhancing the mystery which surrounds the incident he wishes to describe. In removing his personal experience to the past, the poet is able to suggest as well that he has been brooding on the meaning of the tableau of spider, moth and ritual death which he has observed, even though he has failed to come to a conclusive answer (at least for himself) on the question of design. The introduction of the poet's personal voice (as subject) into the first line, moreover, turns the spider into the object of sight and contemplation. It gives the poet more prominence than he had in the manuscript version, which begins with a sentence fragment (no verb) in apposition to the noun "sight" in the fourth line.

There is not much that survives intact from one version of the poem to the other. Notably, only the ninth line of the early version—"What had that flower to do with being white"—survives without change in "Design." Lines two, six and eleven are largely repeated, with changes only in capitalization or line-end punctuation. The remaining ten lines, however, offer substantive changes, which must be taken up line by line.

The simile in the first line, "A dented spider like a snow drop white," which is purely and neutrally descriptive, disappears along with another descriptive word "dented." In their place Frost offers adjectives: "dimpled," "fat," and "white." The first two are unexpectedly appropriate to this murderous spider. Cannily placed in the poem, these terms are normally far more appropriate to a baby than an insect. So, replacing neutrally descriptive terms by terms that normally would seek another context and would offer a different sentiment, Frost both announces his theme and reveals that his approach is basically ironic. In line three the moth, described "Like a white piece of lifeless cloth—" becomes "rigid satin cloth." "Lifeless" is only vaguely descriptive of the moth's state; but it is not at all accurately descriptive of the tableau of the spider holding up the moth. The moth may in fact be "lifeless," but the poem is more accurately descriptive in comparing the moth to "rigid" cloth. Hovering over this image is the hint of rigor mortis and that satin fabric that customarily lines the inside of coffins.[6]

Line four in the manuscript version is rather limp, lifeless. The semirhetorical question "Saw ever curious eye so strange a sight?" seriously deflects the central argument of the poem. In the final version Frost moves the second half of the original fifth line, "assorted death and blight," up to line four, and extends it to "Assorted characters of death and blight," thereby introducing the important metaphor of kitchen domesticity that he will pursue through line seven. So, too, does he decide to drop the first phrase of line five ("Portent in little"), this time, I would suggest, because "portent" strikes us as too potent a word for the poem at this point. Line six stays almost intact, except that it no longer asks a question. Indeed, the two questions which dominate the octave in the manuscript version are strategically dropped, so that the only questions come in the sestet closing the poem. Lines four through seven are intended, then, to suggest kitchens, cakes and cookies ("Assorted," "ingredients," and " Mixed ready")—all as if drummed up by advertisers "to begin the morning right." The only sour note is that the whole thing resembles "the ingredients of a witches' broth." Still, it is *broth* and not *brew* (as we might expect in everyday witchcraft); *broth* echoes closely the culinary metaphor.

The single change in line seven turns "beady spider" into "snow-drop spider," picking up the adjective which Frost had discarded from his original first line. At this point the earlier poem was still fundamentally descriptive, but something was needed, apparently, to keep the idea of coldness and death before us. "Snow-drop" accomplishes this. "Beady," however, does something else. The word, less than precisely descriptive, is morally loaded. A seemingly less neutral word would keep the poem from becoming at all moralistic. In the last line of the octave "moth" turns into "dead wings," but the simile "like a paper kite" is happily retained. The simile carries us back to the implicitly "childlike" description of the spider in the opening line. "Dead wings," on the other hand, moves toward precision, for it is not the "moth" in its entirety that looks like "a paper kite"; it is only its "dead wings." Furthermore, both "wings" and "kite" suggest the idea of flight; the image of white "dead wings" moves toward paradox.

The ninth line ("What had that flower to do with being white") is retained intact. That much about his basic poem Frost had been sure of all along. But if the appositive clause which constitutes the tenth line ("The blue prunella every child's delight") adds the new information that the heal-all is also known as the prunella, it nevertheless adds nothing to the argument of the poem. Indeed, because the content of the lines is not at all functional other than as a bit of information, it can do no more than disrupt the poem's discourse. On the other hand, repeating the fact that it is a "heal-all" despite its not being blue (as are most heal-alls) pushes the argument a step further. The next line is substantially the same. But the twelfth line of the manuscript version is dropped completely, and fittingly so. "(Make we no thesis of the miller's plight)" is wasteful and repetitive, seeming to exist only for the final word ("plight") which maintains the pattern of the same end rhyme throughout the six lines of the sestet. In replacing the entire line, Frost chooses to deepen the question that he asks about the tableau he has witnessed. Not only does he ask, "What brought the kindred spider to that height," but also what "Then *steered* the *white* moth thither in the *night*?" (italics added). What power, then, actually "steered" the moth (white) in the darkness of "night" to a heal-all which is preternaturally "white"? Rather than the somewhat disingenuous admonition that avoids making a thesis out of this tableau, Frost chooses to extend the mystery of the "witches' broth" that he has cautiously witnessed.[7]

In the penultimate line of the poem the first five words are retained ("What but design of darkness"), but the last three words ("and of night") are revised: "to appall?" In the original, "of night" merely repeats the idea in the phrase "of darkness." There is a relatively pointless, if harmless, repetition of meaning. But the phrase "darkness to appall" suggests the appalling effect that the close conjunction of two ideas—"darkness" and "design"—might well have. Moreover, "appall" is a particularly suitable word, in that it suggests both a specific color or the lack of color (pallor) and death (pall).

Because it, too, is inconclusive and somewhat wasteful, the last line of the manuscript poem gives way to a conditional clause in the final version. "Design, design! Do I use the word aright?" is crudely rhythmic, but the simple device of ending a poem with a disingenuous question does little toward formally resolving the poem. On the other hand, to end the poem with the tentative clause "if design govern in a thing so small" offers thematic resolution even as it enhances poetic resonance. "Govern" develops from "steered," of course, which in turn grows out of "brought." The effect is cumulative.

Our conclusion is that a comparison of the earlier definitive versions of "Design" helps to define the poet's final intention. It remained fundamentally consistent. From version to version Frost worked towards a clarification of his idea that the philosophical argument from design was endemically ironic. Another conclusion. Both the first published version of the poem (1922) and the manuscript version (1912) are in sonnet form. Despite internal revisions and the reshaping of several lines, the overall poetic form remained over the years. That the poem was conceived in the form of a sonnet, I would propose, is the poet's final irony, for the strict formal design which characterizes the sonnet apes and mimes the internal argument of the poem.[8] Does the same guiding power, the steering force, which works through the tableau of spider, moth and stylized death, work through the poetic process as well? After so much whiteness, have we experienced, after all, still another variant of that scriptural blackness of darkness that fascinated so many American writers, including Poe and Melville? These questions—good ones, I think—are no more rhetorical than the question that closes out Frost's sonnet.

5

An Occupation Gone

According to Robert Frost, a visitor once said that she understood that he was "many years deciding how to end 'The Death of the Hired Man.'" And she added that this fact was "in a book." But Frost denied the suggestion: "You know how stories get corrupted," he said, and then went on to retell it his way: "[T]here was a book I never read and a teacher I never had that did more for me than anybody else in the world. The book I never read was *Piers Plowman* and the teacher I never had was William James. And both of those acted on me. *Piers Plowman* acted on me this way. I always wanted to do something about the kind of American hired man, you know, that I'd lived with and worked with and been." But he did not know "just how to get it," he admitted. "I didn't have any definite idea about it. It was just a lingering sense about it. I thought that might be what *Piers Plowman* was and so I better let that alone for fear it would take the wind out of my sails. And I let it alone until I'd written, 'The Death of the Hired Man.' And then I read it and I needn't have worried. It's another thing entirely—satire and all that."[1]

It is a curious (and puckish) admission, that a book he had not read influenced the poem he did write, but one made in character. Admitting influence in this way could serve him by deflecting attention away from another text that might have influenced him; namely, an essay entitled "The Hired Man," which appeared in the *Atlantic Monthly* in 1894, just about the time that Frost was beginning to look to magazines of national circulation as possible outlets for his poetry.[2]

This anonymous piece portrays the New England Hired Man (already lamented as having passed from the scene) in ways that foreshadow Frost's own quite different portrait of the type in two long narrative poems that he would publish in *North of Boston* in 1914—"The Death of the Hired Hand" and "The Code."

There are several ways "The Death of the Hired Man" has affinities with the *Atlantic* account. The essay, for instance, presents a genesis of the Hired Man: "In primitive New England, farmers hired men to assist them only in particular seasons, especially at haying time." Later, "in the larger towns, as business and wealth increased, it became the custom for well-to-do persons, such as the lawyer, the doctor, the gentleman of leisure (not unknown fifty or even one hundred years ago), to have a Hired Man to do the chores" (283–84). The duties of this Hired Man were

> to milk the cow, to take care of the horse or horses, to wash the carriage, to saw and split all the wood used by the family, to feed the pig and hens, to shovel snow in winter, to raise vegetables and flowers, to cut the acre or two of grass appurtenant to the house, to drive boys out of the apple orchard, to weed the paths, to mend the fences, to "tinker" the various tools and household utensils used on the premises, to beat carpets, to wash windows, to act as coachman on Sundays and at funerals, and, finally, to educate and bring up all the children of the family [284].

Perhaps this description recalls more closely Stephen Crane's Henry Johnson, retained by Dr. Trescott in "The Monster," than it does Silas, who has returned to Warren and Mary's farm, in Frost's poem. There are enough touches here—milking, cutting wood, apple orchards, mending fences—to suggest Frost's poetry. Nonetheless, it is a touch like that of the Hired Man's having a roll in educating the young that brings the *Atlantic* account and Frost's poem into close alignment. The unnamed author of "The Hired Man" offers his credentials for recording the Hired Man's traits: "I have a special knowledge of the subject. I was brought up, in no small measure, by a Hired Man; I have summered and wintered with him; from him, largely, I imbibed the tastes and principles which have inspired and guided me through life..." (283). In "The Death of the Hired Man" Frost, who was once and always a teacher, makes the point that what bothers Silas most in his final hours is that he did not succeed in teaching the "young [Harold] Wilson" such things as how to build a load of hay or in persuading him that he was adept at water witching. Silas would like one more chance to teach the young boy (who, Silas finds it hard to believe, studies "Latin like the violin / Because he liked it") how "to build a load of hay" (42). He would teach him the secret of what even Warren admits is "Silas' one accomplishment." "He bundles every forkful in its place, / And tags and numbers it for future reference, / So he can find and easily dislodge it" (43) when unloading. "He takes it out in bunches like big birds' nests. / You never see him standing on the hay / He's trying to lift, straining to lift himself." (43) And then, in lines conveying sentiments close to the poet's own, Mary concludes: "He thinks if he could teach him that, he'd be / Some good perhaps to someone in the world. / He hates to see a boy the fool of books" (43). She looks on with pity for "Poor Silas, so concerned for other folk, / And nothing to look backward to with pride, / And nothing to look forward to with hope" (43). Is not Silas' fear analogous to that of the poet who would teach what he knows, but who might at the end find himself without pride or hope?

The author of the *Atlantic* account of the passing of the hired man presents one other piece of information about him that would make Silas an exception: "Hired Men commonly went away, not because they were dissatisfied or because they were dismissed, but on account of some change in their circumstances" (286). Frost's hired man not only leaves because he is dissatisfied but he commits the farmer's unpardonable sin, moreover, of leaving during haying time. That desertion is the cause of Warren's principal complaint. To Mary's request that he "be kind," he replies: "'When was I ever anything but kind to him? / But I'll not have the fellow back,' he said. / 'I told him so last haying, didn't I?" (40). Moreover, "What good is he? Who else will harbor him / At his age for the little he can do?" Warren continues: "I shouldn't mind his bettering himself / If that was what it was" (40–41). The problem is that "when he begins like that, there's someone at him / Trying to coax him off with pocket-money— / In haying time, when any help is scarce" (41). And then, "in winter he comes back to us. I'm done'" (41). Certainly Silas, whatever his character, is not at all like the Irishman singled out in the *Atlantic* account as "a type of the Hired Man," whom the writer extols rather superficially "for his fidelity, for his good nature, and lastly for a certain raciness of character. A friend as well as an employee..." (286).

The pleasing picture of the type painted by the writer in the *Atlantic* contrasts sharply with the portrayal of Silas, coming "home" to die. In Frost's poem the Hired Man has come, pathetically, to his end, but in the generalized figure presented in the *Atlantic* article the Hired Man prospers and when he does not it is because some misfortune or other has befallen him.

It was the poet's great fortune, of course, that his view of the Hired Man would not only prevail but would become widely disseminated. Indeed, the public's great familiarity with this much anthologized piece would in time become something of a burden to the poet. The great difficulty, as he saw it, was that the sentiments expressed in the poem by Warren and Mary (Silas, too, by indirection) were too readily taken to be the poet's own subjective "truths." "It would seem soft for instance to look in my life for the sentiments in the Death of the Hired Man," he complained to Sidney Cox. "There's nothing to it believe me. I should fool you if you took me so." The danger, he warned, was that in being "too subjective with what an artist has managed to make objective is to come on him presumptuously and render ungraceful what he in pain of his life had faith he had made graceful."[3] It is logical to surmise, therefore, that neither of the well-known definitions of "home" that have jumped out of the poem to enjoy a hearty life of their own expresses, at least not exactly, the author's own subjective sentiments. That is to say, each of the definitions of "Home" ("the place where, when you have to go there, / They have to take you in" and "Something you somehow haven't to deserve" [43]) is an objective statement. These statements are made to serve the overall drama of the situation depicted by being attributed to one of the two personages whose dialogue constitutes the heart and bulk of the poem. But Frost could not resist having it the other way, too. A given objective sentiment might also be subjective. At least that is one inference that can be drawn from his admission on another occasion: "In my 'Death of the Hired Man,' that I wrote years ago, there's this line: 'He hates to see a boy the fool of books.' It's interesting to see how country folks are sometimes wise without books."[4] Although it is presented indirectly, the sentiment Frost endorses is the one attributed to Silas, the Hired Man.

What the "town-bred farmer" in "The Code" (first published as "The Code—Heroics" in *Poetry* in 1914) does not know (presumably because the information is not in books) is that his farm-bred hired men possess a code defined in the lines—"The hand that knows his business won't be told / To do work better or faster— those two things" (72). They share as well an unspoken understanding that the wrong kind of talk or talk at the wrong time violates the code. The poem presents two such violations, one in the present-tense narrative and the other in the parable-like "story" told by the worker who stays behind after the other worker has walked away from the field where the three of them have been making hay. Discussion over the first troublesome incident leads to an imbedded narrative presentation of the earlier incident.

In the present-tense narrative we read, "Suddenly / One helper, thrusting pitchfork in the ground, / Marched himself off the field and home." "'What is there wrong?'" asks the farmer of the helper who stays behind. "'Something you just now said,'" is the answer. "'What did I say?'" he asks. "'About our taking pains,'" he is answered. "'To cock the hay?— because it's going to shower? / I said that more than half an hour ago,' adding: "I said it to myself as much as you," he says incredulously. The

5. An Occupation Gone

worker explains that James, "one big fool," "thought you meant to find fault with his work. / That's what the average farmer would have meant." But James "would take time, of course, to chew it over / Before he acted: he's just got round to act" (71). The helper would have done the same, he reveals, except that he knows that the "town-bred farmer" doesn't, as he puts it, "understand our ways" (72). The helper then tells a story about himself and an old boss named Sanders that no one liked. The boss was himself a hard worker, the helper will not deny, one for whom, as far as work was concerned, "daylight and lantern-light were one." But his problem was that he was full of "bulling tricks": "Them that he couldn't lead he'd get behind / And drive, the way you can, you know, in mowing— / Keep at their heels and threaten to mow their legs off" (72). Knowing this about his boss, the helper is keenly alert to any potential for "bulling" from that quarter.

> So when he paired off with me in the hay field
> To load the load, thinks I, Look out for trouble.
> I built the load and topped it off; old Sanders
> Combed it down with a rake and says, "O.K."
> Everything went well till we reached the barn
> With a big jag to empty in a bay....
> But the old fool seizes his fork in both hands,
> And looking up bewhiskered out of the pit,
> Shouts like an army captain, "Let her come!"
> Thinks I, D'ye meant it? "What was that you said?"
> I asked out loud, so's there'd be no mistake,
> "Did you say, Let her come?" "Yes, let her come."
> He said it over, but he said it softer.
> Never you say a thing like that to a man,
> Not if he values what he is. God, I'd as soon
> Murdered him as left out his middle name [72–73].

So far the helper's "story" serves as nothing more than an analogue for the "town-bred" farmer's violation of the code that has led to this "story" in the first place. But now it swerves away to tell in loving detail of the quite different outcome for Sanders, the "bulling" boss.

> I'd built the load and knew right where to find it.
> Two or three forkfuls I picked lightly round for
> Like meditating, and then I just dug in
> And dumped the rackful on him in ten lots.
> I looked over the side once in the dust
> And caught sight of him treading-water–like,
> Keeping his head above. "Damn ye," I says,

> "That gets ye!" He squeaked like a squeezed rat.
> That was the last I saw or heard of him.
> I cleaned the rack and drove out to cool off.
> As I sat mopping hayseed from my neck,
> And sort of waiting to be asked about it,
> One of the boys sings out, "Where's the old man?"
> "I left him in the barn under the hay.
> If ye want him, ye can go and dig him out" [73].

The other workers go straight to the barn, to look for the boss. They cannot find him, even considering perhaps (or so the guilty helper thinks) that he was "spiked ... in the temple" (73) before being buried under an avalanche of hay. But it turns out that he does not lie buried under the hay. Totally disgusted and humiliated, he now sits in the farmhouse kitchen "with both his feet / Against the stove, the hottest day that summer" (73). "He kept away from us all afternoon," says the helper. "We tended to his hay. We saw him out / After a while picking peas in his garden: / He couldn't keep away from doing something" (74).

Here ends the helper's narrative. Following it there is a short exchange between him and the farmer that concludes the poem:

> "Weren't you relieved to find he wasn't dead?"
> "No! and yet I don't know—it's hard to say.
> I went about to kill him fair enough."
> "You took an awkward way. Did he discharge you?"
> "Discharge me? No! He knew I did just right" [74].

The imbedded narrative of the poem—the helper's—may serve to educate the "town-bred farmer" as to the rules governing the Hired Man's code, to the way in which ill-advised speech can violate it, and to the potentially dire consequences to which such violation can lead. This parable-like narrative has designs as well on the reader. Like the French-Canadian farmer of "The Ax-Helve" and like Silas of "The Death of the Hired Man" (who prides himself on his ability to build a load of hay), each of these workers wants credit for "knowing his business." Denying them that credit can have serious consequences. "The Code" displays enough images of violence and potential murder to make the point. Not only does it occur to the helper, as we have seen, that the other workers might think that he has "spiked" the boss "in the temple," but the helper who walks away from the "town-bred farmer" announces his disgust by "thrusting" his "pitchfork in the ground." Significantly, the whole event (including the narrative involving Sanders) takes place under a sky in which "an irregular sun-bordered cloud / Darkly advanced with a perpetual dagger / Flickering across its bosom" (71). Surely, of the Hired Men in this poem, Frost could have as appropriately said, as he did of Silas (the line bears repeating): "It's interesting to see how country folks are sometimes wise without books."[5]

6

Adam's Curse

Frost fancied the notion that Nature in his adopted New England put forth its own annual analogy for the biblical Fall of Adam and Eve. Out of this fancy he created some of his most fetching poems, such as "Nothing Gold Can Stay," "The Oven Bird," and "After Apple-Picking."

First published in *North of Boston* in 1914, "After Apple-Picking" did not immediate catch on with critics or anthologists, garnering relatively little attention until it was singled out in 1938 for supplementary reading by Cleanth Brooks and Robert Penn Warren in *Understanding Poetry*, their "new critical" textbook-anthology.

> My long two-pointed ladder's sticking through a tree
> Toward heaven still,
> And there's a barrel that I didn't fill
> Beside it, and there may be two or three
> Apples I didn't pick upon some bough.
> But I am done with apple-picking now.
> Essence of winter sleep is on the night,
> The scent of apples: I am drowsing off.
> I cannot rub the strangeness from my sight
> I got from looking through a pane of glass
> I skimmed this morning from the drinking trough
> And held against the world of hoary grass.
> It melted, and I let it fall and break.
> But I was well
> Upon my way to sleep before it fell,
> And I could tell
> What form my dreaming was about to take.
> Magnified apples appear and disappear,
> Stem end and blossom end,
> And every fleck of russet showing clear.
> My instep arch not only keeps the ache,
> It keeps the pressure of a ladder-round.

6. Adam's Curse

>   I feel the ladder sway as the boughs bend.
>   And I keep hearing from the cellar bin
>   The rumbling sound
>   Of load on load of apples coming in.
>   For I have had too much
>   Of apple-picking: I am overtired
>   Of the great harvest I myself desired.
>   There were ten thousand thousand fruit to touch,
>   Cherish in hand, lift down, and not let fall.
>   For all
>   That struck the earth,
>   No matter if not bruised or spiked with stubble,
>   Went surely to the cider-apple heap
>   As of no worth.
>   One can see what will trouble
>   This sleep of mine, whatever sleep it is.
>   Were he not gone,
>   The woodchuck could say whether it's like his
>   Long sleep, as I describe its coming on,
>   Or just some human sleep [70–71].

In his guise as farmer the poet describes his worry over the "coming on" of sleep which will end his long day's labor.[1] For he knows that his meet and reward are troubled sleep and repetitive dreams, resulting directly from the daytime activity that has brought him the harvest and the "wealth" he covets. The remembered sensations of apple-picking will prevail in his sleep and will disturb his rest. In memory, but seemingly even stronger than memory, there will nag the "scent" of apples, the "sight" through the skimmed morning-ice, the "ache" and "pressure" on the instep arch, the "hearing" of the "rumbling" from the cellar bin. In sum, he knows not whether that sleep will be like the animal hibernation (the "long sleep") of the woodchuck, or, as the poet puts it ironically, "just some human sleep." It was the "ache" and the "pressure" on the instep arch that Joyce Carol Oates, who grew up on a farm in upstate New York, singled out in this poem. "This poem of surpassing beauty and melancholy had a particular significance for me," she writes, "since I did pick apples, pears, and cherries in my family's fruit orchard, standing on a ladder, though I was never allowed to climb as high as my father on his 'long two-pointed ladder.' I understood from experience how the poet's 'instep arch not only keeps the ache, / It keeps the pressure of a ladder-round.'"[2]

Apples have long been a huge enterprise in New England. During the years that Frost farmed in Derry, New Hampshire, beginning in 1900 and lasting until he moved his family to England in 1912, occupational journals directed at a clearly defined rural population, offered an abundance of news about kinds of apples, the size of annual harvests, and fluctuations in market prices. One such journal was the very successful and long-lasting *New-England Homestead*, published in Worcester, Massachusetts, but circulated throughout New England and parts of Canada. Each fall, it ran a story about the harvesting of apples, frequently illustrated with photographs of apple-pickers at work, some of them standing beside filled or half-filled baskets, the long ladders poking up through the tops of trees.[3] Among the journal's features was poetry, some of it reprinted from newspapers and other journals, but the larger portion of the poetry that appeared in its pages was original to the *Homestead*. If, from time to time, the *Homestead* chose to remind its readers, "The sleep of a laboring man is sweet," a bit of filler presented simply with no rubric or comment,[4] it ran poetry that elaborated on this comforting message from Ecclesiastes. One such poem is L. C. Seal's "The Sleep of the Laboring Man":

> The sleep of the laboring man is sweet!
> When the trudge of the day is o'er
> God measures to him the repose that's meet
> To rank with the toil before.
> The stars filter down from ethereal sheen,
> Through the shadowy watches of night,
> A shimmer of hopes that abide between
> His margins of daily light.
>
> The sleep of the laboring man is sweet!
> When the brain of the tradesman wakes,
> When the pulses of merriment throb and beat,
> No stir on his slumber breaks;
> The woof of his dream is the subtle blend
> The whisper of wind, the voice of a friend,
> And call of the night-bird near,
> Of the sounds which he last gave ear—.[5]

Equally relevant to Frost's "After Apple-Picking" is "The Curse," a *Homestead* poem proposing that the relationship between human "labor" and the flowers and "luscious fruit" it helps to produce is religious or mythic.

> God said, "Let thorns and briars spring up,
> For man has sinned. Let labor be a curse."
> But God's great heart of love could not content
> Itself with justice done. His mercy yearned
> O'er wretched man, so helpless in his fall.
> The briars, God made bloom and bear
> Sweet, fragrant flowers and luscious fruit,

6. Adam's Curse

> And labor, man's great primal curse, He made
> A blessing great, as he who labors with his hands has found.
> So great, that he who labors, finds
> Rich health, sweet peaceful rest, and grand content.
> And as each day, he tills the fertile soil,
> He feels, in every fiber of his being, God is good![6]

Linking the poets of "The Curse" and "After Apple-Picking" are their quite different takes on the notion that "he who labors, finds / Rich *health*, sweet *peaceful rest*, and *grand content*" (emphasis added). The cause-and-effect link between "labor" and "rest" is seen in "The Curse" as beneficial to the laborer, with the divine curse on humankind confirmed but only as a preliminary to God's choice to be merciful and provident. In Frost's poem, however, the apple-picker's labor has not brought on "rest" or "content" but "troubled sleep."

Taken simply with no suggestive extension, the country details of Frost's "After Apple-Picking" tell a story of work and fatigue, but those details are also in the service of another story: the mythic consequences of the Fall. If Eve's curse, after she tasted of the fruit of the forbidden tree, was that she would "bring forth children," Adam's curse, after joining Eve in the risk, was that he would live henceforth by the "sweat" of his "face," that is, his life would be sustained only by his own labor. The irony beyond this curse is Frost's subject. Adam's curse was to labor, but another way of putting it is that Adam and his descendants were doomed to live within, and at the mercy of, the senses. Significantly, Frost defines that curse still further: man will not cease to labor even in rest.

In the very desire to profit from his long hours of work, the poet has made himself vulnerable, in a wry sense, to the dictum that "the sleep of a labouring man is sweet, whether he eat little or much; but the abundance of the rich will not suffer him to sleep" (Ecclesiastes, 5: 12). The rub is that the poet is both laborer and "rich" man. He has the "great harvest" he desired; but he has labored long and arduously to bring in that harvest—certainly too long and possibly too faithfully to enable him to reap that reward of peaceful, untroubled rest promised to the diligent laborer.

In this sense the poem can be seen as an elaboration of Genesis: Adam's curse was not merely that his doom was henceforth to live by the "sweat" of his "face," but that the curse to labor would follow him into his rest and his dreams. Such, inevitably, is the way after apple-picking. And such is the paradox of Adam's curse, exemplified tellingly in the working-life of the poet-farmer of New England. Yet Joyce Carol Oates is equally justified in describing the poem's "powerful subtext" as "the inevitability of loss." While "in its understated way the poem is a tragic work of art," she adds, "yet there remains a defiant human resilience beneath, as in us all."[7]

Not surprisingly, when, in 1920, Frost moved to "a stone cottage on a hill at South Shaftsbury in southern Vermont on the New York side near the historic town of Bennington," he had a plan to plant apples. He told a friend that he would "plant a new Garden of Eden with a thousand apple trees of some unforbidden variety."[8]

7

The Passing Glimpse

"The time draws near for going to press and I must get as many editors as possible implicated in the book beforehand. Ain't I wily?" So wrote Robert Frost on October 15, 1935, to Louis Untermeyer, a friend and fellow-poet, one who also happened to be a reviewer, an editor, and an influential anthologist.[1] Vintage Frost, this statement emanates from his predictably mischievous, puckish, and deceptively businesslike self. Frost's relationship to Untermeyer, however, was hardly unique. It was anticipated by his early dealings with numerous editors, publishers and reviewers, Susan Hayes Ward of *The Independent*, for example, and William Stanley Braithwaite of the *Boston Evening Transcript*. A third example is Frost's complex, less-than-candid relationship with his fellow-poet and influential editor, Ridgely Torrence—a relationship neglected in Frost scholarship. It is the subject of this chapter.

Frost and Torrence had encountered each other's poetry in print years before they met. A late bloomer, Frost knew about Torrence and his work as early as 1906, and perhaps even earlier, while Torrence, an early success, first became aware of Frost's poetry perhaps as late as 1915, when he recommended it enthusiastically to Harriet Moody. On the first of December, that year, he wrote: "I don't know whether you are familiar with [Frost's] work or not. I am not well versed in it myself, but from the few things I have lately had I have conceived a large regard for his reality and power. His poetry has come to stay and must be attended to. I feel sure of that. There were three poems by him in the August *Atlantic* that impressed me greatly. One of them called *The Road Not Taken* quite carried me off my feet."[2] Only three months later, incidentally, Frost would write coyly to this new and powerful friend who had recently become poetry editor of the *New Republic*: "I am enclosing four poems, but you must reject two of them and may reject three or four.... I know you won't try too hard to like these poems. That would be not to give them a fair chance."[3]

It is not clear just when Torrence first met Frost, but it is known that not until March 1919 did they talk, in Torrence's words, "real heart to heart"; to Harriet Moody he wrote the next day that he had been "quite carried away" by Frost, concluding: "He is surely one of the finest things this country has produced. He is a man, a noble character in addition to being a noble poet...."[4] On the same evening Frost wrote, also to Miss Moody, "I had the good evening ... in New York with the great-faced noble Ridgely."[5]

Eighteen months later, in the first Frost to Torrence letter printed in the Thompson edition of the letters, Frost begins: "You'll begin to think I don't see the beauty of having a friend on the editorial staff of *The New Republic*. But I do and I mean to show it by sending you some poems I have on hand just as soon as I can find time and peace of mind to write them all over."[6] He then concludes this short letter with a suggestive, telling notion: "You're not going to be where I can run across you in my first descent on the settlements this week. I must see you, though, when I am down in December if we are going to continue to be anything more to each other than respecters of each other's poetry."[7] Of course they became friends, and fortunately for Frost, Torrence became a valuable and influential ally as well. During Torrence's tenure as poetry editor of the *New Republic*, from 1920 to 1934, many of Frost's poems appeared in that journal.

There seems to be little question that Torrence was a loyal and consistent admirer of Frost's work down through the decades. And it was not the case, one hastens to add, that he was an uncritical reader of contemporary poetry. As Willard Thorp has insisted, under Torrence's direction the *New Republic* published the work not only of "poets already well known, such as Hardy, Sandburg, and De La Mare," but of poets—"early, before they had become 'accepted'"—like Elinor Wylie, Wallace Stevens, Louise Bogan, Hart Crane, Léonie Adams, Yvor Winters, and Allen Tate.[8] And of the late work of Edwin Arlington Robinson, for whom he had had high respect, Torrence told Frost that Robinson's "'fire was gone' 15 years ago."[9]

When we turn to the matter of Frost's opinion of Torrence's poetry, we cannot be so sure of his evaluation of it. As we know, Frost had become aware of Torrence as poet as early as 1906. In the September issue of the *Atlantic Monthly* that year Frost came across a piece entitled "Three American Poets of To-day." Its author was May Sinclair, a novelist and essayist; and the three poets who stand out among the day's "born aristocrats of literature," according to the writer, are William Vaughn Moody, Edwin Arlington Robinson, and Ridgely Torrence.[10] "They are all three rich in imagination," she insists, "but Mr. Moody is distinguished by his mastery of technique; Mr. Robinson by his psychological vision, his powerful human quality; Mr. Torrence by his immense, if as yet somewhat indefinite, promise."[11] For Ridgely Torrence it was, as Sinclair saw it, an optative matter, promise for the future. In 1906, he had to his credit a slender first collection of poems, *The House of a Hundred Lights*, a volume of twenty-seven unnumbered pages published by Small Maynard of Boston in 1900; *El Dorado*, a verse play, in 1903; and nine poems published in periodicals: five of them in college journals, one in the *New England Magazine*, one in the *Critic*, one in the *Gazette* (of Xenia, Ohio) and one in the *Atlantic Monthly*.[12] In her remarks on Torrence's poetry Miss Sinclair concentrates on *El Dorado*, refers to *The House of the Hundred Lights*, which she calls the author's "Rubaiyat" ("a slender volume of quatrains written in frank imitation of Omar Khayyam"[13]) and concludes with "The Lesser Children," an ambitious poem published just twelve months earlier in the *Atlantic Monthly*.[14] Miss Sinclair concludes her piece:

> Mr. Torrence, having left Omar Khayyam far behind him, is inspired by no spirit but his own, and he is forming, a little too deliberately, a style of his own. With all his reverence for old traditions, he is in his own way an iconoclast, a breaker of revered metrical forms. The old rhythms, made malleable by the touch of many masters, become yet more plastic in his hands.

She concludes her panegyric by assuring the reader that "there is no doubt that he has before him a brilliant future. He works in the spirit which great art inexorably demands, the spirit of reverence and of sacrificial patience. But because his art is precious, let him beware of preciosity."[15]

Frost knew the Sinclair essay, and he remembered it vividly for years. He was affected by Miss Sinclair's temerity in naming just three poets and on settling on these three. Years later, when on a visit with Ezra Pound to May Sinclair sometime after the publication of his own first volume of poetry, *A Boy's Will*, in 1913—a book he knew she had been "showing" to "people"[16]—Frost was pleased with her reaction to his question: Shouldn't she have put Robinson ahead of Moody and Torrence "in her article of a few years back in the *Atlantic*?" She agreed with him, adding further that "Robinson was the only one of the three she still cared for."[17]

Two years later, having at last met Edwin Arlington Robinson, Frost chose to bring up the Sinclair article still again in an answer to a letter from Robinson: "It may not pain you to hear that as long ago as May Sinclair's paper in *The Atlantic* I marked you down as one of the few people I intended some day to know.... What has kept me from seeking your friendship all these years is the fear you might be troubled to find anything to like in my work." Of course, he insisted, "I should never actually seek a fellow author's friendship unless everything was right, unless he saw something in me as I saw something in him and there was little or nothing to cover up and lie about in our opinions of each other."[18] It was a high moral principle Frost espoused in meeting Robinson as an equal, in extrinsic poetic merit and in friendship. It was also a principle, admittedly, that he could, need being need, shelve at want.

It is of course possible that, fostered by handy friendship in subsequent years, Frost would change his mind about Torrence's poetry. But there is nothing in the published Frost letters to indicate that he ever thought much of Torrence's verse. It is true that while Torrence was poetry editor of the *New Republic*, Frost sent him "Stopping by Woods on a Snowy Evening," inscribing it "for Ridgely,"[19] a poem that promptly appeared in the *New Republic* on March 7, 1923. Three years later Frost sent him the poem "A Passing Glimpse," which begins: "I often see flowers from a passing car / That are gone before I can tell what they are." He has named "all the flowers I am sure they weren't," not fireweed, not bluebells, not lupine. For, as he concludes his poem, "Heaven gives its glimpses only to those / Not in a position to look too close" (227).

"A Passing Glimpse" was freighted with a public inscription, "To Ridgely Torrence On Last Looking into His Hesperides." What has not been adequately noted is that the poem and its inscription were sent along with the injunction—a mocking injunction?—that the poem was not sent to Torrence for publication.[20] Of course Torrence knew what Frost actually wanted, and the poem appeared in the *New Republic*, in its issue for April 21, 1926. Yet one would not want to overstate the extent to which in "A Passing Glimpse" Frost was playing up to his friend as poetry editor. There was considerable logic in the inscription, for Frost, using the image of flowers seen only from a passing car and then lost forever, echoes the notion in Torrence's *Hesperides* that faith, heaven-given, is rarely glimpsed. Indeed, Frost's poem was a harder, oven-bird–like reply to the more melodic laments of Torrence's poems. Whether the inscription was meant to flatter Torrence or to mollify him before Frost's own temerity in "answering" his poetry or whether the motivation behind the act lay elsewhere, I shall not speculate. Suffice it to say that "A Passing Glimpse" was an "answer" to a question asked or a challenge thrown down unwittingly, even inadvertently, by another poet, this time a contemporary.

7. The Passing Glimpse 71

For despite Frost's feelings about Torrence, or because of them, he found some of his poetry challenging enough to confront its concerns in his own poetry. Torrence's "The Lesser Children," for instance, is an unacknowledged precursor of images, phrases, and words appearing in some of Frost's own, rather more famous poems. "The Lesser Children" first appeared in the *Atlantic Monthly*, was highly praised in the *Atlantic*'s "Contributors' Club" two months later, and then quoted extensively by May Sinclair in her article, "Three American Poets of To-Day," in 1906.

According to May Sinclair, "The Lesser Children: A Threnody at the Hunting Season" has for its subject "The slaughter of the birds."[21] The poem, an ode, runs for nearly 200 lines—198, to be exact. In the slaughter of birds at hunting season, Torrence sees the threat of the apocalyptic demise of man, who would destroy "the lesser children," those "weaker brothers of our earthly breed; / Watchmen of whom our safety takes no heed; / Swift helpers of the wind that sowed the seed." In short, "Warriors against the bivouac of the weed; / Earth's earliest ploughmen for the tender root." The poem is prophetic in that it lashes out at those who wantonly kill off "the lesser children," presenting mankind a dark vision of an earth populated by death sown by his "own dishonor" and inherited, in its "curse of blight," by the "locust [who will] have his fill" and "the blind worm [that will] lay tithe." In this world devoid of man, "The unfed stones rot in the listless mill. / The sound of grinding cease. / No yearning gold would whisper to the scythe." These lines bear comparison to several in Frost's "Mowing": "There was never a sound beside the wood but one. / And that was my long scythe whispering to the ground. / What was it whispered?" (26). The poet of "Mowing" attributes the sound, not to the "yearning gold" but to the scythe, to be answered aphoristically: "The fact is the sweetest dream that labor knows. / My long scythe whispered and left the hay to make" (26). If the whispering scythe (in a world where men do exist) and the scythe that is no longer whispered to (in a world where man has disappeared) are not coincidental coinages, "Mowing" is not an "answer." Rather it is a poem that borrows an image, a notion, for its own purposes. In fact, in "Mowing," as Frost once said, "I come so near what I long to get that I almost despair of coming nearer."[22] This admission comes in the same letter, incidentally, in which Frost comments on his exchange with May Sinclair over the relative merits of Robinson, Moody, and Ridgely Torrence.

And what of the "yearning gold" that no longer whispers to the scythe? Perhaps in "Nothing Gold Can Stay" (first published in the *Yale Review* in 1923) we have another poem coming out of a trace in "The

Lesser Children." It begins: "Nature's first green is gold, / Her hardest hue to hold," and continues "Her early leaf's a flower; / But only so an hour" when "leaf subsides to leaf, / So Eden sank to grief, So dawn goes down to day," leading to the concluding line: "Nothing gold can stay" (206). Of a mated bird, Torrence had written: "Yet speeding he forgot not of cloud / Where he from glory sprang and burned aloud," but took "a little of the coloured sky, / And of the joy that would not stay / He wove a song that cannot die." Surely these lines anticipate the theme of "Nothing Gold Can Stay," and, in a sense, with differences that matter, of the theme of "The Oven Bird."

Just how much of Torrence's "The Lesser Children" remained with Frost as a store of thematic hints, serviceable words and images, I shall not venture to say. That the poem influenced him rather extensively and over a long period covering decades, can be indicated further by a look at two other instances. Torrence writes of "wings broken or a fledgling dead" or the death "underfoot" of " meadows that wore gold" and leaves that "go mourning to the mould / Beneath poor dead and desperate feet / Of folk who in next summer's meadows shall not meet?" The soft, almost lachrymose complaint of these lines was countered by Frost's characteristic toughness in "A Leaf Treader," a poem published thirty years after the appearance of Torrence's poem: "I have been treading on leaves all day until I am autumn-tired. / God knows all the color and form of leaves I have trodden on and mired." Perhaps, he thinks, he has "put forth too much strength and been too fierce from fear." All summer long the leaves have been over his head and now "to come to their final place in earth they had to pass" him by. "All summer long I thought I heard them threatening under their breath. / And when they came it seemed with a will to carry me with them to death. / They spoke to the fugitive in my heart as if it were leaf to leaf." The encounter takes on an even more personal note, as the poet says, "They tapped at my eyelids and touched my lips with an invitation to grief. / But it was no reason I had to go because they had to go. / Now up my knee to keep on top of another year of snow" (270–71).

Another possibility. Torrence sets his poem at sunset in mid–August when the wind blows "through the leisuring air, / And on the sky nightly the mythic hind / Leads down the sullen dog star to his lair."[23] Does the "mythic hind" that "leads down the sullen dog star to his lair" anticipate the dog visit, a visit that Frost celebrates in "One More Brevity" and that he "might even claim" was paid to him by the dog star Sirius—"Heaven's greatest star," an avatar—"who had made an overnight descent / To show by deeds he didn't resent / My having depended on him so long," but had not yet done anything "about it in song" (432–33). Torrence had used the words "lair" and "loneliness." In all his published poetry Frost would use these words a total of only four times: "lair" (more exactly, "lairs") once and "loneliness" three times. In three of the four instances the terms appear in "Desert Places," the poem published immediately preceding the publication of "A Leaf Treader."

Before turning to "Desert Places," however, it may be useful to quote the lines in "The Lesser Children" that center upon the way in which a bird's song brings loneliness. "Who has not seen in the high gulf of light," he asks; "What, lower, was a bird, but now / Is moored and altered quite / Into an island of unshaded joy"? His mate "below upon the bough / Shouts once and brings him from his high employ," weaving "a song that cannot die," one that bids "the radiant love once more beware, / Bringing one more loneliness on the world. / And one more blindness in the unseen air." In Frost's poem, "Loneliness" (the first of five lyrics put together under the umbrella rubric of "The Hill Wife") the young wife speaks: "One ought not to have to care / So much as you and I / Care when the birds come round the house." These birds that have come, apparently, "To seem to say good-by; / Or care so much when they come back / With whatever it is they sing." For the truth is that the two of them "are as much / Too glad for the one thing" as they are "too sad for the other here— / With birds that fill their breasts / But with each other and themselves," and "their built or driven nests" (122). It is almost as if Frost and Torrence are conducting a discordant dialogue in which they use the same terms to talk differently about similar matters. Here again is Torrence. "The weaker brothers of our earthly breed" are "with starry eyes not even raised to plead"; they are "winged mysteries of song that from the sky / Once dashed long music down." This observation leads to the poet's plea: "O who would take away music from the earth? / Have we so much? Or love upon the hearth?"

> The great trees bending between birth and birth
> Sighed for them, and the night wind's hoarse rebuff
> Shouted the shame of which I was persuaded.

Compare these lines with Frost's fourth poem in "The Hill Wife" sequence, "The Oft-Repeated Dream," where Frost once again echoes eerily, even as it particularizes, parts of Torrence's poem. "She had no saying dark enough," begins the poem, "for the dark pine that kept / Forever trying the window latch / Of the room where they slept." The tree outside the window is moved by "tireless but ineffectual hands" that with "every futile pass / Made the great tree seem as a little bird / Before the mystery of glass!" The tree had never made it into the room, but one of the two of them "was afraid in an oft-repeated dream / Of what the tree might do" (123–24).

"Desert Places," first published in the *American Mercury* in 1934, has become one of Frost's iconic poems, partly because it has been so widely anthologized and partly because Frost himself recited it so often in his public readings. The poet looks out, as he goes by, at "snow falling and night falling fast" in a field. The ground is "almost covered smooth in snow, / But a few weeds and stubble showing last." Loneliness. "The woods around it have it—it is theirs. / All animals are smothered in their lairs." The poet recalls that he was "too absent-spirited to count"; yet the "loneliness includes" him "unawares." And lonely as it is, that loneliness "Will be more lonely ere it will be less— / A blanker whiteness of benighted snow / With no expression, nothing to express." Then comes a shift in his thinking, a change in key and scope. "They cannot scare me with their empty spaces / Between stars—on stars where no human race is." For he has it in him "so much nearer home," he reveals, "To scare myself with my own desert places" (269). Torrence's poem "The Lesser Children" is a poignant call for man to face whatever it is within himself that keeps him from seeing his true and benevolent relationship to the beasts and birds of his world. Frost's "Desert Places" swerves from this position not at all. Indeed, it closely builds on one important aspect of Torrence's theme: that the basic fear and loneliness that threaten to dehumanize man may be turned to his advantage—that it might lead to his salvation. Torrence spells out the human situations "when Fear watched at our coming and our going / The horror of the chattering face of Whim," and "hates, cruelties new fallen from the trees / Whereto we clung with impulse sad for love." He continues his litany of "shames we have had all time to rid us of, / Disgraces cold and sorrows long bewept," along with "unmeaning quarrels, blood-compelling lust, / And snarling woes from our old home, the dust." And then he bucks up, rife with hope, "one saving shape may rise." "Fear may unveil our eyes," for we do not know "what curse of blight would fall" upon a land "lorn of the sweet shy races / Who day and night keep ward and seneschal / Upon the treasury of the planted spaces?" Frost had described his wintry scene as "a blanker whiteness of benighted snow / With no expression, nothing to express," concluding his poem with lines ending with the rhymes "spaces," "race is," and "desert places." Two of these are rhymes in Torrence's lines on the function of "Fear": "races" and "spaces." The third rhyme, the concluding rhyme that also gave Frost the title of his poem, Torrence had already used in another line from "The Lesser Children," which refers to "the solemn and compassionate desert places."

Perhaps without Frost's full, conscious knowledge, Ridgely Torrence's poem "The Lesser Children" was for Frost something of a limited preserve for themes, felicitous phrases, and images. There is debt here that Frost neither acknowledged nor, one surmises, ever felt the need to repay. "I had one of my great times with Ridgely last week," he said in a letter in 1923; "I always keep seeing a light as I talk with him—and of course losing it as quickly; the thing is the seeing it."[24] On the matter of literary influence, however—for Frost at least—turn it around: in Torrence's poetry he kept "seeing a light," and then, of course, losing it quickly—but losing it not entirely, only, it seems, to consciousness and to memory.

8

Solitary Griefs

Along with the poets John Davidson and Ernest Dowson, and the artist Aubrey Beardsley, Lionel Johnson (1867–1902) belongs among those young men William Butler Yeats describes as the great losses of his "tragic generation."[1] Tragic, because they died young and, presumably, unfulfilled. Yet it cannot be said that their work went unappreciated. Dead at thirty-five, Johnson left behind a body of work that, though modest in size, was widely read by appreciative readers on both sides of the Atlantic. Edward Thomas, Robert Frost's friend, admired Johnson's poetry and said so publicly. So did Ezra Pound, who contributed a preface to the 1915 edition of Johnson's *Poetical Works*. The poet Louise Imogen Guiney memorialized Johnson in the *Atlantic Monthly*. Her 1902 essay was later used to introduce an edition of Johnson's poems marking the tenth anniversary of the poet's death.

In a 1932 letter Frost alludes to Johnson's poetry. He questions, in particular, the poet's brave resolution in "The Dark Angel": "Do what thou wilt, thou shalt not so, / Dark Angel! Triumph over me: / Lonely, unto the Lone I go; / Divine, to the Divinity." Frost demurs: "it is almost too hard for anything to succeed in being divine, although Lionel Johnson sware [sic] the opposite.... I expect to look backward and see the last tail light on the last car," he continues. "But I shall be going the other way on foot."[2]

Much like the Catholic Francis Thompson, author of "The Hound of Heaven," Johnson was driven by his furies. "Historic Catholicism, with all its councils and its dogmas, stirred his passion like the beauty of a mistress," thought Yeats.[3] It is all the more interesting, then, that Johnson wrote poems that Frost echoes in lines and poems of his own. Consider, for instance, Johnson's "By the Statue of King Charles at Charing Cross" (1889) and "The Precept of Silence" (1893) in the context of Frost's

"Acquainted with the Night" (1928) and "Desert Places" (1934). Here is Johnson's "The Precept of Silence":

> I know you: solitary griefs,
> Desolate passions, aching hours!
> I know you: tremulous beliefs,
> Agonized hopes, and ashen flowers!
>
> The winds are sometimes sad to me;
> The starry spaces, full of fear:
> Mine is the sorrow on the sea,
> And mine the sigh of places drear.
>
> Some players upon plaintive strings
> Publish their wistfulness abroad;
> I have not spoken of these things,
> Save to one man, and unto God.[4]

Johnson's decision in the first line to characterize his complaints as "solitary griefs" would have been especially interesting to Frost, striking him, perhaps, as evidence of the British poet's weakness shown by a willingness to put his self-commiseration on display. Distinguishing between "grief" and "grievance," Frost assigned them, respectively, to poetry and politics. "I find in my old writing the creeping idea coming up that the difference was between grievance and grief," said Frost. "Now, politics is grievance. Something that something can be done about, or you think it can. And poetry is about 'immedicable woes,' as the old poem says, 'immedicable woes.' Woes that you can't do anything about. Grief, real grief."[5]

The sentiments expressed in the middle stanza of Johnson's "The Precept of Silence" stand significantly between Pascal's famous sentiment—a line greatly admired by Johnson: "Le silence eternel de ces espaces infinis m'effraie"[6] and those of Frost in the fourth stanza of "Desert Places." "They cannot scare me with their empty spaces / Between stars—on stars where no human race is," he writes; "I have it in me so much nearer home / To scare myself with my own desert places" (269). Lines 13–14 of Frost's poem—"They cannot scare me with their empty spaces / Between stars"—can be read as a responsive redaction to line six of Johnson's poem—"The starry spaces, full of fear."[7] In these four lines Frost employs the word "scare" (twice) to evoke Johnson's "fear" and, more discursively, opens out Johnson's noun phrase "starry spaces" to read "empty spaces between stars."

It is said that "Johnson spent his life mostly as a recluse, shut up among his books," making "every effort to shut out what he considered a crass and feverish world"; because he suffered from insomnia, he made it a "practice to sleep in the daytime and come alive only when the hush of evening descended upon London."[8] It was then that this isolato took "his solitary walks," holding, as Guiney asserted, "that any walk is the richer for being companionless."[9] It is within what purports to be a paean to the London night, experienced during one of his customary walks, that Johnson pays his tribute to the bold and forthright statue of King Charles I. "The great men of action, namely the saints," as Johnson might have said, "crown themselves with night and the stars, and anoint themselves with silence and solitude."[10] Indeed, sainthood of a different sort is embodied, as Johnson discovers, in the once "discrowned" Charles I. Here are several stanzas, in trimeter, from Johnson's "By the Statue of King Charles at Charing Cross."

> Sombre and rich, the skies;
> Great glooms, and starry plains,
> Gently the night wind sighs;
> Else a vast silence reigns.
>
> The splendid silence clings
> Around me: and around
> The saddest of all kings
> Crowned, and again discrowned.
>
> Comely and calm, he rides
> Hard by his own Whitehall:
> Only the night wind glides:
> No crowds, nor rebels, brawl.
>
> Gone too, his Court: and yet,
> The stars his courtiers are:
> Stars in their stations set;
> And every wandering star.
>
> Alone he rides, alone,
> The fair and fatal king:
> Dark night is all his own,
> That strange and solemn thing.
>
> ....
> Armoured he rides, his head
> Bare to the stars of doom:
> He triumphs now, the dead,
> Beholding London's gloom.
>
> ....
> King, tried in fires of woe!
> Men hunger for thy grace:
> And through the night I go,
> Loving thy mournful face.
>
> Yet, when the city sleeps;
> When all the cries are still:

> The stars and heavenly deeps
> Work out a perfect will.[11]

It will be noted that it is the monumentalized figure actually, not the remembered historical person, who is judged to be the "proud and lovely thing."[12]

In expressing his own admiration for Charles I, Frost linked the king's comportment at that moment of death to John F. Kennedy's theme in *Profiles in Courage*. "Charles I, he was that way," Frost thought, "and he paid with his life for it. It's a beautiful thing, the description of his death. He was wrong, of course, but he was more answerable to God than to any constituents."[13] As Frost said, it will be recalled, "it is almost too hard for anything to succeed in being divine."[14] Johnson himself linked Charles I with Pascal, quoting the French philosopher's benevolent view of humankind: "His very infirmities prove man's greatness: they are the infirmities of a great lord, of a discrowned king," having himself applied the adjective "discrowned" to Charles I.[15] The peaceful vision projected by Johnson in the final stanza, that of a sleeping city, still and silent, and—a singularly un–Pascalian thought—the stars and heavenly deeps working out a perfect will is countered by Frost's account of his own experience as a lonely walker of the city, one who has been "acquainted with the night," having "walked out in rain—and back in rain," beyond "the furthest city light." He has "looked down the saddest city lane"; he has "passed by the watchman on his beat" and dropped his "eyes, unwilling to explain." The list continues. He has "stood still and stopped the sound of feet / When far away an interrupted cry / Came over houses from another street." But such cries were not, he says, "to call me back or say good-by." And then, "further still at an unearthly height, / One luminary clock against the sky / Proclaimed the time was neither wrong nor right" (234).

"Acquainted with the Night," as Randall Jarrell pointed out long ago, is "in Dante's own form and with some of Dante's own qualities."[16] Joseph Brodsky went so far as to insist: "without Dante's *Commedia*, this poem wouldn't have existed."[17] By the mere fact of adopting the *terza rima* of the *Divine Comedy* (*aba, bcb, cdc*, etc.) Frost links it to Dante's poem, especially its famous opening lines. But the great Catholic poet's walk in a "dark wood" (*selva oscura*) has become, in Frost's poem, a walk at night, like, in a limited sense, one of Johnson's "nightly walks"—a gesture of what has been called his "noctambulism."[18] To be one of those who are acquainted with the night, Frost seems to insist, wryly underestimating the matter, is to belong (as he says in "Desert Places") to that blanket of "loneliness" that "includes" him "unawares." To know the night one must be out in it, not viewing it from indoors or, even less satisfactorily, imagining it or spinning words out of whole cloth. From Frost's vantage—within the night itself, so to speak—there is little or nothing that expresses "a perfect will," as Johnson's "stars and heavenly deeps" seem to do. With irony, the skeptical Frost trumps the religious poet Johnson's symbol of quiescence—a boldly silent statue of a triumphant and saintly King Charles I—with an ominously blank "luminary clock against the sky."

"Acquainted with the Night" also provides more specific correlatives for the nominative grief Johnson claims for himself (and proclaims) in "The Precept of Silence." Typically, conclude his academic editors, "Johnson was not able to dramatize his material or to embody his conflict in language living or precise enough to give it permanent significance."[19] The opening stanza of "The Precept of Silence" offers a good example of his characteristic weakness in this regard: "I know you: solitary griefs, / Desolate passions, aching hours! / I know you: tremulous beliefs, / Agonized hopes, and ashen flowers!"

A different approach to the matter of how closely Frost occasionally echoes Johnson in some of his better known poems is to look at Frost poems in which the diction and end rhymes are anticipated by Johnson. For example, take "Fire and Ice" (1920): "Some say the world will end in fire, / Some say in ice. / From what I've tasted of desire / I hold with those who favor fire. / But if it had to perish twice, / I think I know enough of hate / To say that for destruction ice / Is also great / And would suffice" (204). In "The Dark Angel" (1893) Johnson contrasts "flame" and "Ice": "The ardour of red flame is thine, / And thine the steely soul of *ice*"; in "The Church of a Dream" (1890) he pairs the words "spice" and "*suffice*"— the latter a term that occurs only once in Frost's published poetry; and in "The Destroyer of a Soul" (1892) Johnson rhymes "hate" with "great": "I hate you with a necessary *hate*. / First, I sought patience: passionate was she: / My patience turned in very scorn of me, / That I should dare forgive a sin so *great*."[20] It is of no little interest that in "Fire and Ice" Frost also rhymes "fire" and "desire"; it is only the second time he does so but it is also, significantly, the last.[21] Johnson, of course, was hardly the first poet to employ this rhyme (it was already in use in Shakespeare's day), but he was uncommonly devoted to it. In "To a Spanish Friend" (1894)—the friend was George Santayana—Johnson writes: "Clad in everlasting fire, / Flame of one long, lone desire."[22] While in "Brothers" (1900), a poem dedicated to a close friend "killed in the South African War," and, as such, one that would have meant most to Frost after Edward Thomas was killed in France in 1917, Johnson writes: "Now had Death dealt a generous violence / Calling thee swiftly hence / By the like instrument of instant fire / To join thy heart's desire."[23] Elsewhere, in a poem about the "mighty house of hate," Johnson rhymes "desire" or "desires" with "fire" or "fires" three times. Incidentally, in "Brothers" the line—"Earthward you long and lean, earthward"—suggests both Frost's title—"To Earthward" (1923)—and lines in "Vision": "I long for weight and strength / To feel the earth as rough / To all my length" (210).[24] Of the just-dead friend—"Edward Thomas was the only brother I ever had"—he wrote: "His concern to the last was what it had always been, to touch earthly things and come as near them in words as words would come."[25]

One of Lionel Johnson's great luminaries among the Western poets was Dante. To him he was "the mighty Catholic" whom "readers not wholly unworthy of him" eagerly adapted "to their spiritual wants."[26] He is the "pilgrim Dante" in the poem "Sortes Virgilianae" (1891), a guide for Frost in such georgic poems as "Stopping by Woods on a Snowy Evening" (1923), "The Road Not Taken" (1915), and "The Draft Horse" (written *ca* 1920).[27] The situation depicted in each of these poems bears a familial resemblance to the situation rendered in the Catholic poet's famous opening to the *Commedia*:

> Midway upon the journey of our life
>   I found myself within a forest dark,
>   For the straightforward pathway had been lost.
> Ah me! how hard a thing it is to say
>   What was the forest savage, rough, and stern,
>   Which in the very thought renews the fear.
> So bitter it is, death is little more.[28]

The "forest dark" in which the poet finds himself has its analogue, as well, in "Acquainted with the Night." Taking the poet through city streets and beyond, the poem works as a dark, troubled inversion of Johnson's *terza rima* poem "By the Statue of King Charles at Charing Cross." Notably, too, both poems display variations on Dante's *terza rima*.

Future work on Johnson and Frost, whether in the areas of influence, parallels or affinities, might take the path of noting further similarities in word choice and rhyme, as well as thematic differences. In the matter of rhyme it would be interesting to go deeper into Frost's forbearance in employing only twice the rhyme "fire-desire" in the light of its more frequent use by Johnson. Perhaps Frost's choice is no more than an indication of his stated intention to write poems "to see if I can make them all sound different."[29] Johnson, on the other hand, repeats his "master words" to "arrive at a cumulative effect."[30] Just as the words "stars," "night" and "skies" are reiterated for the overall effect of their accumulation in the poem "By the Statue of King Charles," so, too, I would suggest are his reiteration of rhymes from poem to poem, such as "fire-desire," especially when such rhymes occur, as they do in the poem "Plato in London" (1889), among the words he is wont to associate with Pascal—"stars," "starry," "skies," and "sphere."[31]

Another matter. Johnson's editor calls attention to the poet's "most favoured rhetorical figure": "simple repetition: *anaphora*." He offers such examples of this "irritating habit" as "Man's life, my life: of life I am afraid" and "Only the rest! the rest! Only the gloom, soft and long gloom."[32] Frost, too, resorted to anaphora, sometimes to the detriment of individual lines or stanzas. One example will suffice, I think. In the poem "On Talk of Peace at This Time," sent to Edward Thomas at the front in France shortly before his death, Frost writes, as if he will make repetition do the work of feeling: "France. France, I know not what is in my heart," he writes. "But God forbid that I should be more brave / As watcher from a quiet place apart / Than you are fighting in an open grave," although he will admit, "Not mine to say you shall not think of peace. / Not mine, not mine: I almost know your pain." (531) He would do better in the future. Still ahead was his efficacious use of anaphora to marshal the first-person assertions that help to structure "Acquainted with the Night" and the canny use of repetition to close out the last stanza of "Stopping by Woods on a Snowy Evening."

This preliminary examination of the presence of Lionel Johnson in Frost's poetry offers but a beginning. Not only can it be extended in its particulars but it can be opened out to include the larger question of Frost's reading of the other British poets of the 1890s, including the Decadents John Davidson, Ernest Dowson, and Arthur Symons—as well as Francis Thompson, whose poem "The Hound of Heaven" exerted a powerful, lasting force on Frost's spiritual life as well as his poetry. There has not been enough scholarship, in my opinion, dedicated to discovering what Frost's reading of the work of his contemporaries and his betters meant to him and his poetry during the first decade or so when he committed himself to the vocation of poet and the everyday practice of poetry.

9

An Art of the Possible

Shortly before Robert Frost's death on January 29, 1963, *County Government Magazine* published in its December 1962 issue the poet's response to its request for his participation in a symposium on the theme "The Cold War Is Being Won." Its tone is less that of the disheartened cold warrior that he is sometimes taken to have been than of the resigned, though still optimistic, poet-diplomat he had become in the last ten years of his life. "I hate a cold war of sustained hate that finds no relief in blood letting but probably it should be regarded as a way of stalling till we find out whether there is really an issue big enough for a big show-down," he began. "We are given pause from the dread of the terribleness we feel capable of. I was sometimes like that as a boy with another boy I lived in antipathy with. It clouded my days" (901).

But Frost had not always resigned himself to being limited to verse and talk. And thereby hangs the tale of a poet who although he had always had his mind on politics, from the early times when his father taught him politics in San Francisco, would get an extraordinary chance in his eighty-ninth year to play the Cold War diplomat at the highest level.

In 1932, a year of increasing social pressures and widespread political turmoil, both Robert Frost and Walter Lippmann were honored at commencement exercises by the Phi Beta Kappa chapter at Columbia University. Lippmann spoke on "The Scholar in a Troubled World," and Frost read "Build Soil," a poem that branched out from his principal theme of the poet in the world to offer counsel to intellectuals, scholars, artists, and politicians. Sharing a principle he would follow for the rest of his life, Frost advised his young scholars and the rest of the world as well to slow down its rush to take action, "Build soil," he advised, depending on his audience to interpret correctly his metaphor. He advised: "turn the farm in upon itself / Until it can contain itself no more, / But sweating-full, drips wine and oil a little." He himself would, as he said, "go to my run-out social mind / And be as unsocial with it as I can." His first thought and his first impulse was "to take to market," but no, he would "turn it under." "I will turn it under. / And so on to the limit of my nature," he said. For "We are too much out, and if we won't draw in / We shall be driven in" (295). Lippmann, for his part, offered advice to the scholar that seemed, at least at first look, to be in consilience with Frost's. He cautioned against the excesses of the scholar's involvement in matters "outside" the library. As the *New York Times* reported, "Mr. Lippmann contended that the 'scholar' who deserts his books and his research to heed the importunate demands of the present does not do justice to himself and the world." "For this is not the last crisis in human affairs," acknowledged Lippmann; "the world will go on somehow and more crises will follow." Actually, "It will go on best, however, if among us there are men who stood apart, who refused to be too anxious or too much concerned, who were cool and inquiring, and had their eyes on a longer past and a longer future. By their example they can remind us that the passing moment is only a moment; by their loyalty they will have cherished those things which only the disinterested mind can use."[1]

    Frost might go so far as to agree that the scholar (or poet or statesman) must not leap into the middle of things in reaction to the pressures of the moment. But that he should permanently refrain from direct involvement, if that was what Lippmann advocated, was anathema to the poet who continued to harbor ancient thoughts about the poet's responsibilities to the world as he found it. If he had stoically awaited the recognition due his poems until he was nearly forty, Frost would await patiently for the time when he might be called upon to perform some meaningful public service on his country's behalf. Meanwhile, in the 1930s, during Franklin Delano Roosevelt's first two terms as President of the United States, Frost would take on the role, at times, of the loyal opposition. He would speak out against the national government's meddling in the affairs of the individual American citizen, who should be independent of such organized manipulation and control as the Founding Fathers and as Henry David Thoreau had insisted he be. In his most strikingly political poem of the 1930s, "Two Tramps in Mud Time" (published in the *Saturday Review of Literature* in 1934), Frost questioned the basic premise of practicing social welfare to the detriment of an individual's right to well-being. For instance, should he give over the pleasurable and gratifying task of chopping his own wood to the two tramps whose creature needs staked their claim to the task and the compensation that goes with it? Or do his

9. An Art of the Possible 85

quite different needs justify his insistence on continuing with the task himself? It becomes a question of pitting the needs of spirit, aspiration, and self-fulfillment against the need for working for food. The poem's celebrated conclusion sums up explicitly the poet's answer to this antinomy. Although "nothing on either side was said," the tramps "knew they had but to stay their stay / And all their logic would fill" the poet's head: that he had "no right to play / With what was another man's work for gain." He will admit that his "right might be love but theirs was need / And where the two exist in twain / Theirs was the better right—agreed." But he gives himself the last word. "My object in living is to unite / My avocation and my vocation / As my two eyes make one in sight." After all, only when love and need are joined as one, "and the work is play for mortal stakes, / Is the deed ever really done / For Heaven and the future's sakes" (252). Only when the two rights at question here—those of love and those of need—exist apart and come into conflict will he capitulate: need comes first. But the poet will take an even higher road on the matter by revealing that the greater principle (reflecting Thoreau's basic argument in "Life Without Principle") is that the needs of the self are paramount in its constant struggle against the destructive pressures of socialization—or, as Frost put it elsewhere, socialism. The aim was always to bring love and need into consilience, to turn work and play into one thing indivisible. Frost fully agreed with Thoreau when he warned: "Do not hire a man who does your work for money, but him who does it for love of it," for "if the laborer gets no more than the wages which his employer pays him, he is cheated, he cheats himself."[2] It was on this basis that Frost questioned Roosevelt's New Deal domestic policies, which were based, as the poet saw it, on unreasoned and indefensible principles of political economy that resulted in hasty, wavering, and vacillating, yet invariably dangerous measures. In *The New Frontier* for September 1934, eighteen months after Roosevelt took office, Frost published "Provide, Provide," a poem inspired by the strike of charwomen at Harvard University that satirizes the principles, policies, and practices of the welfare state implicit in the New Deal. "Die early and avoid the fate. / Or if predestined to die late, / Make up your mind to die in state," is his wry advice. Do what you can to avoid the state's provision. Indeed, it is "better to go down dignified," he says with a snarl, "With boughten friendship at your side / Than none at all. Provide, provide!" (280).

Frost liked to tell the story of his having once recited the poem to an audience in Washington, with "a very important friend in front." "To rub it in," after reciting the final three lines, he repeated, "'Provide, provide!'"

adding ominously, "Or somebody else'll provide for you!" And then—"to make it deeper still"—he asked, "And how'll you like that?"[3] Frost's highly placed friend was Henry Wallace, who served as Vice-President during Roosevelt's third term, ran for the Presidency as the Progressive Party's candidate in 1948, and stood out as the most socialist-minded politician of prominence in the Washington of his day.

In the *Saturday Review* in January 1936, shortly after Roosevelt was elected to his second term as President, Frost published "To a Thinker in Office" (collected the next year, in *A Further Range*, as "To a Thinker"). His theme was the inconstancy and vacillation demonstrated by those currently exercising political power in and out of office. It was widely taken to be an anti–Roosevelt poem. "The last step taken found your heft / Decidedly upon the left. / One more would throw you on the right." In fact, "just now you're off democracy" and "leaning on dictatorship." There seems to be no direction in this thinker, an observation to the poet's confession: "I own I never really warmed / To the reformer or reformed." So much for the government policies of the times. Frost offers one last bit of advice: "At least don't use your mind too hard, / But trust my instinct— I'm a bard" (298).

Frost revealed later that he had not originally had Roosevelt in mind, but that he would not deny the identification when others read the poem that way. He wanted his poems put to use. In fact, "the pleasantest use of a poem," he said, was "seeing a fragment of it quoted in an editorial, we'll say, in a New York paper." "That's a very great triumph." "To a Thinker" had been put to a definite political use that he approved of. As he said at the age of eighty-four, he didn't want to run for office, but did want to be a politician.[4]

Frost's long-standing desire to be of public use, along with his hope that his work be useful to the common good, comes to the fore in the more explicit political aspects of his poetry of the 1930s. This turn away from the more purely subjective lyrics and narrative poems of his first five volumes was widely regretted and deplored by many of his critics. Indeed, so marked was the academic and intellectual repudiation of Frost, especially after the publication of *A Further Range* in 1937, that it took two remarkable revisionary essays by Randall Jarrell a decade or more later, in the late 1940s and early 1950s, to recall Frost's readers to what Jarrell pointed to as constituting Frost's genuine contributions to poetry. Focusing on poems that showed Frost at his lyrical and narrative best, Jarrell significantly made no case for Frost's more public poetry. He did not mention "Build Soil," with its profoundly conservative message, for instance, or "Departmental," a satire on regimentation, specialization, and socialism. For a generation or more, in fact, much of Frost's political poetry was dismissed as "telling" rather than "showing." Frost's sententiousness in such poems, it was asserted, diminished the poet's overall achievement—a charge that would stick to Frost for the rest of his life and beyond. Still, while the critics disapproved, Frost continued to write his political poetry. At the conclusion of a network television interview conducted when he was serving as Consultant in Poetry at the Library of Congress, he complained that while the half-hour was up, they had not yet "settled anything!" Frost's larger complaint about his stay in Washington was that no member of Congress ever consulted with him. He did not know, of course, that what lay ahead of him was something better than talking things over with one or two members of the United States Congress.

There was a long lead-time before Frost was put to his nation's use by being sent on a cultural mission to the Soviet Union. He first represented the United States, in a small way, in South America. In 1954, under the aegis of the United States Information Agency, the Department of State had sent him to South America as a delegate to the International Writers' Conference in São Paulo, Brazil. In improvised remarks to the assembly he noted that there was a tendency to see the United States as something of a monster. "I won't say anything about Russia, which perhaps does want to dominate the world," he continued, "but I do want to make it very clear that my country does not in any way want to rule the world."[5] Frost's successful mission to South America encouraged the Department of State to send him to England in 1957, which turned into a series of opportunities for Frost to visit his old friends and the places he had lived in over four decades earlier. His English tour, which saw him honored with degrees from Cambridge, Oxford, and the National University in Dublin, seemed to whet further his appetite for serving his country. Next followed the Soviet Union.

The idea to send him to the Soviet Union may have begun with his friend Stewart Udall. Their friendship dated from the late 1950s when Udall was serving in Washington as a congressman from Arizona and Frost was finishing his stint as Consultant in Poetry to the Library of Congress. When Udall heard Frost's complaint that during his term not a single member of congress had asked him for advice, he did his best to redress this slight by having Frost come to dinner. Over the next several years, largely through Udall's good offices but not entirely so, Frost would come to enjoy his closest associations ever with powerful politicians. Frost was capable of helping his own cause. He made it known that he admired

Kennedy's book, *Profiles in Courage*. "That fine book, the *Profiles* is about," he would continue to insist to the end of his life, "being somewhat arbitrary, being more answerable to God than you are to your constituents.... That's a fine idea."[6] And on his eighty-fifth birthday Frost had helped himself further by "predicting" (that is how the press construed his not so explicit remarks) that Senator John Fitzgerald Kennedy would be elected the next President of the United States. This "prediction" evoked first a letter from the young Senator Kennedy and led to what was seen later as something of a friendship. But it was not Kennedy who first thought of inviting Frost to participate in his inauguration as President. That honor falls to Udall, who was by that time Kennedy's choice for Secretary of the Interior.

The world saw Frost's performance at the Presidential inaugural ceremony on January 19, 1961.[7] The glaring winter sunlight so annoyed and distracted the seemingly disorganized, somewhat disheveled old man that he gave up his attempt to read the poem he had composed for this most public of readings before his greatest audience ever. He set his new poem aside and went on to recite "The Gift Outright," a piece—tried-and-true—that he knew by heart. But so clearly superior is "The Gift Outright" to the poem he wrote for John Kennedy that some of Frost's readers wondered whether, not only welcoming the opportunity in that moment of confusion to skip his new poem, he had somehow engineered the whole thing (if only subconsciously). Frost's popularity with politicians running the so-called New Frontier administration ran unabated into the next year. Congress voted Frost a Congressional Medal "in recognition of his contributions to American letters," which the President awarded at White House ceremonies on the poet's eighty-eighth birthday. That evening Stewart Udall, along with Frost's publishers, Holt, Rinehart and Winston, celebrated the poet's birthday with a dinner in his honor.

All that day, however, Frost had something up his sleeve. Nikita Khrushchev was on his mind. The premier of the USSR had visited the United States in September–October 1960, mainly to attend sessions of the United Nations General Assembly. It was at this time that, to the consternation of some of their readers but mainly to the amusement of many others, the world's newspapers reported on Khrushchev's homely, colloquial, even crude language, his generous use of proverbs, and his nonverbal shenanigans, such as taking off his shoe and pounding it on the desk before him in an effort to bring the assembly to attention.[8]

Khrushchev's use of his shoe as a parliamentary gavel was amusing. Probably only a person well used to walking would have the natural resourcefulness to see that a familiar shoe might be put to uses that had nothing to do with feet. In the poem "The Objection to Being Stepped On" Frost talks about such useful conversions: "At the end of the row / I stepped on the toe / Of an unemployed hoe." A question arises. Was there evidence of intention here? "It rose in offense / And struck me a blow / In the seat of my sense." He wonders: "*was* there a rule / The weapon should be / Turned into a tool?" The evidence points that way. "And what do we see? / The first tool I step on / Turned into a weapon" (460). Later, in an interview in Moscow, Frost's comments on the splitting of the atom and how that might be used in warfare repeated the argument of his poem. "I often think about words now: weapon, tool." "A tool can turn into a weapon," he said. "When the peasants rebelled, they turned their tools of labor into weapons. I often hear that the atom has to become a tool for peace. But you always have to keep in mind that it can be a weapon for war too."[9]

Khrushchev's "shoe" also recalls one of Frost's California poems from the early 1930s. In Los Angeles for the Olympics in 1932, amidst many of the world's greatest living athletes (though not the Russians), Frost remembered that he, too, had accomplished an "Olympic" feat and had only recently written a poem to commemorate it. He called it "My Olympic Record Stride," although he would later shorten the title to "A Record Stride." The poem tells the story of a pair of shoes, "Old rivals of sagging leather, / Who once kept surpassing each other, / But now live even together." Each one was soaked in a different ocean, the Atlantic and the Pacific. He wet one, he says, "last year at Montauk / For a hat I had to save." The other he wet "at the Cliff House / In an extra-vagant wave." Now when he touches his "tongue to the shoes," he can taste both Atlantic and Pacific salt. "One foot in each great ocean / Is a record stride or stretch." The poem concludes with a boast. Forgive him if he is "over-elated" as if he "had measured the country / And got the United States stated" (267–68).

Shoes, tools, proverbs, competition, rivalry, games, Olympics, the United States, the Soviet Union, Khrushchev and Frost—all these are counters in the story of Frost as a poet-statesman. Frost could not have been unaware that the Soviet Union had been rejected *de facto* by the 1932 Olympics committee, which refused to invite that country to participate in the games in Los Angeles. In 1962 things were different. Once, in a discussion about disarmament, Frost had thrown out the suggestion, not entirely facetiously, that the United States might consider entering into a baseball competition with the Soviet Union. Now, perhaps they—

the premier and the poet—could get their respective countries on the way to what Frost called one hundred years of magnanimous rivalry. After all, Frost had said of this "grand man," Khrushchev: "With all the fears of us, and fears of what's behind him and round him there, it doesn't seem to touch him at all.... He's my enemy," Frost concluded, "but it takes just a little magnanimity to admire him."[10]

It is not clear whether the notion to send Frost to Russia originated with Udall or Frost himself, though most reports credit it to a third party, Anatoly Dobrynin, the Russian Ambassador to the United States. In any event, when the proposal reached the President, he approved it. Udall would accompany Frost, along with Frederick Adams, the director of the Pierpont Morgan Library in New York and a longtime friend of the poet's, and F. D. Reeve, a specialist in Russian literature and culture who taught at Wesleyan University. Ultimately, each of Frost's three companions would write accounts of the trip. Frost, who died within six months of his return from the USSR, did not. Although Frost's visit was entirely cultural—never diplomatic, of course—it is obvious that it was the possibility that he would meet with Khrushchev—or, as he might have thought it, the thing that he could believe into being—that compelled him to make this long journey and to subject himself willingly to a physically and mentally demanding schedule of public readings and events.

Shortly after arriving in Moscow, Frost began to worry that the meeting would not take place. The entire project—despite the warm and enthusiastic reception he received everywhere he went—was, as he began to fear, doomed to fail. His momentous talk with Khrushchev would not take place. The story of how it was finally arranged for him to meet the Premier in the final days of the trip, though the poet was almost too ill to travel at all, has been well told elsewhere.[11] What needs to be emphasized here is that finally Frost was able to discuss—face-to-face with the Premier—matters such as cultural exchanges, negotiations over the Berlin wall, the desirability of engaging in magnanimous international rivalries in art, sports, science, and democracy, to maintaining the sterile coexistence of a Cold War. He had met with the enemy and though Khrushchev was a "ruffian" (as Frost would call him rather admiringly) he was nevertheless, Frost was certain, a statesman who understood the nature of words, language, and serious play.

Like everyone else, Frost had seen the signs of all this. On Khrushchev's visit to the United States in 1960 the newspapers had picked up on his penchant for peppering his conversation and cinching his arguments with proverbs and what Frost called "dark sayings." "We drink out of a small glass, but we speak with great feelings," he directed at President Kennedy and himself. The newspapers collected his sayings. On changes in the nature of capitalism, he said, "A black frog cannot be whitewashed." On the production of butter and meat for the Soviet Union, he came up with "A dry spoon will scrape the tongue." On nuclear weapons as a deterrent to war with the West, he said, "A gale of words will not make a windmill turn." And on the decay of Western capitalism, he prophesied, "If you cannot hold on by the mane, you will not be able to hold on by the tail."[12] The American poet's own books had always been studded with aphorisms. No exception was *In the Clearing*, a copy of which he would inscribe for Khrushchev in Moscow, just as he had for Kennedy back in Washington. That, too, would be a record stride.

The affinity Frost first felt with Khrushchev might have come through their shared confidence in aphorisms, proverbs, and other "dark sayings." It might be useful, therefore, to look into what Frost meant when he used the term "dark sayings," along with his reasons for considering them as spirit-enhancing challenges to those who would interpret not just literature but life itself.

We might begin this investigation by looking at some lines from the poem "Mending Wall" (first published in *North of Boston* in 1914):

> There where it is we do not need the wall:
> He is all pine and I am apple orchard.
> My apple trees will never get across
> And eat the cones under his pines, I tell him.
> He only says, "Good fences make good neighbors."
> Spring is the mischief in me, and I wonder
> If I could put a notion in his head:
> "*Why* do they make good neighbors? Isn't it
> Where there are cows? But here there are no cows.
> Before I built a wall I'd ask to know
> What I was walling in or walling out,
> And to whom I was like to give offense.
> Something there is that doesn't love a wall,
> That wants it down."
> ...
> He will not go behind his father's saying,
> And he likes having thought of it so well
> He says again, "Good fences make good neighbors" [39–40].

Most readings of "Mending Wall" have been based on the decision as to which of the two voices in the poem—the speaker's or his taciturn neighbor's—speaks the "truth" or, at least, expresses the poet's own view of things. At Bread Loaf in 1955, as recorded by Cook, Frost talked about the old practice of "mending" walls. "It's about a spring occupation in my day. When I was farming seriously we had to set the wall up every year. You don't do that any more. You run a strand of barbed wire along it and let it go at that." It was different then. "We used to set the wall up. If you see a wall well set up you know it's owned by a lawyer in New York—not a real farmer. This is just about that spring occupation, but of course all sorts of things have been done with it and I've done something with it myself in self-defense. I've gone it one better—more than once in different ways for the Need of it—just for the foolishness of it."[13]

Then Frost read "Mending Wall," only to follow its reading with more commentary. The "first person that ever spoke to me about it was at that time becoming the president of Rollins College," Frost started out. He "took both my hands to tell me I had written a true international poem." "And just to tease him I said: 'How do you get that?'" asked Frost. "You know. I said I thought I'd been fair to both sides—both national [and international]. 'Oh, no,' he said, 'I could see what side you were on.' And I said: 'The more I say I the more I always mean somebody else.' That's objectivity, I told him. That's the way we talked about it, kidding. That's where the great fooling comes in." Then, warming to the task, Frost explains that his "latest way out of it is to say: I've got a man there; he's both [of those people but he's man—both of them, he's] a wall builder and a wall toppler." The maker of walls suggests to the poet the maker of boundaries. "He makes boundaries and he breaks boundaries. That's man. And all human life is cellular, outside or inside. In my body every seven years I'm made out of different cells and all my cell walls have been changed. I'm cellular within and life outside is cellular. Even the Communists have cells. That's where I've arrived at that."[14]

He noted, too, that "Mending Wall" was "very much taken as a parable."[15] Indeed, since his comments over the years suggest that he agreed with that characterization of the poem, it is profitable to approach the poem as a parable that is centered on the ambiguity of a troublesome proverb. Frost never calls "Good fences make good neighbors" a "dark saying" *per se*, but in a notebook he attributes it to the Spartans. In the same entry he links the Spartans' verbal devices for keeping their wisdom secret from outsiders with St. Mark's parable on the secrecy characteristic of parables. It is Frost's own little secret that "dark saying," related to the proverb, was synonymous with "parable." The linguistic and etymological tracing of these identifications is rehearsed by Frank Kermode in *The Genesis of Secrecy: On the Interpretation of Narrative* (1979). But the matter

9. An Art of the Possible 93

is put succinctly and clearly in Richard Chevenix Trench's *Notes on the Parables of Our Lord*, an influential nineteenth-century study.

> Partly from the fact which has been noted by many, of mere being but one word in the Hebrew to signify both parable and proverb; which circumstances must have had considerable influence upon writers accustomed to think in that language, and itself arose from the parable and proverb being alike enigmatical and somewhat obscure forms of speech, "dark sayings," speaking a part of their meaning and leaving the rest to be inferred. This is evidently true of the parable, and in fact no less so of the proverb.[16]

Now, though there is already a good deal written about Frost as a parablist, his identification of the "dark saying" with the parable has been pretty much overlooked. It is not important at this late date that, as Theodore Morrison reports, Frost's friend Hyde Cox had to point out to him, in the early 1940s, that his memory of St. Mark's explanation of why Jesus spoke in parables was faulty. "R. F. did *not* remember" recalled Cox. "Like many other people, it was his recollection that Christ said something about parables being easier to understand. I gleefully pointed out that this was just the opposite of what Jesus had said, and I read to R. F. the 4th Chapter of the Gospel according to St. Mark." Frost "was delighted and said at once 'Does that occur anywhere else?' I then read him the thirteenth Chapter of Matthew especially verses 11–13! The rest of the evening was spent discussing the wisdom and the hardness of this thought. R. F. pointed out that it is the same as for poetry; only those who approach it in the right way can understand it. And not everyone can understand no matter what they do because it just isn't in them. They cannot 'be saved.'"[17]

In effect, what seems to have happened that night is that St. Mark's own parable about parables came alive for Frost in a new way. He discovered it as an old "dark saying," new to him, which he could fathom precisely because he was a poet who worked in exactly the same way. In his essay "The Prerequisites," which introduces *Aforesaid* (a well-made collection commemorating his eightieth birthday), Frost laid out his theory of the "dark saying," along with its implications for reading and, in a negative way, for teaching. I shall limit myself to some excerpts and an observation or two. First of all, the essay is itself a parable about how not to teach poetry, or, better still, how poetry is usually mis-taught. For Frost there are no prerequisites for reading poetry. As he put it in "The Prerequisites," "A poem is best read in the light of all the other poems ever written," he begins. "We read A the better to read B (we have to start somewhere, we may get very little out of A). We read B the better to read C, C the better to read D, D the better to go back and get something more out of A.

Progress is not the aim, but circulation. The thing is to get among the poems where they hold each other apart in their places as the stars do."[18] Frost does not say, in so many words, why, having read poem D one might want to go back to poem A. But it can be inferred that there was something in A that one did not understand then but might become clear now after one had experienced other poems. He didn't like obscurity or obfuscation, but he did like dark sayings that were left to time for clarification, Frost once revealed. He could just as easily have said "dark poems."

It cannot be said that Frost's colloquy with Khrushchev, the Russian farmer and man of "dark sayings," had made a palpable difference in the confrontational policies of the United States and the Soviet Union. Frost's not entirely accurate comments to reporters awaiting him as he deplaned in New York were reported as unequivocal statements by Khrushchev about American weakness. "Khrushchev said he feared for us modern liberals. He said we were too liberal to fight. I suppose he thought we'd stand there for the next hundred years saying, 'On the one hand—but on the other hand.'"[19] Frost's New York interview became big news and that angered Kennedy. "Why did he have to say that?" the President asked Udall.[20]

The immediate result of Frost's well-meant but misfiring remarks was that Kennedy cut off all further contact with the poet. He showed no interest in hearing what either his poet-diplomat may have had to say in his own defense or in any messages Khrushchev might have asked Frost to relay to an American president.[21] Events, too, grossly overshadowed Frost's mission. Even as he was meeting with Khrushchev, the Soviet Union was placing its missiles in Cuba. A decade later, Udall would intimate that Khrushchev's meeting with Frost (and separately with Udall) was part of his audacious plan to turn Cuba into a fortress armed against the United States. Be that as it may, Frost's last gesture to claim a grand public role for poetry and for the poet's power to influence policy had melted away before the hard political facts and unexpected world events.[22]

Frost had traveled to the Soviet Union with a plan. On the eve of his departure he set down the lines of that general plan for the benefit of his biographer and as a contribution, perhaps, to history itself. On the fifteenth of August he briefed Lawrance Thompson: "The issue before Russia and us is which comes nearer—their democracy or ours—placating everybody. I may tell them what the issue is but won't claim it is nothing to fight about. Let's be great about it, not petty with petty twits." He allowed that both countries had "a mighty history" and hoped that "we can show ourselves mighty without being ugly. I get round once in so often to the word magnanimity, don't I?" He had a plan: "I shall be prophesying not just predicting from statistics—talking of the next hundred years ahead," he starts out. "I may tell them theirs is an imperial democracy like Caesar's Rome, ours a senatorial like the Roman republic. I have been having all sorts of ideas but as I say for dignity I shall depend on the poems few will understand. I guess you pretty well know my attitude. I shall praise them for art and science and athletics." He might speak to them "of the severity they've been easing down from towards socialism and our liberality we've been straining up from to the same socialism. And then again I may not. I go as an opportunist on the loose. I'd like a chance to ask the great Khrushchev to grant me one request and then ask him a hard one."[23]

Of peculiar interest to the student of Frost, however, is that the poet, who believed that the thing lost in translation was poetry itself, should have put himself and his poetry in the position of being inevitably lost or—at best—misunderstood. A computer translation would render into Russian the English saw "the spirit is willing but the flesh is weak" as "the whiskey is strong but the cow is dead."[24] There are no indications that anything as dramatically distorted happened to Frost's poems when he "said" them in Moscow and Leningrad or when he spoke with Khrushchev in Gagra, but it was readily apparent that getting his poetic messages across was a hit-or-miss affair at best. Nevertheless, he took chances. He read "Departmental," his tale in couplets of the death of the ant Jerry and of the "special Janizary / Whose office it is to bury / The dead of the commissary," which, among other targets, satirizes bureaucracies and all forms of collectivism—the line "our selfless forager Jerry" (262), Frost said, "sums up all socialism"[25]—and should have been readily understood as such by any literate citizen or leader of the Soviet Union. And seemingly on the spur of the moment (and to the surprise of his American companions) he once read a comic anti-war poem that parodies the nursery rhyme "Hey Diddle Diddle." He had just published "Lines Written in Dejection on the Eve of Great Success" in his latest book and, as it turned out, his last one, *In the Clearing*. The section of the poem labeled "Postscript" concludes with a keen observation about how we handle blame for starting a war: "'Well, who begun it?'" is asked aggressively, for "that's what at the end of a war / We always say—not who won it, / Or what it was foughten for" (471).[26]

Only Frost would have run the risk of taking on the Russians with a comic anti-war fable that had to run the gauntlet of translation. It did not work. "It meant nothing to his audience, though there was a scattering of polite applause," reported his friend Frederick Adams.[27] But perhaps Adams missed something. For, although Frost might not have known why, his choice of a poem parodying the nursery rhyme "Hey Diddle Diddle" would have undoubtedly struck a familiar note for some of his Russian listeners. In fact, it has been noted, "English nursery rhymes *en masse* seem to appeal to the children of Russia." "Colourfully illustrated collections have been published in Moscow," write Iona and Peter Opie, with translations made by eminent poets."[28] Frost was decidedly more successful with "Mending Wall." His Russian audiences already knew the poem (it had been translated in the 1930s) and often requested it. If, as will be recalled, Frost had claimed that "the pleasantest use of a poem" was to see "a fragment of it quoted in an editorial," one can only surmise the number of times "Mending Wall" had been put to use in political discourse, especially in the protracted controversy over the Communist-built wall that divided Berlin. "Perhaps Frost's most apposite line for the present moment in history is his famous: 'Something there is that doesn't love a wall,'" read the *New York Times* review of *In the Clearing* five months before Frost went to Russia. "Old-stone savage or new-power-hungry savage," the reviewer concludes, "the good-fences-make-good-neighbors philosophy is riddled again in Berlin."[29] That Frost was reading the poem in the Soviet Union became news when the *Times* printed a page of photographs of the poet in audience among the Russians. Several pictures—under the title of "'Mending Wall' in Moscow"—carried a single caption: "Some of the gentlest mockery the Soviet Union has endured came recently from the 88-year-old poet, Robert Frost, a cultural-exchange visitor. Among other things, he read from his poem, 'Mending Wall,' in Moscow: 'Before I built a wall I'd ask to know / What I was walling out. / And to whom I was likely to give offense.'" The reference to Berlin seemed clear; but Frost would not interpret.[30]

Frost, like everyone else, knew America's official position on the wall, and he was in agreement with his President that the wall should come down. It was, after all, consonant with his dictum that nations must be nations before they could go international. But he was also aware that his poem—indeed, all poems—could be put to different uses, just as jokes told on different occasions to different audiences might aim at different purposes and convey different meanings. It is doubtful, therefore, that Frost read the poem merely because his audiences had asked him to include it in his reading. It seems ingenuous to think, therefore, that he did not read it, as Reeve insisted, "as a commentary on Berlin, which one reporter unfortunately interpreted it to be."[31]

For some unstated reason Frost had come to trust this man of power who could turn a shoe into a weapon and a proverb into a tool. It was that

9. An Art of the Possible   97

trust and a considerable faith in himself that took Frost at the end of his life to Russia. He had no wish to confront the Premier of the Soviet Union before a worldwide audience as President Eisenhower's Vice President Richard Nixon had ended up doing. He wanted no equivalent of a kitchen debate with Nikita Khrushchev. Rather, he would talk with the Premier—on a very high plane—of national accomplishments such as the flight of the Wright Brothers at Kitty Hawk. He had entitled one of his latest poems "How Hard It Is to Keep from Being King When It's in You and in the Situation," and now, in his eighty-ninth year, he found himself in the rough equivalent of such a situation. Knowing that words are deeds, he now had an opportunity to prove that grand deeds can also be poems. In fact, even when it became public knowledge, almost immediately after his return from Russia, that things had turned dark for the two superpowers, he remained preoccupied with what he considered to have been his wondrous trip to the Soviet Union and his one-on-one meeting with Khrushchev. At the National Poetry Festival in Washington in October 1962, still hoping for a debriefing meeting with the President, he went over those recent events: "Everything was so nice, with the great man, too," he started out. "Just what I wanted him to be; and talked, and went the whole length, everywhere—the greatness of it."

> The biggest thing about it was that he wanted—he agreed with me that the great thing was to make the issue great; not to have petty squabbles decide it. The great issue between our two kinds of democracy, we called it. I called it that myself, in courtesy, and he agreed to that. Big—make it magnificent, you know, the great world thought—next hundred years. And whatever came, we didn't name the word "war."

Nor, for that matter did they "talk about love or peace or any of those silly things," he concluded, they had taken to the high road, as Frost saw it, and stayed the course. "All talk big, but splendid, and the kind of thing that we could rest in, with big trials—trials of athletics and science and all that—and about democracy: who's produced the greater men, the greater leaders, and all that," he offered. "And the showdowns, I wasn't, talking about those, you know, and he wasn't, but we knew what we meant."[32] And when Norman Thomas, the best-known American Socialist of his time, asked him for clarification or explanation of what he had been reported as having said upon his arrival in New York, he set down carefully his answer. "I can't see how Khrushchev's talk got turned into what you quote that we weren't men enough to fight," he began. "I came nearer than he to threatening: with my native geniality I assured him that we were no more afraid of him than he was of us." "We seemed in perfect agreement that we shouldn't come to blows till we were sure there was a big issue remaining between us, of his kind of democracy versus our kind of democracy, approximating each other as they are, his by easing downward towards socialism from the severity of its original ideals, ours by straining upwards toward socialism through various phases of welfare state-ism. I said the stage or arena is set between us for a rivalry of perhaps a hundred years." For Frost was ever hopeful that something good would come about between the U.S. and the U.S.S.R. "Let's hope we can take it out in sports, science, art, business, and politics before ever we have to take it out in the bloody politics of war," he suggested. "It was all magnanimity—Aristotle's great word. I should have expected you to approve. Liberal in a good sense of the word…. If only a word would stay put in basic English."[33]

Frost dictated his reply to Thomas, but, keeping it, apparently, for revisions, he did not get to mail it. "Decency, honor, and not too much deceit," he had cautioned diplomats when leaving Brazil in 1954, "are about the best one can aspire to in international relations."[34] But in his one attempt at high international diplomacy, one that was both quixotic and exemplary, this "opportunist on the loose" (as he called himself) had set aside his own advice to diplomats and tried to believe in his country's future.

10

His Best Bid for Fame

"My definition of literature would be just this, words that have become deeds," wrote Frost in 1915.[1] A case in point is "Stopping by Woods on a Snowy Evening"—sixteen lines set down one fine June morning. The poem has had an extraordinary career—varied and uncommonly useful. With tongue in cheek, Frost described this, perhaps his most beloved New England georgic work, as "the short poem with the long name." That there was "a whole room devoted" to that short poem brought the poet Robert Pinsky "unexpected delight" on his visit to the Frost Stone House Museum in Shaftsbury, Vermont.[2] In *Pale Fire*, Vladimir Nabokov's fictional literary scholar, Charles Kinbote, annotates three lines (424–26) in John Shade's poem, "my name/ Was mentioned twice, as usual just behind / (one oozy footstep) Frost": "Frost is the author of one of the greatest short poems in the English language, a poem that every American boy knows by heart, about the wintry woods, and the dreary dusk, and the little horsebells of gentle remonstration in the dull darkening air, and that prodigious and poignant end—two closing lines identical in every syllable, but one personal and physical, and the other metaphysical and universal," writes Kinbote. "I dare not quote from memory lest I displace one small precious word."[3]

Pale Fire, with its 172 pages of commentary devoted to a poem running to fewer than a thousand lines (999 to be exact), appeared just months before Frost's death. Oddly, Frost had remarked, many years earlier, "that 'Stopping by Woods on a Snowy Evening' was the kind of poem he'd like to print on one page, to be followed with 'forty pages of footnotes.'"[4] He was joking, of course, though one can easily imagine his actually carrying out the threat, if for no other reason than to poke fun at the practice of the learned, showy Modernists, as in T. S. Eliot, and his "Wasteland."[5] But literary scholars (as Nabokov so perfectly dramatizes) do not often joke about such matters. What the poet did not do—that is, provide the "forty pages of footnotes" to a sixteen-line lyric such as "Stopping by Woods"—the happy drudge that is the scholar will gladly do. So, here, I offer you "footnotes" to what is perhaps Frost's most celebrated poem.

Composition

Frost once described the conditions under which he wrote poems, not why he wrote them but how they came to be: "People always askin' me how I write poetry. Might as well ask a frog how he jumps. How do I know? I feel somp'n here—in my breast—and pretty soon I'm sweatin' over an unborn thought. Birth pains for poetry are the worst of all pains. Worse than real childbirth, I should say. I've said before that the poems of mine that are delivered the easiest are the ones I like to think about—say to people—like my 'Stopping by Woods.'"[6] That something in his chest was also something he was willing to talk about, as he did to the same friend, on another occasion: "I can manage a poem in the singular very well and not feel the strain, not too much. In the midst of my work at the farm I could handle such a task. Sometimes one would grow out of an idea, leaving me relaxed. At other times the idea would produce a second growth, forcing itself as a Siamese twin on its predecessor. That would bring trouble of spirit, and more than likely right in harvest time." He "would be in a terrible stew, fever, likely. My legs would ache," he wrote, "my head would ache. Eating was out of the question. Sleep? There wasn't any." In fact, as he remembered it, "'Stopping by Woods on a Snowy Evening' was written in just about that way," after he had been working all night long on a different poem, "New Hampshire." Yet, he had to admit, "it was written in a few minutes without any strain." As a matter of fact, he continued, "critics think I had that sort of all-night struggle before I could write the little poem I'm talking about. They must have heard me say, something or other, years back, that I wrote all night, in connection with 'Stopping by Woods.' But the thing I worked on all night had no struggle in it at all. It's in print, called 'New Hampshire.' I sat in the same chair and wrote all night." He'd had "a good time writing scatteringly about New Hampshire—how the state has nothing to sell in commercial quantities." Then, having finished "New Hampshire," he "went outdoors, got out sideways and didn't disturb anybody in the house, and about nine or ten o'clock went back in and wrote the piece about the snowy evening and the little horse as if I'd had an hallucination—little hallucination—the one critics write about occasionally." By way of finishing his account of how "Stopping by Woods" came into being, he cautioned: "You can't trust these fellows who write what made a poet write what he wrote. We all of us read our pet theories into a poem."[7]

The desire to be understood but not being understood and the need to fend off those critics who read *their* pet theories into *his* poems offered Frost a perennial challenge. It became a question of audience. "There is an old school of art that insists on the right to be entirely misunderstood by everybody," he allowed. "Some say that we must insist that we write for no audience at all. There must be an audience, an audience invisible, a blend of all the interesting people whom I have dealt with."[8] The question of Frost's audience—not the one he had somewhere in the back of his mind when he wrote but the audience he acquired over the course of his long career—has perplexed, and sometimes vexed his critics. More than those of any other poet of his time, Frost's poems have appealed to all sorts of readers—from the vulgar (in the old sense of the word) to the erudite. This stretch has not bothered the so-called "vulgar," I suspect, but it has disturbed some of the "elite." Let one of Frost's leading interpreters speak for all those who are so disturbed. His examples are "The Pasture," "Birches," "Mending Wall," and "Stopping by Woods." "[H]aven't these poems been so much exclaimed over by people whose poetic taste is dubious or hardly existent," he asks, "that on those grounds alone Frost is to be distrusted?"[9] The question, as Pritchard poses it, is both rhetorical and strikingly egregious—rhetorical because Pritchard goes on to insist on the many legitimate poetic virtues intrinsic to these great poems and egregious because it is utterly condescending, so certain is he that he and the happy few, perhaps, alone possess "poetic taste" that is not "dubious."

Publication

On March 7, 1923, the *New Republic* published, on the same page, poems under the catchall title of "Two Winter Poems." The first poem was "Stopping by Woods" and the second was "Moon Rider," by the once widely-read poet, William Rose Benét. Benét's poem is typically romantic in sentiment, exemplifying in its figures a linguistic artifice typical of the common poetic language of the day. It begins "A sky of deepening bronze / Seemed tolling like a bell. / Blue ice filmed shrivelled ponds," ending with the line that introduces its central image: "Snow whispering fell." It continues with elaborate descriptions: "Trees traced a frieze of black. / One window's spark / Flecked gold upon the farmyard track," but then turns to an action: "He cinched the saddle on the colt / That snuffed his hand," in preparation for a ride over "the open land" that "lay ghostly still from hill to hill" while below them the snow "tossed" like "foam." Then follows a rather intense description of a ride while "stars crackled overhead," giving way to several stanzas of filler, until the final lines invoking a "frosted heaven" and "the moon's shell / filled" to overflow with light, "welling like ringing of a bell / through the lingering night."[10] That in 1923 Frost was already the more highly regarded of the two poets is indicated by the fact his name—not Benét's—appears on the magazine's cover: "A Winter Poem by Robert Frost."[11] Frost did not think much of Benét's poem. "Bill Benét's is a terrible example of really first rate poetical words and lines that come to nothing in the aggregate," he wrote in a letter to Sylvester Baxter at the time. "In detail he is a little like De la Mare (in this particular poem). But with De la Mare the whole poem is always the thing. He is never just a texture."[12] Unlike "Stopping by Woods," Benét's poem, it has been judged, "lacks unity; it contains details whose fanciful nature distracts or irritates us; the rhythm is uneven to no purpose, and the poem as a whole spills out of the ballad-stanza which might allow it to become more than 'just a texture.'"[13] When the collection *New Hampshire* appeared, "Stopping by Woods" was singled out as a "poem of the month" by both Jean Starr Untermeyer (who reprinted the poem) and Babette Deutsch, who, getting the poem exactly right, extolled its "cool simple sufficiency."[14]

The Oxford Comma

The first version of the poem, published in the *New Republic*, differs from most of the subsequent versions in punctuation. This is important, since punctuation in this poem would become, after Frost's death, a matter of contention among students of Frost's poetry, becoming, for a while, one of the two great "Stopping by Woods" controversies. It stems from the publication of *The Poetry of Robert Frost* in 1969, six years after Frost's death. The most widely publicized of the numerous emendations by its editor, Edward Connery Lathem, is the comma he inserted in line thirteen of the poem on page 224. Although the poet Donald Hall was not the first one to spot these changes, he laid out the most elaborate case against Lathem's emendations, especially the by then infamous "comma." "Frost wrote the line: The woods are lovely, dark and deep," Hall starts out. "We do not find this line" in Lathem's edition of Frost's poetry; "instead we

10. *His Best Bid for Fame*

find: The woods are lovely, dark, and deep. To say that the woods are 1) lovely, 2) dark, and 3) deep differs considerably from claiming that they are lovely *in that* they are dark and deep." Hall continues to make his case: "In Frost's line, the general adjective *lovely* is explained by the more particular modifiers *dark* and *deep*. In the editor's line, the egalitarian threesome is non-parallel"—as if "we proclaimed that a farmer grew apples, McIntoshes, and Northern Spies."[15] What Hall advocates, of course, is a return to punctuating the line as it appears in *New Hampshire*, as well as the several selected or collective volumes that followed over time.

Since Lathem adduced no textual authority for his emendation, it can be reasonably concluded that he was guided in the matter by his understanding of the meaning of Frost's line to provide proper punctuation. He saw in the line, as Hall surmises, a sequence of three items, each term to be set off by commas. The question to be asked, of course, is whether or not it can be determined that the poet intended to put before the reader three items in a series.

In his note to the poem as emended, Lathem lists a variant for the first word of line five in the poem's first appearance in the *New Republic* in 1923: "The" instead of the later "My." He does not mention that in that first appearance of the poem, there is no comma in line two between the words "village" and "though"; that there is a period, not a comma, at the end of line thirteen; and, more importantly, that there are no commas in the same line, which reads, thus, "The woods are lovely dark and deep." Nor does he mention that the *New Republic* text is duplicated, a month later, in London, in Harold Munro's *Chapbook* for April 1923.[16] That these appearances, on opposite sides of the Atlantic, are textually identical suggests that the poem as printed conformed to the poet's exact intentions at the time. (It is possible to argue, unlikely though it seems to me, especially given the closeness in dates of publication, that Harold Munro lifted the poem from the pages of the *New Republic*. There is no evidence I know of to indicate that the poem was so pirated, something that Frost was sure to complain about to someone or other.)

That there was no punctuation in line thirteen is of course uncharacteristic of Frost's overall poetic likes and dislikes, both at the time and subsequently. But in eschewing the punctuation normally employed in such instances, was he reaching out for a transcription of a cluster of sight and feeling in the manner, perhaps, of his younger contemporary e. e. cummings or the nineteenth-century proto-modernist Gerard Manley Hopkins? Did he venture to employ the word "lovely" adverbially to modify the predicate adjective "dark"? That he did so may not be entirely convincing, perhaps, for arguing against such an interpretation is Frost's recorded disapproval in 1935 of poets who would be "new" by "subtraction—elimination," by trying it "without punctuation."[17] But this does not conclude the matter, for into the mix must go the evidence provided by the text of "Stopping by Woods" used in facsimile as frontispiece for *From Snow to Snow*, Henry Holt's mensal anthology of Frost poems in 1936. This holograph reverts to the text of both the *New Republic* and *Chapbook* appearances, showing no commas in line thirteen: "The woods are lovely dark and deep." That this holograph derives from a date later than those of the copies used for the first magazine publications in 1923 seems to be established by the fact that the fifth line of the poem reads, not "*The* little horse must think it queer," but "*My* little horse must think it queer" (italics added), a change repeated in all printings after 1923. Yet, it is also notable that line thirteen of the printed text for the poem, representing the month of December, as it appears in *From Snow to Snow*, in contrast with the manuscript version used as frontispiece, reads, "The wood are lovely, dark and deep."[18] What seems conclusive at this point is that Frost, at different times, authorized two versions of line thirteen—the one-comma version in *New Hampshire* and the selected and collective volumes, and the no-comma version published in the *New Republic*, the *Chapbook*, and in at least one manuscript. Should other transcriptions of the poem turn up—inscribed in readers' copies of Frost's poems, for instance—a count might be kept of which version of line thirteen Frost was wont to set down when recalling the poem and just when he did so. Incidentally, when the *New York Times* reached Lathem "at his home in Hanover, N.H." and asked him about the Library of America volume's restoration of Frost's punctuation in the poem, he told them "he stood by his commas. 'The reading I've given it is the accurate one,' he said of 'Stopping by Woods.'"[19] But the public has also spoken; a recent piece in the *New York Times* on the Library's online collection of images raging from prints and maps to dust jackets and menus characterized the Library's digital gallery as "lovely, dark and deep"—with no comma after "dark."[20]

Repetition

In teaching "Stopping by Woods" I occasionally exorcised my students by asking them this question: Which of the last two lines of the poem do you think the poet set down first? The fifteenth line: "And miles to go before I sleep" or the sixteenth: "And miles to go before I sleep." It was, on my part, a pretext for getting at something about the rhyme scheme of the poem—aaba, bbcb, ccdc, dddd. Having committed himself, in the first stanza, to a demanding rhyme scheme in which the rhymes of each succeeding stanza were dictated by the sound of the end-word of the third line of each stanza, the poet found himself with something of a problem when he came to end his poem. He decided not only to rhyme all four end-words of the final stanza but to do so by writing in identical lines for lines three and four. One knows, in reading the poem, that line four repeats line three, of course. But do we know which of the two lines—three or four—Frost set down first? The answer, it seems logical enough, is line four. This seems logical because, unless Frost knew the solution to the problem of closing out his poem in advance, he would undoubtedly have hit on the last line first. The brief discussion, always spirited, got them to focus (for once, at least) on rhyme-schemes—that there was such a thing. There is a way to answer the question definitively. An early draft of stanzas two through four of the poem has long been available in facsimile.[21] The revisions are instructive. While Frost's change from "horses" to a single horse squares with Lesley Frost's memory that the "little horse" was named "Eunice,"[22] one might reasonably wonder about the identity of the other horse included in Frost's reference to "steaming horses" in the early manuscript. The manuscript shows five lines for the final stanza with the original third line crossed out. The original line defies exact transcription, though its last four words are clear enough—"and there are miles." Had he retained the end-word, his rhyme scheme for the last stanza would have been dded, leaving "e" hanging fire as a rhyme. Use of the same line for lines 3 and 4, brought the poem's rhyme scheme to an ingeniously devised close—dddd.[23] With the recent publication, however, of *The Collected Prose of Robert Frost* we have Frost's own words on the matter, written in 1950 for a new edition of Cleanth Brooks and Robert Penn Warren's *Understanding Poetry* but not used: "I might confess the trade secret that I wrote the third line of the last stanza in 'Stopping by Woods' in such a way as to call for another stanza when I didn't want another stanza and didn't have another stanza in me but with great presence of mind and a sense of what a good boy I was I instantly struck the line out and made my exit with a repeat end."[24]

Christmas Poem

For many years Frost chose a poem as his Christmas poem to send out to friends. "Stopping by Woods" was not one of the poems so chosen.

Surely soon after its publication in *New Hampshire* in 1923 the poem became so widely known that that fact itself may have discouraged Frost from using it as his Christmas poem. Yet there is no poem more suitable to be so used, I would imagine, than "Stopping by Woods." I would not suggest, however, as letters to the *Saturday Review* and the *New Republic*, reflecting the December tinge of the poem, have suggested, that the owner's "house" in the village is a church and that the woods the poet stops before are owned by God.[25] Interestingly, when (probably in 1955, when he read at Brown University) Frost was asked about pretty much the same reading of the poem, by Sharon Brown, an English professor, the answer he received, according to a student who heard the story, was an inconclusive "Perhaps."

Of course, "Stopping by Woods" need not be about "God" (or Santa Claus, the bright idea of at least one reader, possibly with tongue in cheek) to be recognized as belonging to the sub-genre of the "Christmas Poem." It would be considered one even if we did not have the poet's much-later revelation (to his daughter and to one, otherwise, obscure reader) that the situation depicted in the poem had its basis in Frost's experience as a disappointed and distressed father returning home empty-handed, with nothing to show for his trip to town to sell his wares just a few days before Christmas. That he knew, however, that it could not be published as a Christmas poem, at least not at the Christmas season, when it was customary for journals and newspapers to publish seasonal verse that was invariably up-lifting, is suggested by his offering it to the *New Republic*. Standard fare in more popular publications—I have in mind the *New-England Homestead* and other occupational journals of that type—included poems about the baby Jesus, and Santa Claus, with snow and snowflake imagery in abundance, along with references to Christmas music, gifts and dinners. Typical is a poem called, simply, "Christmas," the first stanza of which is replete, as was customary in such poems, with exclamation points:

> Christmas music, Christmas greens,
> Mistletoe and holly!
> Happy faces, festive scenes.
> All the world grown jolly!
> Santa Claus with reindeer fleet,
> Sleigh-bells gaily ringing,
> Cupboards full of viands sweet
> Gifts that love is bringing,
> 'Tis of all the year the prime.
> Merry, merry, Christmas Time![26]

It is not known that Frost subscribed to this weekly journal or even saw it occasionally, but a survey of the contents of this publication for the years 1900 to 1910, the years during which Frost was living on the Derry farm in New Hampshire, turns up poems that, after the fact, recall some of Frost's own poems in subject matter, situation, language or imagery. The poems that I shall adduce appeared in Christmas issues of the *New-England Homestead*. "December" is typical.

> Happy little snowflakes,
> Flitting everywhere;
> Dancing down so gaily
> Through the chilly air,
> Resting on the fir trees
> Branches, here and there;
> Purer and more fair,—
> in December.
>
> Soon the ground is covered
> With a mantle white;
> Now the sun, appearing,
> Sheds a radiant light;
> Fluttering gently earthward
> Snowbirds cease their flight;
> Holly berries, crimson,
> 'Gainst green leaves shine bright;
> Someone darts by, laughing,
> To see the world so light,—
> 'Tis December![27]

Particularly Frost-like is the line "fluttering gently earthward."

Or take "Christmas at the Farm" with an imagistic description of the snow and the woods: "swirling snow is falling" in "the forest dark and still"—Frost's surviving manuscript shows that the line "between the woods and frozen lake" first read "between a forest and a lake."[28] But occasionally there was a notable exception to the predictably sweet Christmas poem in the *New-England Homestead* during the first decade of the twentieth century, buoyant in tone and up-lifting in sentiment. Such a poem, temperamentally much closer to Frost but hardly comparable in technique or language, is the eight-line poem "A Christmas Hardship."

> Through all the year I dwell content,
> And take the frugal lot that's sent
>
> For mine. But ah, when chiming bells
> Breathe Christmas gladness in their knells,—
>
> On that one day, for earthly gold
> I'd almost turn a pirate bold!

'Tis hard in poverty to sup,
When children hand their stockings up![29]

Children's Poem

Ever alert to defend his poem against what might be called the Dreiserian reading of "Stopping by Woods" (more about that in a moment), Frost ended one such defense with an anecdote. "I'm going to get up a children's book of my poetry pretty soon," he promised. "'Stopping by Woods' will be in it." The book would be made up of "short poems to see who can learn 'em at one hearing. Always girls first." Then his anecdote: "A teacher tried these out to see how many could get them memorized by hearing 'em once. One little girl remembered 'Stopping by Woods' at one hearing. She went home and said it to her mother. The mother said,

"Why, dear, I knew that before you were born."
She spoke right up: "Then, why didn't you tell me!"

That was a nice adventure," Frost sums up. "The poem's on my mind lately, I suppose because of the fuss it has stirred up."[30]

This was evidence, of course, that despite its beginnings and the audiences to which he first addressed it—the readership of the *New Republic* and the *Chapbook*—the poem had become a children's favorite. The matter bothered Donald Hall, who, as editor of *The Oxford Book of Children's Verse in America*, wrote apologetically as late as 1985: "I include Robert Frost's 'Stopping by Woods on a Snowy Evening,' because anthologists of children's verse have used it for several decades; it has even been illustrated and published as a children's book by itself," Hall explains. "Does it belong in *The Oxford Book of Children's Verse in America*?" he asks rhetorically. "If we know anything about Robert Frost we know he did not write it for children. I reprint the poem because it has *become* a poem for children— but I do not include it without doubt. It is a poem passed on to children for their own good, not because of an intrinsic or structural intention, like a pipe for crawling through."[31]

When these sentences were quoted in the *New York Times*, they appeared under the heading: "What Do Children Really Like?" Well, one thing that fascinates children is death—which accounts, perhaps, for the Dreiserian subtexts found in the poem by John Ciardi and others—that I shall turn to next. And what, by the way, was Donald Hall thinking, particularly when his collection for children opens with the Twenty-Third

Psalm, followed a page later with extracts from Michael Wigglesworth's "The Day of Doom"?

Death Wish Poem

The proposal that Frost's poem has as it sub-text the suppressed expression of a death wish has caused a major controversy among some of Frost's most serious-minded readers. When John Ciardi suggested in the *Saturday Review of Literature* that "Stopping by Woods" was the dramatized expression of a death-wish, he received a flood of letters, most of them taking issue with his reading. The most famous of these letter-writers in 1958 was Philip Wylie, the author of *A Generation of Vipers* and the virulent warrior against American "momism." He chose to chastise Ciardi for his piece in the *Saturday Review of Literature* by "addressing" Frost in a parody of his familiar poem, which he titled "Stopping to Write a Friend on a Thick Night." It concludes that Frost's "blanket snow's thus double-crossed" by one "who should be blanket-tossed," for "he has miles to go to Frost / And years to learn it's Frost he lost."[32]

But the controversy over "Stopping by Woods" as the expression of a death-wish has never been entirely resolved. "Somebody's been reading Dreiser or something" was Frost's way of dismissing of what he considered to be inappropriate doom-and-gloom readings of his most widely quoted poem.[33] He brushed aside the idea that "Stopping by Woods" was about anybody's death-wish, a suicide considered and rejected or at least put off. In support of Frost's position, it has been noted that Frost once explained to a stranger, in 1947 (though the explanation had also been made to his daughter Lesley, as she recalled, "sometime in the forties"), that the poem derived from the poet's own sadness one Christmas eve as he returned home alone with no gifts for his children.[34] The "woods" that are "lovely, dark and deep" may tempt him to tarry before them but that they stand for the attractions of death is not part of the poet's intention, it seems. This existential dilemma is simply not, as Frost might have put it, in the situation. In fact, Frost took his case to his readers, explaining the simple meaning of the poem over and again when he did his lectures and readings. This is how he put it in his lecture-reading at Brown University on December 7, 1955: "There's not a single anecdote you can tell but has alteriority to it, or you wouldn't call it significant. That's what you mean its significance is. And the funny part of it is, you can use an anecdote in two or three different ways, at different banquets. You can make it mean one thing by a little touch here and another thing somewhere else. And just so with the poems." Then he brought up "Stopping by Woods." "You know what I could use it for, offhand? It says in it, 'The woods are lovely, dark and deep, / But I have promises to keep.' Now I might just say it at the end of this evening: 'This is all very fine, 'the woods are lovely, dark and deep,'—this is all very fine, being with you, but I best be getting' along back to Cambridge. There are other things." Of course, he insisted, "that doesn't mean Cambridge is any worse that Providence. Just means that's the way you part often, with that very expression. This is all very fine, but I got to be gettin' along. Some people have turned that into an ugliness. I'm just willing they should, but I think they're off the key of the poem—that you got to go. That somebody's been reading Dreiser or something. Gets the idea, the other thing."[35]

Granted that it may not be possible or even desirable to pin down and define the mystery that is the heart and soul of Frost's poem. Yet it seems to me that the poet protests too much when he denies the "Dreiserian" possibilities in the situation he dramatizes in this poem that is both lyric and monologue. After all, the dark side of Frost, as Lionel Trilling belatedly discovered, was indeed terrible in poems such as "Home Burial," "The Hill Wife," "Desert Places," "Acquainted with the Night," "An Old Man's Winter Night," to mention a few titles among many.

But the death-wish theory can be approached in another way. In the surviving manuscript of "Stopping by Woods," the fifth line of the poem reads: "The steaming horses think it queer"—which gave way, in the final version, to "My little horse must think it queer."[36] The changes seem to indicate that even if the poem recovers a bit of the poet's immediately personal experience, fact at this point gives way to artifice (actuality to art), and memory yields to imagination or fancy. The change also aligns details of the poem closely with details in the source that I shall propose for it. For antecedent to the poet's "little horse" that shakes its bell and recalls the poet from his fixation on the dark woods to the responsibilities he has assumed is the sorrel horse that appears in Edith Wharton's Berkshires novella *Ethan Frome* (1911). In each instance the horse is instrumental in the working-out of the themes of moral-ethical responsibility that link poem and story. The last thing that the unhappily married Ethan notices before the run down the hill that he thinks will snuff out his life and that of his young lover is a tug at his conscience, at his sense of responsibility. "Suddenly he heard the old sorrel whinny across the road, and thought: 'He's wondering why he doesn't get his supper.'"[37] Then "just as they started he heard the sorrel's whinny again, and the familiar wistful call, and all the confused images it brought with it" (183). In the moments after the crash that has not taken either his or Mattie's life, Ethan's high sense of responsibility and his dreadful and depressing mission as caretaker of the weak and the injured comes again to his full consciousness as he hears not the whinny of his horse this time but the sound of "a little animal twittering somewhere near by under the snow.... It made a small frightened cheep like a field mouse, and he wondered languidly if it were hurt. Then he understood that it must be in pain: pain so excruciating that he seemed, mysteriously, to feel it shooting through his own body" (185). He discovers that the sound made by the small animal he hears is really coming from the seriously injured Mattie.

> He got his face down close to hers, with his ear to her mouth, and in the darkness he saw her eyes open and heard her say his name.
> "Oh, Matt, I thought we'd fetched it," he moaned; and far off, up the hill, he heard the sorrel whinny, and thought: "I ought to be getting him his feed" [186].

Just as concerned with the dictates of conscience and responsibility, Frost's poem is less theatrical in incident and gesture than is Wharton's tale, but it is no less dramatic. In Frost's poem the woods—"lovely, dark and deep"—are as dangerously attractive to the speaker of the poem as is the long sled run, increasingly treacherous at dusk, in *Ethan Frome*. Yet there is in both instances a "saving grace," if you will, in a non-human sound or gesture that recalls both Wharton's Ethan (the sorrel's whinny) and Frost's speaker (shaking the harness bells) to their human responsibilities, to an act of consciousness or thought dictated by a triggered conscience. When we consider Frost's poem in the context of *Ethan Frome*, we are encouraged to stress the ethical nature of both works. Each of them illustrates how difficult choices, especially those made to accord with the mandates of a righteous conscience, are enacted, even when they serve only to intensify the conditions of life at their seemingly most unbearable. To recognize in *Ethan Frome* a literary source for "Stopping by Woods" lends support to the argument of those who find that Frost's poem, on some level at least, is about a death-wish. In fairness, Frost can be given a last say on "Stopping by Woods." At Bread Loaf, on July 5, 1954, he followed up his reading of the poem: "That one I've been more bothered with than anybody has ever been with any poem in just the pressing it for more than it should be pressed for. It means enough without its being pressed. That's all right, you know. I don't say that somebody shouldn't press it, but I don't want to be there."[38]

I note, in passing, that the Ciardi reading of "Stopping by Woods" has standing in the culture at large. *The Sopranos* (HBO television) would show us that Frost's poem is indeed about death, or so goes the reading Meadow, the college-age Mafioso daughter, gives the poem. Her reading, however, brings not clarity to her younger brother but promotes confusion. When she explains to A. J., who is struggling with the poem, a class assignment, that "white" is the color of death, the information serves only to puzzle A. J., who complains that he thought the color of death was "black."

Parody

Whether or not "Stopping by Woods" was Frost's personal favorite among his poems, few would dispute that it remains his most readily-recognized and beloved poem to the public at large—though, as Frost complained, it was also the most over-analyzed.[39] Its verses are still "sung" to the tune of a popular song, amusing and delighting hordes of students, who always seem not to know whether such performances brought down the aesthetic value of the poem. Check the internet and read the following: "Anyway, as far as fitting music and lyrics, did you know you can sing Robert Frost's 'Stopping by Woods on a Snowy Evening' to the turn of 'Hernando's Hideaway' from the musical *The Pajama Game*? Go ahead, try it: 'Whoooooose woods / These are / I think I know' (etc.). Maddening—you'll never read the poem again without hearing that Broadway tango. But hey, that's intertextuality for ya!"[40]

"Stopping by Woods" has made it to greeting cards. Complementing "Promises to Keep," an email card reproducing the poem as Frost wrote it and that can be sent at no cost,[41] there are parodies. Consider "Birthday Poems by Robert Frosting," which contains the following homage (with a hint of Frost's "Fire and Ice"): "Whose cake this is I think I know, / With scads of candles giving glow, / A conflagration growing higher, / It must be yours, based on the fire!"[42] And an unidentified somebody seems to be familiar with the extant draft of stanzas two through four of "Stopping by Woods," for a card sold in shops supplies a draft, showing obligatory cross-outs, of the missing first verse.

> Whose woods these are ~~i a'int /~~
> ~~sure~~ i think i know his ~~apartment~~
> ~~building~~ house is ~~downtown~~[43]

Nor has "Stopping by Woods" escaped the pen of the comic-strip cartoonist. An installment of Brian and Greg Walker's "Hi & Lois" strip (available on the internet) displays two figures walking through a snowy wood.

> FIRST FIGURE: Robert Frost is my favorite American poet!
> SECOND FIGURE: What did he write?
> FIRST FIGURE: I'm glad you asked! Let me recite a few lines.... "Whose woods these are I think I know his house is in the village though. He will not see me stopping here to watch his woods fill up with snow."

This pleasant exchange is punctuated by a loud BOOM!—followed by a hunter (or farmer) holding a gun and yelling "Get offa my property!"—to which the Second Figure reacts—"Show him your poetic license, Dad!"[44]

Parodies are a sub-set of adaptations, Linda Hutcheon points out, adding that "an adaptation is not vampiric; it does not draw the life-blood from its source and leave it dying or dead, nor is it paler than the adapted work. It may, on the contrary, keep that prior work alive," and in some cases help to give "it an afterlife it would never have had otherwise."[45]

On the Web (and Elsewhere)

What has made "Stopping by Woods" so attractive to Frost's common readers, especially those whose taste in poetry has been questioned by some of Frost's readers? Surely there is nothing remarkable about its language per se or the poet's phrasing. Yet Google "stopping by woods," "promises to keep," "miles to go," "before I sleep" or "miles to go before I sleep"—simple words and commonplace phrasing, after all—and you will be faced with dozens upon dozens of hits. These phrases appear in titles published, not merely in journals such as *Canadian Literature* but in unexpected places such as *Social Science Review, University of Colorado Law Review, Nursing and Health Care Perspectives, New England Journal of Medicine, Science,* and *Wildlife Conservation.* There are borrowings from the poem for book titles: *Miles to Go: A Personal History of Social Policy* (1996) by Daniel Patrick Moynihan; *Promises to Keep: Technology, Law, and the Future of Entertainment* by William W. Fisher; *Promises to Keep: Daily Devotions for Men of Integrity* by Nick Harrison; *Promises to Keep: How Jackie Robinson Changed America* by Sharon Robinson; *Promises to Keep: The United States Since World War II* by Paul S. Boyer; *Promises to Keep: Crafting Your Wedding Ceremony* by Barry L. Stopfel; *Whose Woods*

These Are: A History of the Bread Loaf Writers' Conference, 1926–1992, ed. David Howard Bain and Mary Smyth Duffy (1993); *Whose Woods These Are: The Story of the National Forests* (1962); *Whose Woods Are These?* (Western Massachusetts Small Forest Landowners Creating a Co-op, 2001); and *Before I Sleep* by Dr. Tom Dooley. These phrases have been appropriated for songs, countless stories, sermons, and advertisements. Therapists and grief counselors have appropriated the poem for their own purposes. In Las Vegas the very popular French-Canadian singer Celine Dion sings a song, "Miles to Go," in which she quotes the last lines of Frost's poem twice, just as the poet does.[46] Commonplace the phrases may seem to many when taken separately, they nevertheless appeal to some sort of universal instinct. Who wouldn't want a part of that magic?

(No) Conclusion

Is it the poem's originality in imagery or metaphor that accounts for its success among readers? Maybe not. After all, "the sweep/ Of easy wind and downy flake" echoes Emily Dickinson's "easy sweeps of sky"; "he gives his harness bells a shake" is reminiscent of Sir Walter Scott's "he gave the bridle-reins a shake" in "The Rover"; "and miles to go before I sleep" recalls "And I have many miles on foot to fare" from John Keats's "Keen Fitful Gusts"; and even "the woods are lovely, dark and deep" reworks "Our bed is lovely, dark, and sweet" from Thomas Lovell Beddoes' "The Phantom Wooer."[47] Yet, this is the way poets consciously or unconsciously mine the work of their predecessors and honor the poems of their own traditions. And for that matter, think of Frost's "lovely, dark and deep" when you read "cold dark deep and absolutely clear" in Elizabeth Bishop's "At the Fishhouses," a poem published more than a generation later.

Is it novelty of scene or situation? Longfellow, one of Frost's favorite poets and from whom he took the title of his first book—*A Boy's Will*—wrote a small poem titled "Snow-Flakes":

> Out of the bosom of the Air,
> Out of the cloud-folds of her garments shaken,
> Over the woodlands brown and bare,
> Over the harvest-fields forsaken,
> Silent, and soft, and slow
> Descends the snow.
>
> Even as our cloudy fancies take
> Suddenly shape in some divine expression,

10. *His Best Bid for Fame*

> Even as the troubled heart doth make
> In the white countenance confession,
> The troubled sky reveals
> The grief it feels.
>
> This is the poem of the air,
> Slowly in silent syllables recorded;
> This is the secret of despair,
> Long in its cloudy bosom hoarded,
> Now whispered and revealed
> To wood and field.[48]

Here is similarity, and difference. In the fashion of his day Longfellow discovered outside himself, in an instance of what Ruskin called the pathetic fallacy, that the snow falling from a "troubled sky reveals" the "grief" that "the troubled heart" feels. If the poet will "make in the white countenance confession," the falling snow constitutes, in the "silent syllables" of the "poem of the air," nature's confession of its own "secret of despair" long "hoarded," but "now whispered and revealed / to wood and field." This is Longfellow's intoned account of an earlier instance of meditation; "Stopping by Woods," on the other hand, intones the meditation itself.[49]

This leads me to something said by C. M. Bowra, sixty-five years ago. "The last verse is a complete surprise," he wrote. "Most of the poem is taken up with a situation which has its own charm, but this becomes much more interesting because it is the prelude to something else which is the more mysterious because very little is said about it. Frost marks this change in his subject with a slight change of technique in the last verse, where a single rhyme and the repetition of the last line show that something important is afoot."[50] In my opinion, Bowra puts his finger on just how Frost's particular technique in this poem serves to bring about what he might call its "ulteriority"[51]—the way in which the poem teases the reader into further thought.[52] To Bowra's well-taken point I would add another thought.

In a notebook Frost jotted down the following sentences: "The mind is given its speed of more miles an hour than even the stream of time," so that "it can choose, absolutely how fast it will go with the stream or whether it will stand still on it or go against it. The great thing is that it can stay in one place for a while," and "it is probably the only thing that can."[53] This, in my view, offers a key to how "Stopping by Woods on a Snowy Evening" brings about its ultimate effect. The poet has made time stand still with his tableau of stopped horse, rider, night and even "falling" snow—which, as the only contrast to this stillness—this moment in time—

enhances the "out-of-time" mode of this experience. And the repetition of the line—the master stroke of the poem, however it was derived, whatever poetic difficulty it was designed to resolve—puts off the end of the timeless, "out-of-time" moment, a "momentary stay against confusion," a momentary stay for the mind "weary of considerations" ("Birches").[54] Writing about a moment in which the mind has had its "stay in one place for a while," the poet recreates that almost motionless moment—a gestalt—at one slow swoop—in the reader's experience of the poem. No wonder, he said to Sidney Cox, shortly after the first publication of "Stopping by Woods," "The more I think of it the surer I am of that there poem."[55] He did not change his mind. Decades later, having once asserted that the poem contains "all I ever knew,"[56] he predicted that it is "my best bid for remembrance."[57]

11

Crowe Ransom

"I felt very sad about Frost, though I didn't go to the funeral," John Crowe Ransom confided to Allen Tate. "I generally had the curious feeling about him of being indebted to his achievement, in this sense: he was at his best a fine poet, but he chose not to be at his best generally, and therefore discharged the debt to the less literate society which we can't find it in us to take seriously." In conclusion, he confessed: "That's a sort of missionary feeling, with relief that somebody else is doing the job. But in saying this much I don't mean that I have let the question worry me."[1]

In print Ransom always rated Frost high among poets writing in English. Early on, for example, Ransom countered what he considered to be Gorham B. Munson's wrong-headed simplifying of the poet's thought by insisting on Frost's irony—"the ultimate mode of the great minds," Ransom insisted.[2] He also noted, at another time, that "the important successors to Wordsworth in the poetry of nature have been Keats, and Hopkins, and our own Robert Frost."[3] When he surveyed the literary achievements of English poets in the first half of the twentieth century, Ransom concluded that the period's major poets were Hardy, Yeats, Robinson, Eliot, and Frost.[4] Modesty, one assumes, kept the ironic Ransom from adding himself to this short list.

Frost was aware of Ransom's poetry by 1918 at the latest. It was Christopher Morley—he had published Ransom's poetry in his newspaper column in New York and Philadelphia—who got Ransom's first manuscript a hearing at Henry Holt, Frost's publisher. Ransom's manuscript, *Poems About God*, was sent to Frost for evaluation, as he later recalled the circumstances of his involvement with Ransom's "early exercises in rustic skepticism"[5]: "There was a year when I lost, sort of, my job," Frost wrote, "and I hadn't anything and there was a lull in everything, selling books, around that time and Holt's gave me a hundred dollars a month to live on with the understanding that I'd read any manuscript they sent me. They only sent me two manuscripts for the year—and one was his [Ransom's] *Poems About God*, and the other I won't mention. But John was sort of my discovery," he boasted. "They printed him. John had repudiated those first poems I believe; he doesn't think so much of them." But Ransom "had the art," he allowed, "and he had the tune."[6]

Later on, readers would notice that much of Ransom's *Poems About God* recalled Frost's poetry. The case for Frost's influence on Ransom's early poems is made by Vivienne Koch.

"All of the *Poems About God* are Emersonian in their sense of aspiration and Frostlike in their feeling for the detail of country life," she writes. "This was the time of Frost's great popularity in America.... Ransom's predilection for homely domestic scenes, for a rather refined colloquialism, as well as the bantering humor with which these materials are employed, all suggest a close study of the New England poet." In particular, Koch suggests that Ransom's poem "Grace" is a version of "The Death of the Hired Man." "Its skillful realism, especially in the brutal incongruity of the anti-poetic effects surrounding the hired man's death, makes an honest and fairly interesting narrative," she argues. "Unlike Frost, however, Ransom rarely bothers to employ a dramatic frame. Most of the *Poems About God* are 'I' poems, and transparently autobiographical," she continues. "There are Southern people, the poet's parents, a Southern reverence for women (with the exception of 'drabs ... fondled for pay'), a great deal of talk about eating, some pretty country scenery, and a surprisingly adolescent sense of sin—mostly in relation to sex."[7] Koch does not, however, go into specifics: how a given poem by Ransom is influenced by, or even derives from, a poem by Frost.

Just how profoundly indebted the early Ransom was to Frost is clear, to take one example, in the poem entitled "One Who Rejected Christ." First published in *The Independent* on July 27, 1918, it was shortly thereafter included in *Poems About God*.

> There's farmers and there's farmers,
> There's many a field and field,
> But none of the farmers round about
> Can haul such harvest wagons out
> As I from an acre's yield.
>
> There's plenty and plenty of farmers
> Who leave the ground by the fence,
> Thinking it's nice that a patch of roses

> Should scratch out the hay and tickle their noses
> With nice little wild-rose scents.
>
> I'm not like other farmers,
> I make my farming pay;
> I never go in for sentiment,
> And since the roses paid no rent
> I cut the stuff away.
>
> A very good thing for farmers
> If they would learn my way;
> For crops are all that a good field grows,
> And nothing is worse than a sniff of rose
> In the good strong smell of hay.[8]

The Frost poem Ransom's poem evokes most clearly and obviously is "The Tuft of Flowers" from *A Boy's Will* (1913), where it is explained, on the contents-page, that it is "about fellowship."

> I went to turn the grass once after one
> Who mowed it in the dew before the sun.
>
> The dew was gone that made his blade so keen
> Before I came to view the leveled scene.
>
> I looked for him behind an isle of trees;
> I listened for his whetstone on the breeze.
>
> But he had gone his way, the grass all mown,
> And I must be, as he had been,—alone,
>
> "As all must be," I said within my heart,
> "Whether they work together or apart."
>
> But as I said it, swift there passed me by
> On noiseless wing a bewildered butterfly,
>
> Seeking with memories grown dim o'er night
> Some resting flower of yesterday's delight.
>
> And once I marked his flight go round and round,
> As where some flower lay withering on the ground.
>
> And then he flew as far as eye could see,
> And then on tremulous wing came back to me.
>
> I thought of questions that have no reply,
> And would have turned to toss the grass to dry;
>
> But he turned first, and led my eye to look
> At a tall tuft of flowers beside a brook,
>
> A leaping tongue of bloom the scythe had spared
> Beside a reedy brook the scythe had bared.
>
> The mower in the dew had loved them thus,
> By leaving them to flourish, not for us,

> Nor yet to draw one thought of ours to him.
> But from sheer morning gladness at the brim.
>
> The butterfly and I had lit upon,
> Nevertheless, a message from the dawn,
>
> That made me hear the wakening birds around,
> And hear his long scythe whispering to the ground,
>
> And feel a spirit kindred to my own;
> So that henceforth I worked no more alone;
>
> But glad with him, I worked as with his aid,
> And weary, sought at noon with him the shade;
>
> And dreaming, as it were, held brotherly speech
> With one whose thought I had not hoped to reach.
>
> "Men work together," I told him from the heart,
> "Whether they work together or apart" [30–31].

Disingenuously an "answer" to Frost's "The Tuft of Flowers," Ransom's first-person monologue is expressed in the voice of a plain-speaking, pragmatic, and selfish utilitarian. He wants hay not flowers. But Ransom's title—more reminiscent of Edwin Arlington Robinson, to be sure, than of Frost—tilts the poem toward allegory. The farmer's speech about crops and yields, the full use of his land and the waste in allowing space by the fence for wild-roses, may be, as Frost might have put it, ulterior. It is doubtful that the speaker of the poem speaks for the Christian poet, who seems to have in mind Isaiah (35: 1): "The wilderness and the solitary place shall be glad for them"—the "wild beasts of the desert and the wild beasts of the island"—and "the desert shall rejoice, and blossom as the rose." If Frost's poem is "about fellowship" among men, Ransom's poem is about the utterly practical farmer who denies "fellowship" even of the wild-rose to his harvest of strong-smelling hay.

As such, then, the poem is not to be seen as an "answer" to "The Tuft of Flowers" but as an ironic "statement" fully in accord with Frost's idea that things were done first for glory, then for use. Here, by way of conclusion, is Frost's own directive on "The Tuft of Flowers." This was one of his early poems, he would say, "and it's a farmer one." He had been "a young farmer, twelve to thirteen years old," whose job was "to come after the mower in the morning and scatter the grass to dry in the sun." The mower "liked to mow by hand in the dew—from five o'clock, from four o'clock, from daylight on—while the dew was on it," and then it was the young Frost's "place to turn the grass," as they "used to call it." "And he'd gone, usually," Frost continued, "before I got to work. His work came before mine. Mine was by sunlight, his was by dawn, dawn-light." Frost then recited "The Tuft of Flowers," stopping after the line "But from sheer morning gladness at the brim," to say, "that's the glory of it. Then, the use of it."[9] On that, as in so much else, Frost and Ransom were in accord.

12

Axe and Helve

Behind "Junk," Richard Wilbur's "Anglo-Saxon" poem, first collected in *Advice to a Prophet and Other Poems* (1961), stands Robert Frost's poem "The Ax-Helve." The resemblance of Wilbur's poem to Frost's in theme and image is clear enough throughout, but it is most explicit in the opening lines: "An axe angles / from my neighbor's ashcan," followed by "It is hell's handiwork, / the wood not hickory," and (deplorably) "The flow of the grain / not faithfully followed."[1]

The axe angling from the first line, static and moving again toward what it was, needs no comment. But the rubbish hoard also includes a "cast-off cabinet / Of wavily-warped / unseasoned wood," which, though it echoes Frost as well, stems clearly from Henry David Thoreau's *Walden*. In particular, Wilbur's poem goes back to Thoreau's parable of the Kouroo artist. The epigraph to "Junk," a quotation from a fragmentary Anglo-Saxon poem, is translated by Wilbur: "Indeed, Wayland's handiwork, the sword Mimung, which he made, will never fail any man who knows how to use it properly."[2] Yet, judging by the vision manifested in this poem, it is evident that Wayland's handiwork, along with all of man's "junk," cannot last. If we apply the values of Wilbur's poem, we shall see also that the staff carved by the Kouroo artist cannot endure; nor will Baptiste's ax-helve, perfect ax-helve that it is. What might endure is a poem, if Thoreau is right, a poem "carved out of the breath of life itself." If echoes of Frost and Thoreau give Wilbur's poem a poetic and "historical" context, they do not narrow its meaning, for the poem goes ultimately its own direction, accomplishes some different purposes and in vision moves beyond Frost, the Frost of this poem at least.

"Junk" laments *and* celebrates: it laments the spiritual decay manifested in jerry-built things and it celebrates the return of such things to natural form and pure element. Decrying man's betrayal of his instinct for form and of his bent for art, the poem, in celebrating natural process, a condition for sadness usually, is no less a celebration of "hell's handiwork," nature's ceaseless redemption of matter constantly betrayed by man. Apparently echoing the calculated misanthropy of a Robinson Jeffers, but only initially, Wilbur is here closer in attitude to Frost the leaf treader, the confronter of facts. But his attitude, close as it is to Frost's, is even closer in spirit to the transcendental attitudes expressed by *Walden* and Emerson's *Nature*: if in part his attitude seems to echo Thoreau's occasional bitterness, especially in his *Journals*—"What [man] touches he taints," writes Thoreau[3]—it reflects even more closely one aspect of Emerson's romantic judgment of "Art" (necessarily a lesser thing when compared to nature): Man's "operations taken together are so insignificant, a little chipping, baking, patching, and washing, that in an impression so grand as that of the world on the human mind, they do not vary the result."[4] Wilbur's poem, concerned with "Art" undoubtedly, but more exactly with man's *debasement* of nature through art (recalling Emerson's definition of Art as "nature passed through the alembic of man"[5]) concludes with a version of Emerson's transcendent unity, moving as always in Wilbur through the "things of this world." "The sun shall glory / In the glitter of glass-chips," for it foresees the discovery in "the blistering paint / peel off in patches, / that the good grain / be discovered again." All of it "burnt, bulldozed," shall be buried "to the depth of diamonds," where Hephaestus "keeps his hammer / And Wayland's work / is worn away."

Throughout Emerson's *Nature* the evidence for such betrayal and redemption appears in many ways and virtually on every page, but in the section on "Language" Emerson put the matter as clearly as he ever did (and more directly than Frost would dare, one might add). It is quoted here as a native source for what seems to me a basic principle of both Thoreau's and Wilbur's epistemology and aesthetic. "The problem of restoring to the world original and eternal beauty is solved by the redemption of the soul. The ruin or the blank that we see when we look at nature, is in our own eye," insists Emerson. "The world lacks unity, and lies broken and in heaps," because "man is disunited with himself."[6]

Thoreau deplored the vanity which drives man to build monuments to himself. "As for your high towers and monuments," he writes in "Economy," "there was a crazy fellow once in this town who undertook to dig through to China, and he got so far that, as he said, he heard the Chinese pots and kettles rattle."[7] In "Digging for China" Wilbur writes similarly about a fellow—perhaps the poet—who once undertook the same task, and who in the course of doing so succeeded in losing the world, as

Thoreau advised.[8] Here are the opening lines of Wilbur's poem: "'Far enough down is China,' somebody said. / 'Dig deep enough and you might see the sky / As clear as at the bottom of a well.'" So, the poet says, "I went and got the trowel out of the shed / And sweated like a coolie all that morning, / Digging a hole beside the lilac-bush," watching his hand "Dig deep and darker," as he tried "to dream a place where nothing was the same."[9]

One recalls in this connection Thoreau's winter looks at the bottom of Walden Pond through blue ice, and his eagerness for a sight of the bottom of a neighboring well. And one recalls the quest Frost describes in "Directive," and even more so, the memorable experience of "For Once, Then, Something":

> Others taunt me with having knelt at well-curbs
> Always wrong to the light, so never seeing
> Deeper down in the well than where the water
> Gives me back in a shining surface picture
> Me myself in the summer heaven godlike
> Looking out of a wreath of fern and cloud puffs.
> *Once*, when trying with chin against a well-curb,
> I discerned, as I thought, beyond the picture,
> Through the picture, a something white, uncertain,
> Something more of the depths—and then I lost it.
> Water came to rebuke the too clear water.
> One drop fell from a fern, and lo, a ripple
> Shook whatever it was lay there at bottom,
> Blurred it, blotted it out. What was that whiteness?
> Truth? A pebble of quartz? For once, then, something [208].

Here, like Emerson and Thoreau, Frost is concerned with the possibilities for perception that goes beyond "the blank ... we see when we look at nature." True, Frost's perception in this instance has been minimal. He does not know what, finally, he has seen, but he is certain that he has seen something; something that is not illusory.

Now we can look at the conclusion of Wilbur's "Digging for China." Though his "trowel never did break through to blue," the poet did have his vision. When he tires "of looking into darkness," and of having his "sunbaked head" hang "down a hole," he stands up in a place he has forgotten and is rewarded by seeing that world anew: "Blinking and staggering while the earth went round," he saw "silver barns, the fields dozing / in palls of brightness, patens growing and gone / in the tides of leaves, and the whole sky china blue." And then, until he got his "balance back again," he writes, "all that I saw was China, China, China."

12. Axe and Helve

"For once, then, something." It might be said that Wilbur has himself seen something in Thoreau's incident that Thoreau had apparently not thought of, for Thoreau had ended his account of digging for China, by saying disdainfully: "I think that I shall not go out of my way to admire the hole which he made." But if Thoreau did not see the full possibilities of the experience itself, he knew well enough that the "monument," the hole dug, was in itself worthless. For Wilbur the restoration to the world of "original and eternal beauty" has come, if I read this poem correctly, through the upsetting of the illusory modes of the day-in-day-out habits of sight, through recreating the possibility for original and fresh perception. What the poet learns—and it is his reward—is that the sky in New Jersey is like the sky in China, but only when he really sees the New Jersey sky.[10] Emerson begged us to acknowledge the miracle of each evening's stars. Thoreau, knowing that all miracles are local, would not follow rumors of red snow: he would wait in full certainty to see such snow fall in Concord.

The title poem of Wilbur's third volume, *The Beautiful Changes and Other Poems* (1947), is also about local miracles. It notes that "the beautiful changes as a forest is changed / by a chameleon's tuning his skin to it," for "any greenness is deeper than anyone knows."

And the poem ends with the notion that the beautiful changes, "wishing ever to sunder / things and things' selves for a second finding, to lose / for a moment all that it touches back to wonder."[11]

"The Beautiful Changes" anticipates in vision the transcendentalism of the poem "Junk": the "second finding" of man and man-made things "wast[ing] in the weather / toward what they were" presents proof, and a different kind of proof—but one more difficult to accept easily and gracefully—that "any greenness is deeper than anyone knows." Both poems can be viewed as responses to Emerson's concern with the problem of "restoring to the world original and eternal beauty," but "Junk" confronts the wasting away of all man's "chipping, baking, patching," along with the wasting away of man himself, with an acceptance that even Emerson seldom achieved.

And Wilbur continued to see man's problem as one of vision, even as one of poetry, if you will, poetry in its full sense. In an interview in 1964, stating his preference for the "classical" in poetry, and choosing to make his reference to Blake—not pointedly, I think , to Thoreau or Emerson—he said: "the word romantic makes me think of Novalis, for example, of Jena School German romantic imagination, and its preference for vagueness, and its love of the blue flower that's in the blue distance." But

"I prefer not to situate the beautiful and the spiritual at a vague distance. I prefer William Blake's classical eye. I think of William Blake as a classicist in this sense. He can see all the spiritual truth he needs to see in the sand-grain near at hand, and in the other immediate properties of his world."[12] The significance of Wilbur's statement is not so much that it adds to our understanding of his poems but that it directly reaffirms his commitment to the romantic vision which has always been at the heart of his poetry. "My eye will never know the dry disease / Of thinking things no more than what he sees," concludes "Poplar, Sycamore," another poem in *The Beautiful Changes*.[13] If these lines are uniquely Wilbur's, the commitment they convey Wilbur shares with Thoreau, Emerson and his third fellow New Englander Robert Frost.

13

A Single Peel

Frost was uncommonly well-versed in what readers said about his poetry. Seldom naming his critics, Frost nevertheless, at public readings usually but sometimes in print, was wont to make oblique remarks about the ways in which, in his opinion, his poems were being misread. His umbrage at John Ciardi's famous "death-wish" reading of "Stopping by Woods on a Snowy Evening" led to what are perhaps the best known of his thrusts at a critic. But Ciardi was not the only one; there was always some critic or other with whom Frost would take informed issue. They were simply wrong at times, Frost insisted, and their errors lay invariably in their misapprehension of the poet's own aesthetic intentions. For Frost was no believer in the validity—either before or after its classic formulation of what W. K. Wimsatt, Jr. and Monroe C. Beardsley in 1946 devised as "the intentional fallacy," a critical concept that offers the notion that the ultimate meaning of a literary text is neither controlled nor determined by its author's sense of what he deliberately sets out to achieve. Following logically from this position is the further notion that a writer is not *ipso facto* any more authoritative an interpreter of his own texts than is any other informed reader. There is no indication that Frost knew of Wimsatt and Beardsley's concept of the "intentional fallacy," but one can safely infer that his response to it would have been one of unhesitating dismissal.

Perhaps the best known of all the poems that Frost thought critics had persistently misread was "The Road Not Taken." And in that case there was no Ciardi (or his followers) upon whom to fix his blaming eye, but Frost could and did blame most of the poem's readers he had encountered. Within six weeks of the poem's first publication in the *Atlantic Monthly* for August 1915, Frost lamented to Louis Untermeyer: "I'll bet not half a dozen people can tell who was hit and where he was hit by my 'Road Not Taken.'" He had already acknowledged in the same letter that in that poem he had been "only fooling"; yet he had also hoped that his poem's meaning would not be "too hidden" to be perceived.[1] Surprisingly, Frost was too sanguine even in hoping that less than "half a dozen" would smoke out both his target in the poem and his attitude toward his subject.

It was not Frost's fault that his poem was misread. For years he said publicly that the poem referred less to his own views than to those of an English friend, the poet Edward Thomas. But it was not until 1964, with the appearance of his edition of the *Selected Letters of Robert Frost* that Lawrance Thompson identified Frost's target in the poem as Thomas, and the tone of the poem as one of irony and sly humor. Thompson's description of the circumstances surrounding the composition of the poem warrants quoting. "While living in Gloucestershire in 1914, Frost frequently took long walks with Thomas through the countryside," writes Thompson. "Repeatedly Thomas would choose a route which might enable him to show his American friend a rare plant or a special vista, but it often happened that before the end of such a walk Thomas would regret the choice he had made and would sigh over what he might have shown Frost if they had taken a 'better' direction." But "more than once, on such occasions," Frost "had teased his Welsh-English friend for those wasted regrets," notes Thompson, who continues: "Disciplined by the austere biblical notion that a man, having put his hand to the plow, should not look back, Frost found something quaintly romantic in sighing over what might have been.... In a reminiscent mood, not very long after his return to America as a successful, newly discovered poet, Frost pretended to 'carry himself' in the manner of Edward Thomas just long enough to write 'The Road Not Taken.'" Frost sent "a manuscript copy of the poem to Thomas, without comment, and yet with the expectation that his friend would notice how the poem pivots ironically on the un–Frostlike phrase, 'I shall be telling this with a sigh.' As it turned out Frost's expectations were disappointed. Thomas missed the gentle jest because the irony had been handled too slyly, too subtly."[2]

Thomas' failure to read the poem as Frost intended it to be read turned out to be a harbinger of how the general reader would interpret the poem. A decade later Frost received a letter from a young person from Tennessee asking him about the "sigh" in the last stanza of the poem. His reply was brief but right to the point. Without naming names, he wrote: "No wonder you were a little puzzled over the end of my 'Road Not Taken.' It was my rather private jest at the expense of those who might *think* I would yet live to be sorry for the way I had taken in life. I suppose I was gently teasing them. I'm not really a very regretful person...."[3]

13. A Single Peel

The young Tennessean was neither the first reader nor the last one to find both the content and tone of Frost's poem problematic. What did that "sigh" signify? There is no need to sample the plethora of specific interpretations in circulation that this question—surely a legitimate one—has inspired. Suffice it to say that not one of the interpretations that has achieved print down through the decades appears to have questioned the seriousness, the directness, and even the solemnity of the poet's voice in the poem. If the poet had outfoxed himself by enacting too subtle and too sly a jest, he nevertheless insisted upon the authority of his own poetic intention. *Pace* its readership over half a century, "The Road Not Taken" poked fun at the very notion that the poet should ever sigh, wistfully or reluctantly, over having once made one choice over another. Frost would never have shared his poet friend's nervous-nelly mannerism of dwelling over the desirability or undesirability of a choice irrevocably made in the context of other choices irrevocably not made.

But the story of Frost and the authority of poetic intentions has a second side. There was at least one occasion when Frost's interpretation of another poet's poem was at odds with that other poet's intention. Unfortunately, there was no direct exchange between the poets on the matter of just how to interpret the poem's meaning. Indeed, it was not until several years after Frost's death that the other poet, a friend, would discover that Frost had read his poem in such a way that his own poetic intentions had been subverted.

Robert Francis was that second poet and the story he tells is full of interest. "Frost as Apple Peeler" he calls his account, and it appeared in 1978 in the *New England Review*. Francis' graceful account of Frost's "misreading" of one of Francis' poems as well as Frost's own attendant decision to gain his revenge by composing a poetic attack on Francis deserves to be read in its entirety. For present purposes, however, the account can be safely foreshortened. It must have been immediately following its publication in *New Poems by American Poets* (1953), surmises Francis, that Frost first encountered his eight-line poem, "Apple Peeler." The poem begins: "Why the unspoken spiral, Virtuoso, / Like a trick sonnet in one long, versatile sentence?" The poet asks, "Is it a pastime merely, this perfection, / For an old man, sharp knife, long night, long winter?" It is "solitaire," it's "the ticking clock," it's "the apple / turning, turning as the round earth turns."[4]

Francis was to discover from Frost that as the author of "The Silken Tent," a one-sentence sonnet, he saw the reference to "a trick sonnet" in the second line of the poem as disparaging to himself. Francis' disclaimers were not at the moment rejected, nor were they accepted, apparently. Instead, as Francis would not discover until 1976, thirteen years after the older poet's death, Frost had taken revenge in a poem that attacked his Amherst friend in a particularly personal way. It is true that Frost did not publish his malicious poem, but he did preserve it in manuscript among his papers where it became grist, as he knew it must, for the mill of his designated biographer.

Francis tells this story, in much greater detail than this summary would suggest, for two reasons. He wants to demonstrate two things about Frost: "(1) He could be cruel and kind at the same time: he wanted to punish me [Francis] but he didn't want me to suffer from his punishment. (2) He could misread a poem in the same way that he took other people to task for misreading his own poems; that is, he could find something in a poem that wasn't there at all."[5] The first of these matters can be dispatched with in a sentence. Just how kind Frost was in choosing not to publish his poem about Francis during his own lifetime has already been suggested. He left the dirty public work for his scrupulous biographer. The second of the two things is, in my view at least, both more complicated and more open to question. In the course of arguing that the poem "Apple Peeler" could have nothing to do with Frost, Francis resorts even to an account of the source of the poem and its genesis. The poem was really based on a recollection of "a very old lady," he reveals. "Each night before going to bed she liked to eat an apple," continues Francis, "and she made the paring of it a sort of ritual. She wanted to test the steadiness of her hand." In the poem, however, "the old lady became an old man."[6] If the subject of Frost, the wily old virtuoso, never crossed the younger poet's mind, then, is it not clear that Frost had read a meaning into the "Apple Feeler" that was not there, that had not, so to speak, been intended by the poet? Francis so argues, in so many words. Frost evidently thought he knew better. It seems inevitable that Frost would have thought he was Francis' "apple peeler," particularly since it was Frost who had written "After Apple Picking," arguably the most famous "apple" poem in the language.

One *is* tempted, therefore, to agree with Frost that Francis' poem is "about" him, in an important way; for if Francis seems to insist upon the primacy and the authority of his statement of a poet's intentions in the "Apple Peeler," he is also doing one of three things. (1) He is deliberately concealing his conscious intention long after the fact. (2) He is not acknowledging that his poem says things that he did not intend. (3) He is still denying to himself his and his poem's true intentions. Frost, who was so quick to deny hidden intentions in his own poems but who had insisted nevertheless that "The Road Not Taken" was really a sly thrust at the portentous manner of another poet, here—in his reading of "Apple Peeler"—succeeds in smoking out the hidden intentions in the work of another poet.[7]

14

Poem / Play

In this place I shall say something about the title of the playwright Arthur Miller's most famous play, the possibility that this play is related to a classic poem by Robert Frost, and the further possibility that the familiar New Testament Parable of the Prodigal Son contributes to the form and meaning of both Frost's poem and Miller's play.

Miller on Frost

By the time Miller was a student at the University of Michigan in the 1930s, Frost's official connections to the university as teacher and poet-in-residence had long since ended although he continued to visit the university frequently. In *Timebends* Miller refers briefly to Frost's behavior at President John F. Kennedy's inauguration and he tells us that among the reading he recommended to Marilyn Monroe was Frost's poems.[1] Miller also reports on what may have been the one occasion when he was in Frost's presence. It's something of a shaggy dog story, and it has nothing to do with this chapter, but it is mercifully brief. "One evening," writes Miller, "I saw unusual deference paid" to Louis Untermeyer by "the kingly and much older Robert Frost, who sat still for a lengthy lecture from Louis on etymology." It was that afternoon that "my young springer spaniel, Red—an unteachable animal I later gave away to my Ford dealer, fleeing his showroom before he could change his mind—had rushed through our Willow Street doorway down the stoop and smashed into the side of a passing car, stunning his brain still further and sending him hysterically running, with me behind him, way up to Borough Hall." That evening, "Frost listened to the story of my chase and then, staring out like one of the heads on Mount Rushmore, drawled, 'Sounds like a comical dog.'"[2]

The Word "Death"

When Mel Gussow said to Miller in 1986, "It's curious how much a title affects a public understanding of a play," Miller said, simply, "It tells you what to look for." Gussow followed up: "What if *Death of a Salesman* had a different title?"[3] Miller did not answer the question, preferring to talk about the recent production of the play in Beijing but if others had had they way, the play's title would have been different. As Brenda Murphy tells the story, Kermit Bloomgarden, who ultimately produced the play, worried that its title would hurt receipts, and Robert Dowling, the owner of the theater "where the play was to be produced" agreed. He "wanted to keep the title from appearing on the front of the theatre if the word 'death' was to appear in it." Bloomgarden suggested that "the title be changed to *Free and Clear*, a phrase from Linda's speech in the Requiem." But Miller and Kazan "were adamant about the title," and *Variety* reported finally, at the end of December, that "the 'Death of a Salesman' title for the new Arthur Miller play is being retained at the author's insistence." Noting that the producers disliked the title, "figuring it has a sombre connotation that may tend to repel prospective playgoers, besides being a story tipoff," the article concluded that "Miller has been adamant and under Dramatists Guild rules has final say."[4]

Titles with the word "death" in them had some precedent, surely, as Miller notes in *Timebends*: "*Death Comes for the Archbishop*, the *Death and the Maiden* Quartet—always austere and elevated was death in titles," though in his play, he added, it "would be claimed by a joker, a bleeding mass of contradictions, a clown, and there was something funny about that."[5] Miller does not name them, but there were other uses of the word "death" in titles. There was "Death in the Woods," Sherwood Anderson's story, *Death in the Afternoon*, Hemingway's book about bull-fighting, and "The Death of the Hired Man," Robert Frost's dramatic narrative in verse.[6]

"The Death of the Hired Man"

Published in *North of Boston* (1914), this poem has a simple scenario. An old man, who had more than once deserted for higher wages, now has returned, sick and confused, to ask for his old job back from the couple—man and wife—who had formerly employed him. He never appears on "stage"; we learn about him through the conversation between the husband and wife—Warren and Mary—who are out on the porch. Mary is more sympathetic to Silas's plight, having brought him back into the house where he now sleeps back of the stove. Warren argues that Silas, having left him during haying time, does not deserve to be taken back. He should be in the care of the banker brother, who lives just thirteen miles away. Mary reports what Silas has been saying and thinking. He has come back, as Warren correctly surmises, to "ditch the meadow" and to "clear the upper pasture, too"—tasks he seems to have promised to do in the past but not done. He also wants to have another chance to show the "college boy" long since gone on how to stack hay, for instance, saving the boy from becoming "the fool of books." Mary recognizes that Silas has "nothing to look backward to with pride, / And nothing to look forward to with hope." The dilemma faced by the young couple is whether or not to "take in" the aged, sick Silas, who is obviously no longer useful to them in the economy of the farm. If Mary would take Silas back, if only to give him a "home" in which to die, Warren argues in favor of making Silas endure the consequences of those choices he has made in the past. But at the core of their individual decisions are variant notions of what constitutes one's "home," notions that are presented as contrary definitions. The wife's definition that home is "Something you somehow haven't to deserve" is put into doubt by the husband, who argues that by leaving the farm for the sake of higher wages elsewhere just when he was needed most—at harvest time—Silas has long since forfeited whatever claim he might have had on this "home." This liberal definition, put forth by Mary, is countered by her husband's perhaps harsher view that "Home is the place where, when you have to go there, / They have to take you in." These definitions, taken in conjunction, lead implicitly to the idea that, under scrutiny, notions of "home" have already undergone change and redefinition. At the heart of the discussion are two conflicting views of charity and responsibility or what might be called justice. The matter becomes moot—resolution is no longer necessary—when Warren reveals that when he went into the house to talk to Silas he found him dead.[7]

The Play Is a Poem, the Poem Is a Play

In agreement with the producer-director Tyrone Guthrie, the scholar-critic Christopher Bigsby writes that *Death of a Salesman* is "a long poem by Willy Loman. For much of the play it is he who hears the voices, shapes the rhythms, creates the rhymes. He turns experience into metaphor, bringing together discrete moments to forge new meanings which then dissolve."⁸ In an interview in 1977, Miller makes the same point but in other terms: "The play is really one continuous poem. It has no scenes. It has no interstices."⁹ It is a perfect example of the dramatization of a mind that is at every stage, William James decided in the *Principles of Psychology* in 1890, "a theatre of simultaneous possibilities."¹⁰

Turning to Frost, who described his narrative poem as "a short play, very short,"¹¹ we see that he keeps Silas off stage. He creates our sense of Silas's life entirely from the outside—from the points of view of the husband and wife; while Miller conceives his entire play as scenes playing themselves out within Willy's mind and around him—even though there are scenes that Willy could not possibly have known about (e.g. Linda's dialogue with her son or the conversations at the restaurant before Willy shows up); these scenes parallel the basic situation in Frost's poem in which Silas, always inside, away from view, is invoked in the conversation that takes place between Warren and Mary out on the porch.

The Death of an Old Man

Play and poem both have as their subjective center "old" men who are well beyond their abilities to function at their respective tasks or trades. Reviewing Frost's collected poems in 1949, Charles Poore wrote in the *New York Times*: "'The Death of the Hired Man,' with its poignancies as deep, probably, as the death of any salesman."¹² If poignancy does not make tragedy, this pairing of common men does bring us to Miller's position: "I believe that the common man is as apt a subject for tragedy in its highest sense as kings were."¹³ In a different vein but along the same track the author of a recent book on obituaries and their writers concludes that "Miller's account of the death of Willy Loman can be read as an elevated obit of a common man."¹⁴

The Manny Newman "Story"

In *Timebends* Miller tells of his fascination with Manny Newman, one of his Brooklyn uncles, Manny's wife and children—especially his two sons. So much of *The Death of a Salesman* is there: Manny's prevarications, lies (to himself and others, and dreams; Manny's occupation as a salesman driving "all the way through New England in his little car, which in winter was barely kept above freezing by its primitive heater," driving "through every town, stop[ping] at every traffic light"; the loyal wife, "alternately flushed and paled as she dreaded and was relieved of the fear that he was making too much of a fool of himself," both of them "still in love"; his two sons "a pair of strong, self-assured young men, musketeers bound to one another's honor and proud of their family," neither of them "patient enough or perhaps capable enough to sit alone and study," "both missed going to college"; one son, "filled with the roiling paradoxes of love for me and competitive resentment, of contempt for his late failed father and at the same time a pitying love and even amused admiration for the man's outrageousness"; the revelation that Manny had a dream: "He wanted a business for us. So we could all work together," reveals Miller's cousin, "a business for the boys." "This conventional, mundane wish was a shot of electricity that switched all the random iron filings in my mind in one direction," wrote Miller. "A hopelessly distracted Manny was transformed into a man with purpose: he had been trying to make a gift that would crown all those striving years; all those lies he told, all his imaginings and crazy exaggerations, even the almost military discipline he had laid on his boys, were in this instant given form and point," Miller revealed. "To be sure, a business expressed his own egotism, but love, too. That homely, ridiculous little man had after all never ceased to struggle for a certain victory, the only kind open to him in this society—selling to achieve his lost self as a man with his name and his sons' names on a business of his own. I suddenly understood him with my very blood." But Miller admits that he "had imagined all of this and that in reality he was not much more than a bragging and often vulgar little drummer."[15] The one major item missing from this rich store of memories and imaginings as regards the play—*The Death of a Salesman*—that would emerge from them Miller would find elsewhere: in the narrative Parable of the Prodigal Son—more specifically, in the surprise ending in which the "lost" son who has squandered all that has been given to him returns not to punishment but to the greatest rewards a loving father can heap upon his head. Except for going off to the war, neither of Manny Newman's sons is reported to have gone much farther away from their family home in Brooklyn than lower Lexington Avenue in Manhattan. Oddly, it may have been the Prodigal Son theme (displaced) in Frost's poem that helped Miller fill-out his play.

"The Death of the Hired Man" offers not a father and a son but an old man and his (presumably) younger employers. The hired man, too, goes away—and does it more than once. His recurrent behavior is that he leaves for more money and then returns. He, too, has dreams, and those dreams involve not a son but a young man who has worked alongside him in the fields but has gone off to college. The hired man wants one more crack at him—to teach him something of value, how to "build a load of hay," so as to keep him from being ruined by what he has learned at college; he wants to "ditch the meadow" and "clear the upper pasture, too"—"he has a plan"; but he "jumble[s] everything" (40–45).

The Parable of the Prodigal Son

Since I do not want to take the space to reproduce the entire text of the Parable of the Prodigal Son as it appears in Luke 15: 11–32, I offer you a summary by Roger Stein: "Having squandered his fortune, starving and destitute in a far country..., feeding the forbidden pigs, he [the Prodigal Son] wishes that he could fill his stomach by sharing the food of the pigs he feeds! And how beautifully the father's love is described. Laying aside his dignity, he runs to embrace his son, refuses to hear out his confession, re-clothes him in appropriately filial garments, and joyfully celebrates having regained his lost son." When the son who has stayed at home complains about his father's surprising behavior—his killing of the fatted calf in celebration of the Prodigal's return—his father answers him: "It was meet that we should make merry, and be glad: for this thy brother was dead, and is alive again; and was lost, and is found."[16]

In Frost's poem, the hired man Silas behaves like "family"—even like the Prodigal Son; so, too, does Biff in *Salesman*. Willy's prodigal behavior has long since been revealed to Biff when the son finds the father in a Boston hotel room with a woman. Biff's own prodigal behavior consists of thievery and (out West) jail time. Willy will forgive him these peccadilloes but wants more from Biff than just that. He wants him to be "magnificent." There's no evidence that Biff will forgive Willy his peccadilloes; in fact, he charges him with deceit (at best) when he confronts him with the piece of hose from the cellar. In Frost's poem Silas' prodigal behavior takes the form of desertion—he leaves the "family" at harvest time for employment elsewhere at higher wages. If Mary will forgive him, Warren is reluctant to do so. If Silas is like an animal that has come home to die, so is Willy Loman. It is Willy's fate to kill the "calf" (himself) for Biff's sake (re-ordering the progression of anthropological and religious ritual from human sacrifice to animal sacrifice to symbolic sacrifice).

It would be all too easy to get lost in the literature devoted to the Parable of the Prodigal Son, a good deal of it following closely the story in Luke but much of it displacing the myth in one or many ways. This displacement is especially interesting when it takes place in realistic stories, poems or plays. I use the terms "realism" and "displacement" as they are defined by Northrop Frye: "Realism, or the art of verisimilitude, evokes the response 'How like that is to what we know!' When what is written is *like* what is known, we have an art of extended or implied simile.... The presence of a mythical structure in realistic fiction [or poetry or drama], however, poses certain technical problems for making it plausible, and the devices used in solving these problems may be given the general name of *displacement*."[17] Now I see—no surprise, of course—the presence of the Parable of the Prodigal Son both in Frost's "The Death of the Hired Man" and "The Death of a Salesman," though in neither case is the Parable's structure or its details followed literally or slavishly.[18] It was not possible or desirable to do so. In Miller's case, for starters, there was the necessity "to cling to the process of Willy's mind as the form the story would take."[19] Though, it must be noted, he does avail himself of the triumvirate present in the Parable of the Prodigal Son: the father and the two sons. As another writer has put it, echoing St. Augustine, though less allegorically, "We are all, like the Prodigal Son, seeking our home, waiting to hear the father's voice."[20] In Frost's poem the Prodigal Son who returns home after his desertion is an old man. Silas's faults are defined by Warren and Mary, who are not his parents but employers—who act in loco parentis, in a way. Silas has in the past deserted them at harvest time, going to work for others at higher wages. He has come home to die, becoming himself the sacrifice (a radical displacement of the "fatted calf," as I have said, of the Parable). As Miller said, famously, "the structure of a play is always the story of how the birds came home to roost."[21]

In 1983, in Beijing, Miller described his play: "*Death of a Salesman*, really, is a love story between a man and his son."[22] Certainly this is also one way (if an uncommon one) of interpreting Luke's Parable of the Prodigal Son: the father's love of one son over the other is patent, just as Willy's love for Biff over Happy is clear. In "The Death of a Salesman" the obvious Prodigal Son is Biff, who has come home after his profligacy out West (he has been in jail) and he is greeted by a father who will do anything for his Prodigal (anything he can to bring into evident reality Biff's "magnificence"), while the "good son," who has not gone West ("Me? Who goes away? Who runs off and—," Happy breaks off in his rebuke of Biff)[23] and who—not Biff—actually gives his parents Christmas money that they use to repair the water heater, is excluded from Willy's plans.

In a radical displacement ultimately it is Willy himself who stands in for the "fatted calf" of Luke's Parable, killing himself to give Biff a $20,000 gift in insurance money. But this isn't the only way the Parable operates deep in Miller's consciousness. For Willy is himself a Prodigal Son, one whose return home has taken place over and over again during his adult life, as he goes out into the territory where his prodigal behavior takes place—the incident of the woman in Boston, for instance, is metonymic. That familiar image of the returning Willy—home from the hapless hunt for sales—seen from the back, weighed down by the suitcases he has lugged all over New England lines him up with all the wanderers, from Odysseus to Cain to Parsifal, as well as the less heroic Prodigal Son.[24] But for Willy there is no "fatted calf," neither at home, nor, as he learns to his stupefaction, at the home office either. Now it is of course possible (perhaps probable) that there is no direct link between Frost's displaced use of the Parable of the Prodigal and Miller's similarly displaced use. But they do share one particular displacement: the younger son has become the old hired man in Frost, while he has been duplicated in Miller, with the son dividing or duplicated into two avatars, one of whom is the old, superannuated salesman. Neither Silas nor Willy is of much, if any, use to the farm, in Silas's case, or the firm, in Willy's. By this point each of them, in terms of occupation or job, has become expendable.

Yet just as there is in the Parable of the Prodigal Son, there is an emphasis on the idea of home in both "The Death of the Hired Man" and *The Death of a Salesman*. For the Prodigal Son home is a place of welcome, forgiveness, and celebration. Things are different in the two modern texts. In Miller's play, Linda's cautious welcome to her two sons erodes quickly into disappointing illusion, and celebration turns rancid and ugly—the dinner the boys plan to have for Willy turns into cruel and vicious rejection. (Happy repudiates the father in favor of the girls—"No, that's not my father. He's just a guy."[25]) From that point Willy is totally lost, reversing the text in St. Luke, substituting "father" for "brother": "thy brother was dead, and is alive again; and was lost, and is found." In Frost's "Death of the Hired Man" the husband and wife debate the issue of whether or not to allow Silas, the Prodigal, to come back by offering each other contrary definitions of "home."

Death of a Salesman "grew from simple images," Miller recalled in 1957. "From a little frame house on a street of little frame houses, which had once been loud with the noise of growing boys, and then was empty and silent and finally occupied by strangers. Strangers who could not know with what conquistadorial joy Willy and his boys had once re-shingled the roof. Now it was quiet in the house, and the wrong people in the beds."[26] The mother Linda has the foreboding lines, said to the Prodigal

Son Biff, that express this loss of "home." "You've got to get it into your head now that one day you'll knock on this door and there'll be strange people here."[27] It has already happened with the home office, as Willy so painfully learns when he goes in to the "home" office to beg for the job that he thinks he was once promised.

Summing Up

Frost's poem about the dying hired man anticipates Miller's play about the dying salesman—sometimes by analogue, sometimes by reversal. The old man Silas's returning "home" parallels the young man Biff's returning "home." The wife, Mary, makes a case for Silas; Linda, the wife, makes the case for Willy. Both Willy and Silas want to go back to the past, to correct mistakes, make improvements. Frost writes about Silas from the outside—the points of view are the husband's and wife's—while Miller conceives his play as playing itself out, mostly so, in Willy's head. If all descriptions of Willy are done around him, those of Silas take place in dialogue he does not hear. For Silas, a dying animal returning home to die, the farm is his "home"; for Willy his "home" includes the company (the firm), where the feeling of being "at home" is important, where Willy thinks of himself as part of the family, not as a "hired" hand. If Willy has intimations that he has always been a bit out of sync, he doesn't really understand his situation. He admires the old salesman Dave Singleman, who makes his sales over the phone from his hotel room (a home away from home) and who has the happy fate to die, wearing "his green velvet slippers," in "the smoker of the New York, New Haven and Hartford, going into Boston"[28]—still another home away from home—perhaps the successful salesman's own true home.

15

Nothing Gold Can Stay

It is America's "National Pastime." Arguable though this proposition may be, it nevertheless affirms baseball's link to patriotism. John Philip Sousa saw the game as the very embodiment of the nation's faith in democracy. In *Pipetown Sandy* (1905) the American March King turned novelist cries out in celebration: "Our National Game! What an enemy to nepotism, or any other 'ism' that thrives on the favor of influence!"

> Oh, base-ball! Thou art truly the embodiment of purest democracy; like love, thou does level all ranks. Of what avail is distinguished ancestry, pre–Adamite origin, cerulean blood or stainless escutcheon, when one is at the bat and strikes out! Intellectual superiority, physical perfection, social status, wealth or poverty count for nothing. If you fail to bring in the winning run.[1]

What, then, might Sousa have made of the cancellation in 2003 of the near-ritualistic celebratory showing of *Bull Durham*, the classic baseball movie, at the Baseball Hall of Fame, at Cooperstown, New York, because two of the movie's actors had been called out for their temerity in making public what they found wrong with American political policies and practices. Scheduled to appear at the showing of *Bull Durham*, Susan Sarandon and Tim Roberts were dis-invited and the showing of the movie was canceled. The politics and patriotism of "my country right or wrong!" prevailed over democracy, free speech, and the whiff of the possibility of civil disobedience, turning the Hall into more of a place of exclusion than of inclusion—at least for certain people. To the best of my knowledge, the Hall does not show *Eight Men Out*, a movie about the notorious Black Sox Scandal.

Virtually from its shadowy beginnings, to Americans "baseball" has seemed to be more than a game. Walt Whitman hailed baseball in his poem *Leaves of Grass*, and New England's Brahmin historian Henry Adams attended baseball games, as did the mid-western John Hay, who served Presidents Lincoln, Hayes, McKinley and Roosevelt. As Hay wrote to his wife (June 20, 1880), "As I left the office yesterday Brown asked me if I would like to see a game of base ball. I said yes and we went," continued Hay, "It was between the Washingtons and Baltimores—the Washingtons won after a hotly contested game. One man sprained his ankle, one got hit on the head, one broke his finger." The games must be worth attending, for he had friends who "go nearly every day," he marveled. "Sir Edward and Miss Fanny know all the players in the country, by name and face and record."[2]

In the twentieth century, many authors have written about baseball. Sometimes lovingly, sometimes not so much. Ring Lardner's emotions were mixed. His *You Know Me, Al*, told in the letters of Jack Keefe, a semi-literate pitcher for the Chicago White Sox, is a classic of American humor of the pre-political correctness days. F. Scott Fitzgerald, who thought that Lardner's innate cynicism was enhanced by his baseball writing, introduces rumors about the cynical gambler reputed to be behind the Black Sox game-throwing scandal in the 1919 World Series to cast shadowy light on Jay Gatsby's eventual fall from riches to death. William Carlos Williams devotes a chapter in his novel *White Mule* to a "Fourth of July Double-header" in his story of immigrants and assimilation. Ernest Hemingway imbues his Cuban fisherman with admiration for the heroic achievements of the injured New York Yankee's Joe DiMaggio. John Updike, in "Hub Fans Bid Kid Adieu," apotheosizes Ted Williams of the Red Sox. In *Underworld* Don DeLillo replays Bobby Thomson's heard-around-the-world home run against the Brooklyn Dodgers in 1951. Robert Coover generates a whole world out of baseball statistics in *The Universal Baseball Association, Inc.: J. Henry Waugh, Prop.* Mark Harris devoted a suite of four novels to the game, peaking with *Bang the Drum Slowly*. Others, apart from the novelists, have written much about baseball, journalists such as Roger Angell, Roger Kahn, and James Reston, Jr., historians like Doris Kearns Goodwin and David Halberstam, along with George Will, whose *Men at Work* traces doggedly how the so-called Protestant ethic—the achievement of grace through hard work and good habits—has shaped the careers of a small bevy of hand-picked players.

What this preamble leads me to, by the laws of a personal logic, is a question: "Why has Pete Rose not been inducted into Cooperstown's National Baseball Hall of Fame?" Everyone knows what the principal charge is—that Rose, one of the most notable players of the twentieth century, violated the rules of organized professional baseball by gambling, namely by placing bets to win on the team he was serving as manager. But

15. Nothing Gold Can Stay

this, the most important case to come up during A. Bartlett Giamatti's tenure as Commissioner of Major League Baseball, ended in the harshest judgment and punishment ever meted out to a gambling baseball man in more than half a century. Previous sinners guilty of consorting with gamblers received suspensions—in bad-boy Leo Durocher's notorious case, for example, of one year. But Pete Rose was the first such malefactor in many decades to be banished from everything pertaining to organized professional baseball in the United States. And so far—more than a quarter-century later, and the tenure of two baseball commissioners after Giamatti—who died days after handing down his sentence—the banishment of Pete Rose is still in effect and, despite the perception that there is more than a little public support for his admission he is still excluded from the Baseball Hall of Fame. Even the squeaky-clean, universally applauded Calvin "Cal" Ripkin, who surpassed the untouchable Lou Gehrig's record of consecutive games played, has conceded that Rose should be eligible for election to the Hall of Fame, even though he does not advocate lifting his banishment from all other matters, events, and things pertaining to baseball. There's no forgiveness emanating from this so aptly named player, only the recognition of what Rose accomplished as a major league player—confirmed by the numbers, as they say, that he put up, including the most base hits ever. Yet Bartlett Giamatti, that believer in the power of myth to sustain and redeem, could not have disagreed more profoundly. To understand that his stand was adamant, to say the least, one need only look into Giamatti's character and the circumstances that went into its formation.

Giamatti was the high priest of a religion that praises the relative cool clarity of baseball within its protected and nearly virtual domain. That view is nowhere conveyed more clearly or idealistically than in the words of this literature professor turned university president turned baseball official. In "The Green Fields of the Mind," an essay published in the *Yale Alumni Magazine* in 1977, A. Bartlett Giamatti writes, with heartfelt sentimentality, about the game of baseball and its fatal discontent: "It breaks your heart. It is designed to break your heart. The game begins in the spring, when everything else begins again, and it blossoms in the summer, filling the afternoons and evenings, and then as soon as the chill rains come, it stops and leaves you to face the fall alone." He then makes it even more personal: "It breaks my heart because it was meant to, because it was meant to foster in me again the illusion that there was something abiding, some pattern and some impulse that could come together to make a reality that would resist the corrosion; and because, after it had fostered again that most hungered-for illusion, the game was meant to stop, and betray precisely what it promised."[3]

Whatever else they may have had in common, Bartlett Giamatti and Robert Frost shared an interest in professional baseball as fans and supporters of the same New England team, the Boston Red Sox. And both of them, of course, knew their way around universities. Each had a deep regard for poetry though they might have chosen to talk about it differently. Indeed, if baseball has had its mythologists and poets, no one so far has exceeded Giamatti in his love for the game of baseball as pastoral or his passion for its geometrical clarity or mathematical simplicities or mysteries. To such gem-like devotions the poet Frost does not even come close. His forte is the recognition of the agonistic possibilities of the game, the game as site for the display and exercise of prowess. While Giamatti celebrates baseball in which the object is to return "home," to the "green place in the mind," Robert Frost knew that, as he told a friend during a pickup game at the Bread Loaf School of English in Vermont, "you have to spike them as you round the bases." It was clear to George Kumler Anderson, a long-term teacher at Bread Loaf and the school's historian, that the referent for "them" in the previous sentence was someone or something other than "bases." Notice, too, that Frost's emphasis is on running the bases, not arriving back at home plate. Experience is valued for itself, it may be said, rather than its goal. In a *New Yorker* "Profile" in 1931, one of his friends (the poet Raymond Holden) recalled that Frost sometimes played "a game of scrub baseball" with "his children and a few neighbors, batting just long enough to enjoy it and then sitting down to talk about the prowess of Babe Ruth."[4] In "Perfect Day—A Day of Prowess," a piece on the All Star game commissioned by *Sports Illustrated* and published on July 23, 1956, Frost acknowledges that one of his "unfulfilled promises on earth was to my fellow in art, Alfred Kreymborg, of an epic poem someday about a ball batted so hard by Babe Ruth that it never came back, but got to going round and round the world like a satellite."[5] The same piece introduces Frost as "America's greatest living poet—an old pitcher himself." With "what authority do I speak?" Frost himself boasts playfully. "Have I not been written up as a pitcher in *The New Yorker* by the poet, Raymond Holden? —though the last full game I pitched in was on the grounds of Rockingham Park in Salem New Hampshire, before it was turned into a race track. If I have shone at all in the all-star games at Breadloaf in Vermont it has been as a relief pitcher with a soft ball I despise like a picture window."[6] As a pitcher (even at softball), did he ever "dust" a batter, to get him off the plate with an inside pitch or even deliberately throw at anyone? Who knows? Yet the game was a competition and the object was to win by whatever means it took while staying within the rules. As he confided to his notebooks, "Object in life is to win—win a game" or "win the play of a poem."[7] Born in San Francisco but raised after the age of eleven in a New England mill city (Lawrence, Massachusetts), he learned his baseball early. The *Sports Illustrated* editor who sought him out certainly knew his man.

In "Clark Griffith's gem of a field, gem small, in beautiful weather in the capital of the country," as Frost wrote, he watched a game in which the four homers came from "exactly the four they were expected from, Musial, Williams, Mays and Mantle." "Each team made 11 hits, two home runs and not a single error"—a perfect example of prowess, and "prowess of course comes first, the ability to perform with success in games, in the arts and, come right down to it, in battle." He rates fairness high, but it is not fairness in the ballplayers that he takes up but fairness in the umpires where "the least lack of fairness or the least lack of faith in the possibility of fairness" would damage the game.[8] In Frost's case baseball was less a field of dreams than a place offering opportunities for accomplishment and, as we have seen, the display of prowess and bravery. For Giamatti, however, baseball is the occasion and excuse for the existence of the dream of an eternal, green place that is always desired by the mind and which, when it exists, really exists in the mind. For Frost baseball takes its place among the sites in this world that make it, to borrow the words of the Romantic poet John Keats, a vale of soul-making. For Giamatti, it is the locus of the prelapsarian world that constitutes the "home" we would all go to if we could or come back to when we can. He saw "home" as the goal of Western heroic journeys. Odysseus survives dangers and withstands temptations to make his twenty-year journey back home. It's as if in baseball a player hopes to reenact that ritual voyage out and beyond and then, if successful, all the way back to "home," from which he originally set out.

Frost saw "home' in another way. If he also believes in the necessity behind the risk when one sets out for the unknown and returns, he has the two speakers in "The Death of the Hired Man" express dissimilar notions of what "home" is. The wife's definition that home is "something you somehow haven't to deserve" is put into doubt by the husband who argues that by leaving the farm for wages elsewhere just when he was needed most—at haying time—Silas forfeited whatever claim he had on this "home." This liberal definition is countered by the husband's harsher view that "Home is the place where, when you have to go there / They have to take you in." "The hunger for home makes the green geometry of the baseball field more than simply a metaphor for the American experience and character," writes Giamatti in an essay titled "Baseball and the American Character"; "the baseball field and the game that sanctifies boundaries, rules, and law and engages cunning, theft, and guile; that exalts energy, opportunism, and execution while paying lip service to management, strategy, and long-range planning, is closer to an embodiment of American life than to the mere sporting image of it."[9]

For Pete Rose, one may say, "home" was less a place to get back to, completing a circuit out and back, but a place to "score." The most notoriously regarded run ever scored by Pete Rose came in the All-Star game in 1971 when he crashed into the catcher trying to block him from touching home plate and scoring. Rose said that he could not have faced his father had he not done this. What, one might speculate, would Frost have said? That Pete Rose played the game hard "for mortal sake" as it should be played? That if the game was "meaningless," as it has been argued against Rose—why play it at all? That one must play to win, without cheating and by staying within the rules? What did Giamatti think of the collision at home plate that injured the catcher and curtailed his baseball career? He did not say, but perhaps it is not irrelevant to his general way of thinking that his much admired Odysseus earned his way back all the way home by slaughtering the suitors for Penelope's hand who had made themselves at home while he wandered his way back through the dangers and temptations of the world.

Frost knows that "nothing gold can stay," accepts the misfortune and goes on to become a leaf-treader, stomping leaves into the ground, helping autumn to do its job of preparing us for winter. Giamatti seems to know this, too, recognizes it, but will not personally accept it. As he writes in "The Green Fields of the Mind," "Of course, there are those who learn after the first few times. They grow out of sports. And there are others who were born with the wisdom to know that nothing lasts."

> These are the truly tough among us, the ones who can live without illusion, or without even the hope of illusion. I am not that grown-up or up-to-date. I am a simpler creature, tied to more primitive patterns and cycles. I need to think something lasts forever, and it might as well be that state of being that is a game; it might as well be that, in a green field, in the sun.[10]

At this point Frost's words on the Fall sound a cautionary note: "Nature's first green is gold… / But only so an hour," and thus, in the end, "Eden sank to grief" (206).

Frost and Giamatti both speak out against what Frost calls corruption.

15. Nothing Gold Can Stay

If the poet locates the game's essential need for "fairness" in the umpire, Giamatti comes out against cheating. In a remarkably worked out bit of reasoning and decision-making Giamatti, as president of the National League of Professional Baseball Clubs, denies Kevin Gross's appeal of suspension. A pitcher with the Philadelphia Phillies, Gross had added a piece of sandpaper to his fielding glove, a violation of rule 9.02(b). He was not charged with doctoring the baseball or throwing illegal pitches in a game. Here, in a nutshell, is Giamatti's reasoning in "Decision in the Appeal of Kevin Gross": "It is cheating per se to have such a glove with sandpaper and sticky substance on the field. On August 10, 1987, Mr. Gross cheated by bringing on the field an illegal glove." Then, in the words of the baseball judge he was, Giamatti nails down the verdict:

> It is not necessary actively or even inadvertently (such as could have occurred, given the placement of the sandpaper in the glove) to have defaced a baseball. That contingency is covered elsewhere in the rules. Mr. Gross is neither charged with defacing a baseball nor with throwing a defaced baseball. To be guilty of cheating is enough to have flagrantly and willfully violated [rule] 8.02(b).[11]

Interestingly, it is enough to have broken this rule against merely having such a glove on the field to make it an act of cheating. Cheating, of course, is the essential threat to the game, according to Giamatti as the league's president and one of the most responsible stewards of the game. "Cheating," he continues, "is a very serious offense and merits serious discipline." For cheating "has always been considered destructive of the essence of a contest designed to declare a winner."

> Cheating corrodes the integrity of any game. It undermines the assumption necessary to any game declaring a winner, that the contestants are playing fairly, i.e., under identical rules and conditions. It destroys public and participant confidence, morale, and goodwill. Mr. Gross acted with indifference to these principles.[12]

Turning to the Rose case, we find that he has violated the principle of what might be called democratic individualism. Cheating is a violation even as Rose's behavior—collision at plate, betting on baseball games—serves a rampant individualism that is in conflict with "democratic" individualism. In short, Rose does it—the hard playing—more for himself than for the sake of his team. It is clear that gambling, too, is done entirely for the individual self; it can do nothing to further the chances for a team's success. On the contrary, there is always the danger that betting might affect his playing or the way he manages the team on a given day.

As much as Giamatti had wrestled with the Gross case (he said he worked harder at reaching his decision than he had ever worked in New Haven where, among other jobs, he was president of Yale University for eight years), in the Pete Rose case he found himself with an instance of indifference not to the rules by which individual games are played but to baseball rules for the conduct of participants away, and seemingly apart, from games. There seems never to have been a question as to whether or not Pete Rose had violated the rules against betting on baseball games or even, more specifically, on games played by Rose's own team. But there was a larger issue involved. In violating organized baseball's rules against gambling on baseball games was Pete Rose asserting individuality over the collaborative game itself? Giamatti made it clear that it was Rose's arrogance and destructive character as shown forth in this case of repeated violations that made him a serious threat to the integrity of the game in the eyes of the Commissioner of Baseball. In "Statement Released to the Press on the Pete Rose Matter," he concludes: "The matter of Mr. Rose is now closed. It will be debated and discussed. Let no one think that it did not hurt baseball. That hurt will pass, however, as the great glory of the game asserts itself and a resilient institution goes forward. Let it also be clear that no individual is superior to the game."[13]

What might have Robert Frost decided in the Pete Rose case had he been Commissioner of Major League Baseball? One can only speculate. Might not he have been conflicted, given the claims of individuality and the logic of the rules in effect? He was "particular," he insisted, that "college athletics should be kept from corruption. They are close to the soul of culture."[14] For such athletics, he argued, enabled the enactment of prowess, justice, courage, and knowledge. No one ever questioned Rose's possession of these qualities, not on the field at least. And if Rose was not trying to determine the outcome of games by his proscribed betting on them, how could it be said that he had "hurt" the game? When he bet on his own team to win, was he not, in a small, almost trivial, way, trying to will that desirable bit of future in? As Frost said of them, in an interview conducted by Mark Harris, "The Founding Fathers didn't believe in the future.... They believed it *in*. You're always believing ahead of your evidence. What was the evidence I could write a poem? I just believed it. The most creative thing in us is to believe a thing in, in love, in all else. You believe yourself into existence."[15]

Frost was a baseball fan and player for all seasons or, to be more exact, for all surfaces. "As I say," he concluded his piece on the 1956 All Star game, "I never feel more at home in America than at a ball game be it in park or in sandlot."[16] One might say that Frost, who joked over the couple "Adam and Eve / Put out of the Park" (426), did not need to live with the illusion of that mythic place of green in the mind that so ordered and vitalized Giamatti's very being. After all, for many of the first boys of summer the playing fields were not expanses of green but lots of sand. The beauty of baseball was that it need not be played within the park. For Frost it was "perfect," not because it was Eden-like but because it was an arena for believing the future in. What Frost would have made of the Pete Rose case seems rather likely.

Giamatti lived much of his life in conventionally enclosed spaces—the enclosed green swards of quadrangles at two universities—Yale and Princeton—and the green enclosures of baseball parks. He does not advocate lighting out for the West or even going out into the trees. He knows where the clearings that matter are and those clearings are manmade, predictable, fulfilling (to a degree). Frost, on the other hand, would advocate taking the road less traveled by, striking out for the unknown, finding the unexpected clearing, making new tracks. Giamatti laments, as we have already seen, that the "game" leaves us in the fall, just when we need it most. What to make of a diminished thing, however, is precisely what Frost would have us learn from the song of the oven-bird that midsummer, mid-wood bird that sings its harsh, heuristic song when the dust over all presages the coming of fall. Giamatti sings of beginnings and blossoms. He can elegize elements of the fall, but he can write no ode to autumn. Winter and death go unmentioned.

Nowhere in Giamatti's writings about baseball, collected joyfully as *A Great and Glorious Game*, does he mention the potential for any player's suffering pain and physical injury. But Frost, a serious player himself, notices: "We all winced with fellow feeling when Berra got the foul tip on the ungloved fingers of his throwing hand." After all, all players at any level are full of "bodily memories of the experience" of playing the game—"what we farmers," Frost continues, tongue-in-cheek, "used to call kinesthetic images."[17]

Both Giamatti and Frost equated athletes with artists. Giamatti: "At the moment where an athlete makes something happen, everyone watching is elevated. That's what we say about great works of art. It's done with the body, but it's done with the mind and the spirit too. Whether you're a great ballet dancer or a great singer, athletes and artists have a lot in common."[18] Frost: "Prowess of course comes first, the ability to perform with success in games, in the arts and, come right down to it, in battle. The nearest of kin to the artists in college where we all become bachelors of arts are their fellow performers in baseball, football and tennis."[19] But what would Frost have made of Pete Rose's betting on all the horses in a given race so that he would be a winner and could parade as such before his friends and cronies? This is hardly an example of Frost's notion, it can be contended, that one can believe one's future into being.

To Giamatti's belief in the sustaining mythic nature of this American game—to a passage on "the enclosed green space" of baseball already quoted—we may contrast William Carlos Williams' more naturalistic view of the playing field itself in the novel *White Mule* (1937). "A little self-consciously he wandered toward the pitcher's mound," Williams begins; he hadn't realized how much raised it was above the rest of the diamond."

> And the way they whip that ball in! Walking in toward the plate he looked back to where Wiltze had stood. But when several fourteen to sixteen year old boys approached he turned and walked back across the infield, past second base out into the soft grass beyond. It was coarser than he had thought it to be from the stands, much more uneven and full of worm casts.[20]

Here is we have a close-up look of the playing field as arena, suggesting the fierce if democratic battles between pitcher and catcher, the tears in the fabric of the coarse field replete with its worm casts. The physician-poet Williams took a harder look at baseball than did Giamatti, the scholar of green fields and enclosed spaces, who left us, once again, with this picture: "Such imagery [of 'enclosed green space'] may be one reason why now almost forty-five million people a summer flow to baseball parks in the midst of urban wildernesses, flow in big cities to a place where perfection does not exist but which recalls in some distant way the place that promised perfection and whose name we derive from the enclosed park of the Persian king, paradise."[21] Still, Giamatti saw in himself, as we have seen, "a simpler creature," one "tied to more primitive patterns and cycles." "I need to think something lasts forever," he wrote, it will be recalled, "and it might as well be that state of being that is a game; it might as well be that, in a green field, in the sun."

Maybe the positions taken by Williams and Frost are not reconcilable, after all, with Giamatti's. Maybe, as Wallace Stevens tells us in "The Poems of Our Climate," "The imperfect is our paradise." Maybe, but if so, don't expect Giamatti to act accordingly. For it was his fierce hold on the mythic nature of that green and enclosed place—that paradisal game we others know simply as baseball—that led him, not to suspend Pete Rose—for a short or very long period—but to banish him entirely from the sacred places he had desecrated and all that might be considered to belong to it.

15. Nothing Gold Can Stay

Perhaps Bart Giamatti should have some culminating, prophetic words. In an essay he entitled "Men of Baseball, Lend an Ear," he writes: "It is, this grand game, no game but a work of art fashioned to remind us that we all began in the great green Elysian Field of the New World, with all its terrors and promises," he begins with a caution: "Today, in those enclosed green spaces in the middle of cities, under smoky skies, after days that weigh heavy either because of work or because of no work, the game reminds the people who gather at that field in the city of the best hopes and freest moments we can have." And that reminder brings with it a moral imperative: "the obligation to continue to be the medium for hope, in the season America now is in, is an obligation far weightier than your mercantile spats. Princelings and Sovereignlets of baseball, you speak of the game as an industry. That is your right. Play the game for whatever mercenary motives you wish." But, he concludes, "remember that, from our point of view, you play it so that we may all remember a past—graceful, energetic, free in the order and law of a green field—that never was."[22]

I have almost left out something of enormous importance, in my opinion, to a better understanding of the way Bart Giamatti was virtually compelled—hard-wired, perhaps—to handle and resolve the Pete Rose matter. The son of a renowned Dante scholar, Giamatti was himself by training a professional student of Renaissance literature. Three of the four chapters of *The Earthly Paradise and the Renaissance Epic* (1966), his first scholarly work, bear titles such as, in order, "Gardens and Paradises," "The First Renaissance Earthly Paradises," and "The Earthly Paradise and the Christian Epic." He concludes the book with admiration for the vision of John Milton. "The earthly paradise in *Paradise Lost*, home of Truth, innocence and joy whence came all falsity, sin and pain, blends all the previous images of the beautiful place into one," Giamatti reminds us. "For in telling his ancient story through the ancient image of the garden, Milton has included all he learned from the gardens of his Renaissance predecessors. In this garden, all the conflicts found in the other gardens are held in balance by the Christian-Humanist poet in his 'golden Scales'; and even after disobedience has outweighed innocence, the garden remains as a master image of equilibrium, and a version of the blissful Truth that man has always wanted and by which all other gardens are found wanting."[23] But not "wanting" is the garden green of Major League Baseball, not if he— Bartlett Giamatti—could help it. And if the teacher had introduced his Princeton and Yale students to Dante's circles of Hell, it is doubtful that as Commissioner he had the patience to explain how it would it all work out for the sinner before him.

One of Giamatti's Yale colleagues has reached back to the ancients to characterize the unfortunate consequences of the impasse in the Giamatti—Rose case by taking a long look back to the ancients. "Aimed at each other across the years in the manner of Greek tragedy," he concludes, the antagonists "destroyed each other."[24] Curiously, it is the memory of this single decisive act by A. Bartlett Giamatti that has so far kept his name alive, if not always fresh or green, in the public arena. As for the ageing Pete Rose, he has his records and his numbers, but those, at least for now, will not suffice.

Chapter Notes

Introduction

1. William Hazlitt, "Lecture on the Dramatic Literature of the Age of Elizabeth," in *The Complete Works of William Hazlitt*, ed. P. P. Howe after the edition of A. R. Waller and Arnold Glover (London: J. M. Dent, 1931), 6: 327–28.
2. Louis Mertins, *Robert Frost: Life and Talks-Walking* (Norman: University of Oklahoma Press, 1965), p. 50.
3. Mertins, 310.
4. William Logan, "Early Frost," *New York Times Book Review* (June 22, 2014), p. 14.
5. Ezra Pound, "Modern Georgics," *Poetry* 5 (Dec. 1914): 127–30.
6. Mertins, 351–52.
7. Pound, "Modern Georgics," 127–28.
8. Matthew Parfitt, "Robert Frost's 'Modern Georgics,'" *Robert Frost Review* (Fall 1996), 54–55.
9. See Michael Putnam, "The Future of Catullus," *Transactions of the American Philological Association* 113 (1983): 243–62.
10. "'For Glory and for Use,'" ed. George Monteiro, *Gettysburg Review* 7 (Winter 1994): 94.

Chapter 1

1. *The Notebooks of Robert Frost*, ed. Robert Faggen (Cambridge: Harvard University Press, 2006), p. 137. Incidentally, the word "homestead" appears in Frost's published poetry, in "A Hundred Collars"—in the line "Of late years, though he keeps the old homestead" (*A Concordance to the Poetry of Robert Frost*, ed. Edward Connery Lathem [New York: Holt Information Systems, 1971]).
2. Wallace Stevens to William Humphrey, Jan. 14, 1947, "Six Stevens Letters," ed. Jonathan Strange, *Wallace Stevens Journal* 18 (Spring 1994): 21. Related to Stevens' negative view of farming as a suitable occupation for an aspiring writer is the exchange between Frost and Stevens in Key West in 1940, in which "Stevens teased RF by saying, 'Your trouble, Robert, is that you write poems about—*things*.' RF replied, 'Your trouble, Wallace, is that you write poems about *bric-a-brac*'" (Lawrance Thompson, *Robert Frost: The Years of Triumph 1915–1938* [New York: Holt, Rinehart and Winston, 1970], p. 666).
3. For instances of the use of the phrase "Poetry of Agriculture," see *New-England Homestead* 38 (Mar. 4, 1899): 272; 38 (Mar. 25, 1899): 378); and 44 (Jan. 18, 1901): 89. Trade publishers also appealed to the farmer's sense of poetry and myth surrounding his occupation by assigning titles such as *The Triumphs of Timothy* and *The Book of Alfalfa* to their farming manuals and other agricultural books.
4. Interesting in this regard is what the poet Elizabeth Bishop said, days after Frost's death, to the poet-critic Randall Jarrell after reading and re-reading two of Jarrell's books: "I've read *The Lost World* through, several times—read *The Bat-Poet* again, too—and I think, if you will take it the way I mean it, that you are the real one and only successor to Frost," though she was quick to add: "Not the bad side of Frost, or the silly side, the wisdom-of-the-ages side, etc.—but all the good. The beautiful writing, the sympathy, the touching and real detail, etc. Also your psychology is, of course, much in advance of Frost's! Not *his* kind of idealized 'lost world' of the small farmer at all..." (*One Art: Letters*, ed. Robert Giroux [New York: Farrar, Straus and Giroux, 1994], p. 432).

5. Dr. Debora E. Longshore, "Sanitation for the Farmer's Home," *New-England Homestead* 32 (Apr. 11, 1896); 445.

6. Quotations from Frost's poetry or prose, unless noted otherwise, refer to *Robert Frost: Collected Poems, Prose, & Plays*, eds. Richard Poirier and Mark Richardson (New York: Library of America, 1995). These are indicated in the text by page numbers within parentheses.

7. Sherman Paddock, "Unwritten Poetry," *New-England Homestead* 43 (Nov. 23, 1901): 541.

8. Quoted in Mertins, 399.

9. In the spirit of artistic ecumenism, just before he was named head of the National Endowment for the Arts, Dana Gioia called attention to the popular view of Frost as a regional figure, calling him (all on same page of a sixteen-page essay) "the great poet of Yankee New England," "New England's archetypal bard," "the future poet laureate of Vermont," and "the great poet of rural New England." ("Two Views of Robert Frost," in *Disappearing Ink: Poetry at the End of Print Culture* [St. Paul: Graywolf Press, 2004], pp. 168–84.)

10. John C. Kemp's book is *Robert Frost and New England: The Poet as Regionalist* (Princeton: Princeton University Press, 1979); Gioia, 173.

11. Gioia, 183.

12. *Farm-Poultryman*, eds. Edward Connery Lathem and Lawrance Thompson (Hanover, NH: Dartmouth Publications, 1963), p. 9.

13. *Farm-Poultryman*, 11.

14. Robert Louis Stevenson had also published a poem bidding adieu to a farm, one that the *New-England Homestead* reprinted in 1899. Stevenson's "Farewell to the Farm" differs from Frost's "On the Sale of My Farm" in tone and intention. Frost is moderately playful until, at the end, unquestioned sentiment breaks through, but Stevenson settles for the expected rhyme and the jaunty gait of skilful doggerel, as is apparent in the poem's first and last stanzas: "The coach is at the door at last; / The eager children mounting fast, / And kissing hands, in chorus sing: / Good-bye, good-bye, to everything! / .... Crack goes the whip, and off we go; / The trees and houses smaller grow; / Last, round the woody turn we swing; / Good-bye, good-bye to everything!" (38 [Feb. 25, 1899]: 249). See also the anonymous "Selling the Farm," a first-person narrative about an ageing couple who change their minds at the last moment and decide not to sell the farm (*New-England Homestead* 51 [Sept. 9, 1905]: 245).

15. *Selected Letters of Robert Frost*, ed. Lawrance Thompson (New York: Holt, Rinehart and Winston, 1964), p. 223.

16. To the best of my knowledge there has been no systematic study of Frost's reading published to date.

17. José Enrique Rodó, "How a Newspaper Should Be," in *The Oxford Book of Latin American Essays*, ed. Ilan Stavans (New York: Oxford University Press, 1997), p. 68.

18. *New-England Homestead* 41 (Oct. 13, 1900): 342.

19. The *Homestead* also catered to its more literarily-minded readers by publishing from time to time the work of the well-known poets of the day and reprinting poems by the classic and near-classic poets. In 1898, for example, the *Homestead* featured poems by Eugene Field, Nora Perry, John Hay, Ralph Waldo Emerson, Helen Hunt, Lewis Carroll, Bayard Taylor, Emily Dickinson, William Cullen Bryant, James Russell Lowell, James Whitcomb Reilly, Oliver Wendell Holmes, Omar Khayyam, Shakespeare, Edward Lear, and Henry Wadsworth Longfellow. The journal's thinner stream of original fiction was enriched by the appearance, also in 1898, of two stories by the popular French writer Alphonse Daudet.

20. Mayme Isham, "Pleasures on the Farm," *New-England Homestead* 29 (Sept. 29, 1894): 140.

> Have you never read a poem sweetly told in words that charm,
> All about some happy childhood and the "pleasures on the farm"?
> "Ah! For childhood," you will murmur, "*then* the farm is very well";
> But wonder if for manhood this is just the spot to dwell.
> And you question oft within you what those "pleasures" really mean
> As you think of night and morning and the hard day in between;
> Of the mowing in the meadow with the hot sun scorching down;
> Of the hoeing, and the digging, and the marketing in town.
> Breakfast early in the morning, oftentimes by candle light,
> Then a hustle through the day-time, and a supper late at night:
> That's the story oft repeated of the farmer's toilsome year.

Can we look and find a brightness to this life that seems so drear?"
True there's beauty in the sunshine and a freshness in the air,
But when the sweat is pouring, why, what can a body care
For the beauty round about him, for the murmur of the breeze,
For the distant song of robin, or the rustle of the trees?
But there're two sides to a story if we only read it right;
There's a dark side to the farm life, and another, shining bright.
There's a freedom; there's a gladness; there's a joy, life-giving, great,
In the open-hearted country that we cannot help partake!
There are shouts of children playing, sweeter far than city's din;
And we glory in their freedom far removed from city's sin.
There are kind, warm-hearted neighbors and we grasp the friendly hand,
And we talk our trials over feeling sure they understand.
And we feel repaid for labor when we sit on winter's night
With our dear ones all about us dimly seen in fading light;
And we sing some sweet old ballad calling mem'ries of the past,
And we laugh and talk together, hoping only,—this may last.
There are apples sweet and juicy, and we like them all the more
When we know they're from the "Baldwin" that just hangs the gateway o'er;
We can hear its branches sighing in the breeze that just went by;
And we see those days in autumn when we plucked the fruit on high.
Oh! Too numerous to mention when we stop to count them all
Are the pleasures in the country on the farm, from fall to fall.
To be sure, a minor sadness sometimes stirs this life of ours;
For we know, for we have seen it, that there's sunshine after showers.
And whate'er our occupation, in the shop, or on the farm,
We can find the "silver lining"; and so, now, what's the harm
In this our little life here, to catch these brighter gleams
And hold them ere they vanish like sweet forgotten dreams?

21. D. F. A., "The Fringed Gentian," *New-England Homestead* 43 (Aug. 17, 1901): 64.
22. L. A. Safford, "December," *New-England Homestead* 53 (Dec. 1, 1906): 551.
23. Quoted by Henry Hart, "Richard Ellmann's Oxford Blues," *Sewanee Review* 117 (Spring 2009): 282.
24. *Prose Jottings of Robert Frost*, ed. Edward Connery Lathem and Hyde Cox (Lunenburg, VT: Northeast-Kingdom, 1982), p. 92.
25. *New-England Homestead* 52 (May 26, 1906): 670.
26. *New-England Homestead* 55 (Sept. 7, 1907): 203; (Nov. 16, 1907): 148.
27. Clarence Hawkes, "Keep Up Your Fences," *New-England Homestead* 35 (Sept. 4, 1897): 233.
28. J. L. Henry, "Cost and Waste of Fences," *New-England Homestead* 40 (Apr. 14, 1900): 470.
29. Charles Pierson Augur, "Discard Useless Farm Fences," *New-England Homestead* 41 (Dec. 15, 1900): 600.
30. *New-England Homestead* 52 (Apr. 14, 1906): 510.
31. Anna J. Grannis, "Set Toil to a Tune," *New-England Homestead* 42 (Mar. 2, 1901): 347.
32. Quoted in Mertins, 399.
33. Clarence Hawkes, "Pokin' 'Round," *New-England Homestead* 35 (Aug. 14, 1897): 165.
34. *New-England Homestead* 56 (Jan. 11, 1908): 55.
35. E. W., *New-England Homestead* 40 (June 30, 1900): 778. See also "The Laughing Crow," a poem which tells the story of children who befriend and domesticate a scornful bird (*New-England Homestead* 42 [May 18, 1901]: 692).
36. Paul Rosenfeld, "American Painting," *The Dial* 71 (Dec. 1921): 649.
37. Allen W. Porterfield, "Reluctance of the American Novel to Enter the Barn," *New York Times* (Feb. 11, 1923), p. BR2.
38. M. A. B., "My Good Samaritan," *New-England Homestead* 43 (July 20, 1901): 65.
39. Charles H. Smith, "The Farmer as a Thinker," *New-England Homestead* 40 (Apr. 28, 1900): 539.
40. "A Poet of the Farm: James Whitcomb Riley," *New-England Homestead* 32 (Jan. 11, 1896): 51.
41. Sherman Paddock, "Unwritten Poetry," *New-England Homestead* 43 (Nov. 23, 1901): 541.

42. Mary M. Currier, "An Immortal Song," *New-England Homestead* 44 (Feb. 15, 1902): 261.
43. Quoted in Mertins, 399.
44. Ethelwyn Wetherald, "April Rain," *New-England Homestead* 44 (Apr. 26, 1902): 602.
45. T. W. B., "In the Pasture," *New-England Homestead* 46 (June 27, 1903): 668. See also Mrs. C. W. N.'s "Joy in Living," *New-England Homestead* 52 (May 5, 1906): 605.
46. E. C. Tompkins, "The Springtime Miracle," *New-England Homestead* 44 (Mar. 29, 1902): 482.
47. Grace Irene Chapin, "The White Birches," *New-England Homestead* 44 (Jan. 25, 1902): 144.
48. "Bertha," "God's Healing Breezes," *New-England Homestead* 44 (Jan. 11, 1902): 73.
49. E. A. Brinninstool, "Pretty Good Place," *New-England Homestead* 46 (May 2, 1903): 505.
50. James Buckham, "The Lonesome Old Man," *New-England Homestead* 42 (Feb. 16, 1901): 259.
51. "The Hired Man," *Atlantic Monthly* 73 (Feb. 1894): 283–86.
52. James Buckham, "The Hired Man," *New-England Homestead* 42 (Mar. 26, 1901): 420.
53. William Cary Duncan, "Our Hired Man," *New-England Homestead* 45 (Oct. 18, 1902): 400.
54. For an example of Frost's serious-comic use of dialect or patois, see his portrayal of the French-Canadian neighbor in "The Ax-Helve" (173–76).
55. *New-England Homestead* 41 (Dec. 22, 1900): 661.
56. "Vedo's Tramp," *New-England Homestead* 40 (Mar. 24, 1900): 561.
57. "Fidget's Tramp," *New-England Homestead* 40 (Mar. 10, 1900): 323–24.
58. Eugene C. Dolson, "Her Heart's Domain," *New-England Homestead* 49 (Oct. 29, 1904): 391.
59. Moses Teggart, "Without and Within," *New-England Homestead* 47 (Aug. 29, 1903): 176.
60. Eleanor C. Hull, "The Housekeeper's View," *New-England Homestead* 50 (Apr. 15, 1905): 477.
61. *National Poetry Festival Held in the Library of Congress, October 22–24, 1962, Proceedings* (Washington: General Reference and Bibliography Division, Reference Department, Library of Congress, 1964), p. 238.
62. Mabel Cornelia Matson, "Phoebe," *New-England Homestead* 48 (Apr. 23, 1904): 500.
63. Mary Clarke Huntington, "The Perfect Whole," *New-England Homestead* 48 (Jan. 23, 1904): 99.
64. Mabel Cornelia Matson, "The Flower in Her Hand," *New-England Homestead* 47 (Dec. 5, 1903): 503.
65. Some sense of just how far the editors of *New-England Homestead* would tolerate sexually suggestive poetry can be gleaned from Ione L. Jones's "As the Rain Came Down": "The rain came down / In the little town, / But he did not think of going / From the cosy room, / With its softened gloom, / And fair little Mollie, sewing. / He plead his case / With a loving grace, / His ardor each moment growing; / A 'yes' she stitched / In her apron, bewitched,— / Then Mollie lay down her sewing" (32 [Apr. 11, 1896]: 445).
66. Ethelyn Dyer, "Footprints on the Snow," *New-England Homestead* 52 (Mar. 24, 1906): 415.
67. Jeffrey S. Cramer, *Robert Frost Among His Poems* (Jefferson, NC: McFarland, 1996), p. 181.
68. Frank H. Sweet, "Tell-Tale-Tracks," *New-England Homestead* 44 (Jan. 18, 1902): 109.
69. Elsie G. Baker, "Stories in the Snow," *New-England Homestead* 44 (Mar. 15, 1902): 418.
70. In the context of the tracking imagery of "Closed for Good," consider as well Frank Dempster Sherman's "The Snow Bird," which concludes: "But happiest is he, I know, / Because no cage with bars / Keeps him from walking in the snow / And printing it with stars" (*New-England Homestead* 33 [Nov. 28, 1896]: 509).
71. Alberta Field, "Some Insect Guests on Familiar Plants," *New-England Homestead* 49 (Oct. 22, 1904): 364.
72. Harriet A. Stanton, "Perseverance Conquers Ill," *New-England Homestead* 31 (Dec. 7, 1895): 526.
73. *New-England Homestead* 54 (June 29, 1907): 760.
74. Eliza Bradish, "Spiders," *New-England Homestead* 43 (Dec. 21, 1901): 683.
75. Susan Owen Moberly, "Under the Apple Trees," *New-England Homestead* 31 (Aug. 24, 1895): 156.
76. See *New-England Homestead* 37

(Oct. 22, 1898): cover; 40 (Jan. 13, 1900): 35; and 41 (Aug. 25, 1900): 169.
77. Ethelyn Dyer, "The Curse," *New-England Homestead* 52 (Mar. 24, 1906): 418.
78. L. C. Seal, "The Sleep of the Laboring Man," *New-England Homestead* 60 (May 14, 1910): 720.
79. James Janes, "Gathering Autumn Leaves," *New-England Homestead* 45 (Nov. 15, 1902): 524.
80. Mary F. Butts, "The Roadside Party," *New-England Homestead* 42 (June 22, 1901): 823.
81. Illria Turner, "The Old Homestead," *New-England Homestead* 47 (July 11, 1903): 39.
82. Frank H. Sweet, "The Deserted Homestead," *New-England Homestead* 49 (Aug. 20, 1904): 148. See also Harriet Perley, "The Old Home," *New-England Homestead* 42 (Jan. 19, 1901): 109.
83. Florence A. Jones, "The Road to Anywhere," *New-England Homestead* 57 (Dec. 12, 1908): 572.
84. Lawrance Thompson, *Robert Frost: The Early Years, 1874–1915* (New York: Holt, Rinehart and Winston, 1966), p. 500.
85. George Macdonald, "Which Road Would You Take?" *New-England Homestead* 35 (July 17, 1897): 69.
86. For Frost's intention in "The Road Not Taken" and the failure of readers to discern it, see Chapter 13 ("A Single Peel").

Chapter 2

1. T. S. Eliot, *Inventions of the March Hare: Poems 1909–1917*, ed. Christopher Ricks (New York: Harcourt Brace, 1996), pp. 13–16, 334–35.
2. Jay Parini, *Robert Frost: A Life* (New York: Henry Holt, 1999), p. 363.
3. Parini, 385.
4. Cramer, 14.
5. Lawrance Thompson and Arnold Grade, eds., *New Hampshire's Child: The Derry Journals of Lesley Frost* (Albany: State University of New York Press, 1969), note I: 19, 4–5.
6. Lucinda T. Carlton, *The Legend of Westrunning Brook, in Rhymes and Legends of the Nutfields* (Manchester, NH: Williams Printing, 1919), pp. 14–15.
7. See Cramer, 95–96.
8. Carlton, 40–42.
9. Carlton, 50.
10. Herman Melville, *Moby-Dick*, ed. Harrison Hayford and Hershel Parker (New York: Norton, 1967), p. 43.
11. Along with Thoreau and Emerson, Melville is something of a gray eminence in "Directive." "Let the most absent-minded of men be plunged in his deepest reveries— stand that man on his legs, get his feet a-going," he writes in *Moby-Dick*, "and he will infallibly lead you to water, if water there be in all that region. Should you ever be athirst in the great American desert, try this experiment, if your caravan happen to be supplied with a metaphysical professor. Yes, as every one knows, meditation and water are wedded for ever" (13).
12. Reginald Cook, *Robert Frost: A Living Voice* (Amherst: University of Massachusetts Press, 1974), p. 192.
13. "Closed for Good," in *Complete Poems of Robert Frost 1949* (New York: Henry Holt, 1949), p. 576.
14. "'For Glory and for Use,'" 97.
15. Carlton, 59.
16. *Selections from Ralph Waldo Emerson: An Organic Anthology*, ed. Stephen E. Whicher (Boston: Houghton Mifflin, 1957), p. 438.
17. *Prose Jottings*, 10.
18. Priscilla Paton, *Abandoned New England: Landscape in the Works of Homer, Frost, Hopper, Wyeth, and Bishop* (Hanover, NH: University Press of New England, 2003).

Chapter 3

1. "Speaking of Loyalty," in *Poetry and Prose*, ed. Edward Connery Lathem and Lawrance Thompson (New York: Holt, Rinehart and Winston, 1972), p. 410.
2. "Poverty and Poetry," in *Poetry and Prose*, 366.
3. Vrest Orton, *Vermont Afternoons with Robert Frost* (Rutland, VT: Charles E. Tuttle, 1971), p. 20.
4. *Complete Works of Ralph Waldo Emerson*, Vol. VIII, *Letters and Social Aims* (Boston: Houghton Mifflin, 1904), pp. 151–52.
5. *Selected Letters*, 179.
6. *Interviews with Robert Frost*, ed. Edward Connery Lathem (New York: Holt, Rinehart and Winston, 1966), p. 21.
7. Quoted in Sidney Hayes Cox, "The Sincerity of Robert Frost," *New Republic* (Aug. 1917), 25: 109, and *A Swinger of Birches: A Portrait of Robert Frost* (New York: Collier, 1961), p. 21.
8. *Farmer-Poultryman*, 83.
9. *Farmer-Poultryman*, 17–18.

10. *Farmer-Poultryman*, 19.
11. *Farmer-Poultryman*, 23.
12. "The Quest of the Orchis," *The Independent* 53 (June 27, 1901): 1494.
13. *Selections*, 420.
14. *Early Years*, 270.
15. "The Quest of the Purple-Fringed," *Complete Poems*, 459.
16. For Frost's interest in Mrs. William Starr Dana's *How to Know the Wild Flowers* (New York: Scribner's, 1893), see Thompson, *Early Years*, 218.
17. Dana, 310.
18. Dana, 348.
19. *Early Years*, 530.
20. Thompson and Grade, II, 7, 7–8. My discussion of Frost's change of title in this poem about the orchis appeared in slightly different form in "Frost's Quest for the 'Purple Fringed," *English Language Notes* 13 (Mar. 1976): 204–06. For a defense of Frost's practice in this matter, see Michael West, "Versifying Thoreau: Frost's 'The Quest of the Purple-fringed' and Fire and Ice," *English Language Notes* 16 (1978): 40–47, and Ron Thomas, "Thoreau, William James, and Frost's 'Quest of the Purple-Fringed': A Contextual Reading," *American Literature* 60 (1988): 433–50.
21. *Living Voice*, 264. See also John C. Kemp, who believes that Frost's poem "recreates the observer's response to what he finds in his walks" (207).
22. *American Poetry 1922: A Miscellany* (New York: Harcourt, Brace, 1922), p. 112.
23. J. Henri Fabre, *The Life of the Spider*, trans. Alexander Teixeira de Mattos (London: Hodder & Stoughton, 1912), p. 234.
24. Fabre, 302–303, 306.
25. Compare Charles Darwin. In his *Journal of the Voyage of the Beagle* (a book Frost liked well enough to re-read) Darwin writes:

It is well known that most of the British spiders, when a large insect is caught in their webs, endeavor to cut the lines and liberate their prey, to save their nets from being entirely spoiled. I once, however, saw in a hothouse in Shropshire a large female wasp caught in the irregular web of a quite small spider; and this spider, instead of cutting the web, most perseveringly continued to entangle the body, and especially the wings, of its prey [*Journal of Researches into the Natural History and Geology of the Countries Visited During the Voyage Round the World of H.M.S. "Beagle" Under the Command of Capt. Fitz Roy, R.N.* (New York: D. Appleton, 1833), p. 33.

26. "Remarks Accepting the Gold Medal of the National Institute of Arts and Letters," in *Selected Prose of Robert Frost*, ed. Hyde Cox and Edward Connery Lathem (New York: Holt, Rinehart and Winston, 1966), pp. 101–02.
27. "Remarks," 102.
28. "Remarks," 102.
29. "Remarks," 102.
30. *Living Voice*, 51.
31. *Living Voice*, 232.
32. *Living Voice*, 232.
33. Ralph Waldo Emerson, *Journals and Miscellaneous Notebooks of Ralph Waldo Emerson, Volume III, 1826–1832*, ed. William H. Gilman and Alfred R. Ferguson (Cambridge: Harvard University Press, 1963), p. 12.

Chapter 4

1. Frost's confidence in his poem is indicated by his forthright suggestion to Louis Untermeyer that he include the poem in an anthology he was compiling: "You'll want Design" (*The Letters of Robert Frost to Louis Untermeyer* [New York: Holt, Rinehart and Winston, 1963], p. 143.)
2. *Selected Letters*, 45.
3. The "In White" manuscript, now at the Huntington Library, San Marino, California, was published first in Reginald L. Cook, *The Dimensions of Robert Frost* New York: Rinehart, 1958), p. 85. It was subsequently republished, with slight differences in transcription, in Thompson's *Early Years*, 582.
4. Quoted in *Dimensions*, 85.
5. Three commentaries on "Design" remain indispensible: Randall Jarrell, *Poetry and the Age* (New York: Alfred A. Knopf, 1953), pp. 50–53; Reuben A. Brower, *The Poetry of Robert Frost: Constellations of Intention* (New York: Oxford University Press, 1963), pp. 104–108; and Hyatt H. Waggoner, *American Poets: From the Puritans to the Present* (Boston: Houghton Mifflin, 1969), p. 4 *et passim*. For a cogent and persuasive presentation of the argument that "Design" shows the influence of William James's Pragmatism, see Thompson's *Early Years*, 383–87.
6. See Brower, 105.
7. Thompson suggests that the lines "What brought the kindred spider to that height, / Then steered the white moth thither in the night?" are a mock-echo of the well-known lines of William Cullen Bryant's

poem on providential design, "To a Waterfowl": "He who, from zone to zone, / Guides through the boundless sky thy certain flight..." (*Early Years*, 582).
   8. Frost's puckish attitude toward the sonnet form is instructive. "The sonnet is the strictest form I have behaved in," he wrote to Untermeyer, "and that mainly by pretending it wasn't a sonnet" (*Letters to Untermeyer*, 381).

Chapter 5

1. *Living Voice*, 144.
2. "Hired Man," *Atlantic*. All quotations from this text are identified by page number(s) within parentheses.
3. *Selected Letters*, 385–86.
4. *Interviews*, 219.
5. *Interviews*, 219.

Chapter 6

1. See Daniel Hoffman, "Robert Frost: The Symbol a Poem Makes," *Gettysburg Review*, 7 (Winter 1994), 109–10.
2. Joyce Carol Oates, "First Loves: From 'Jabberwocky' to 'After Apple Picking,'" in *Faith of a Writer: Life, Craft, Art* (New York: HarperCollins, 2003), pp. 13–21.
3. For illustrations of apple orchards and scenes of apple-picking, see *New-England Homestead* 37 (Oct. 22, 1898): cover; 40 (Jan. 23, 1900): 35; and 41 (Aug. 25, 1900): 169.
4. See, for example, *New-England Homestead* 42 (Apr. 13, 1901): 557.
5. *New-England Homestead*, 60 (May 14, 1910), 720.
6. Ethelyn Dyer, "The Curse," *New-England Homestead* 52 (Mar. 24, 1906): 418.
7. Oates, 19–21.
8. *Selected Letters*, 255–56.

Chapter 7

1. *Letters to Untermeyer*, 265.
2. Quoted in Lyman Lee Leathers, "Ridgely Torrence and the Search for an American Identity," Diss. University of Pennsylvania, 1963, p. 195 (note).
3. *Selected Letters*, 265.
4. Quoted in *Selected Letters*, 236.
5. *Selected Letters*, 237.
6. *Selected Letters*, 257.
7. *Selected Letters*, 257–58.
8. Willard Thorp, "The Achievement of Ridgely Torrence," *Princeton University Library Chronicle* 12 (Spring 1951): 109.
9. Robert S. Newdick, *Newdick's Season of Frost: An Interrupted Biography of Robert Frost*, ed. William A. Sutton (Albany: State University of New York Press, 1976), p. 369.
10. May Sinclair, "Three American Poets of To-Day," *Atlantic Monthly* 96 (Sept. 1906): 326.
11. Sinclair, 326.
12. Thorp, 109–11.
13. Sinclair, 333.
14. Ridgely Torrence, "The Lesser Children," *Atlantic Monthly* 94 (Sept. 1905): 326–30.
15. Sinclair, 335.
16. *Selected Letters*, 74.
17. *Selected Letters*, 84. See also Thompson's *Early Years*, 414.
18. *Selected Letters*, 190.
19. Dorothea Kingsland, "The Ridgely Torrence Collection," *Princeton University Library Chronicle* 15 (Summer 1954): 214.
20. Kingsland, 214.
21. Sinclair, 334.
22. *Selected Letters*, 83. Frost also recalled his having once told C. Day Lewis that "Mowing" was "straight goods—all mine" (quoted in Mertins, 343).
23. When Torrence collected the poem thirty-six years later, as "Threnody at the Hunting Season," he revised it extensively—for the worse, in my opinion. In *Poems* (1941) it opens: "In the middle of August when the southwest wind / blows after sunset from the upper air / And through the dusk, Antares toward the west / Leads down the smouldering Scorpion to his lair" (98).
24. Thorp, 109.

Chapter 8

1. W. B. Yeats, *Autobiographies*, ed. William H. O'Donnell and Douglas N. Archibald, Vol. III of *The Collected Works of W. B. Yeats*, ed. Richard J. Finneran and George Mills Harper (New York: Scribner, 1999), IV: 219–66.
2. See Edward Thomas, *Language Not to Be Betrayed: Selected Prose of Edward Thomas*, ed. Edna Longley (Manchester: Carcanet, 1985), p. 160; Ezra Pound, "Preface," *The Poetical Works of Lionel Johnson* (London: Elkin Mathews, 1915), pp. v–xix; Louise Imogen Guiney, "Of Lionel Johnson," *Atlantic Monthly* 90 (Dec. 1902): 856–62; and *Letters to Untermeyer*, 220–21.
3. Yeats, 184.

4. *Some Poems of Lionel Johnson*, ed. Louise Imogen Guiney (London: Elkin Mathews, 1912), p. 67.
5. *National Poetry Festival*, 237.
6. For Johnson's appreciation of Blaise Pascal, see *Post Liminium: Essays and Critical Papers of Lionel Johnson*, ed. Thomas Whittemore (London: Elkin Mathews, 1911), pp. 155–60. For the connection between "Desert Places" and the *Pensées*, see Cook's *Dimensions*, 187–88, and *Living Voice*, 292.
7. For the argument that there are also traces of Torrence's poetry in "Desert Places," see Chapter 7 ("The Passing Glimpse").
8. *The English Literary Decadence: An Anthology*, ed. Christopher S. Nassaar (Lanham, MD: University Press of America, 1999), p. 213.
9. Guiney, "Of Lionel Johnson," *Some Poems*, 19.
10. Fernando Pessoa, *The Book of Disquiet*, ed. and trans. Richard Zenith (New York: Penguin, 2003), p. 138.
11. "By the Statue of King Charles at Charing Cross," *Some Poems*, 48–50.
12. The phrase comes from Yeats, 151.
13. *National Poetry Festival*, 255–56. Frost frequently referred to the behavior of Charles I at his death; see Cook's *Living Voice*, 71, 92, 94.
14. *Letters to Untermeyer*, 220.
15. *Post Liminium*, 157. Emphasis added.
16. Jarrell, 53.
17. Joseph Brodsky, "On Grief and Reason," in Joseph Brodsky, Seamus Heaney, and Derek Walcott, *Homage to Robert Frost* (New York: Farrar Straus Giroux, 1996), p. 18.
18. Iain Fletcher, introduction to *The Complete Poems of Lionel Johnson*, ed. Fletcher (London: Unicorn Press, 1953), p. xxv.
19. Walter E. Houghton and G. Robert Stange, "The Aesthetic Movement," in *Victorian Poetry and Poetics*, ed. Houghton and Stange (Boston: Houghton Mifflin, 1959), p. 720.
20. Guiney, *Some Poems*, 69, 94; Fletcher, *Complete Poems*, 83. Emphasis added.
21. Earlier Frost had first employed the rhyme in "Love and a Question" (1913): "Within, the bride in the dusk alone / Bent over the open fire, / Her face rose-red with the glowing coal / And the thought of the heart's desire" (17).
22. *Some Poems*, 58.
23. *Some Poems*, 61.
24. *Some Poems*, 62.
25. *Selected Letters*, 217. Frost's correspondent was the editor-critic Edward Garnett.
26. *Post Liminium*, 98. Frost echoes Johnson—"The *Purgatorio* is said to be hard"—in "The Constant Symbol," *Selected Prose*, 23.
27. Fletcher, 92.
28. *The Divine Comedy of Dante Alighieri*, trans. Henry Wadsworth Longfellow (Boston: Houghton Mifflin, 1895), p. 3.
29. Quoted in Reginald L. Cook, "Robert Frost's Asides on His Poetry," *American Literature* 19 (Jan. 1948): 359 note.
30. Fletcher, xxxvii.
31. Fletcher, 7.
32. Fletcher, xxxvii.

Chapter 9

1. "Democracy Losing, Lippmann Asserts," *New York Times* (June 1, 1932), p. 18.
2. *The Writings of Henry David Thoreau* (Boston: Houghton Mifflin, 1906), IV: 459.
3. Reported in *National Poetry Festival*, 242.
4. "'For Glory and for Use,'" 94.
5. Reported in *Congresso International de Escritores e Encontros Intelectuais* (São Paulo: Anhembi, 1957), p. 482. My translation.
6. *National Poetry Festival*, 255.
7. Frost's recitation at John F. Kennedy's inauguration is available in *Robert Frost: Poems, Life, Legacy*, CD-ROM, compiled by Joe Matazzoni, ed. Donald Sheehy (New York: Henry Holt, 1997).
8. Benjamin Welles, "Khrushchev Bangs His Shoe on Desk," *New York Times* (Oct. 12, 1960), pp. 1, 14. Khrushchev's shoe-pounding over fifty years ago was still remembered decades later. See "Cold War Satellite Images Are Paying Off," *Boston Sunday Herald* (July 12, 1998; p. 23), which begins: "If former Soviet Premier Nikita Khrushchev were alive, he'd have to eat the shoe he pounded in fits of socialist passion as he vowed that capitalism would perish."
9. *Interviews*, 285.
10. Russell Baker, "Frost Honored on 88th Birthday; Praises His 'Enemy' Khrushchev," *New York Times* (Mar. 27, 1962), p. 39.
11. See, for example, Frederick B. Adams, Jr., *To Russia with Frost* (Boston: The Club of Odd Volumes, 1963); Stewart L. Udall, "'...and miles to go before I sleep': Robert Frost's Last Adventure," *New York Times Magazine* (June 11, 1972); and F. D. Reeve,

Robert Frost in Russia (Boston: Little, Brown, 1964).
12. "A Khrushchev Proverb Begins Second Day of Vienna Meeting," *New York Times* (June 5, 1961), p. 12; and "Khrushchev Gets Off Some More Aphorisms," *New York Times* (Oct. 18, 1961), p. 18.
13. *Living Voice*, 82.
14. *Living Voice*, 82–83.
15. *Living Voice*, 55.
16. Richard Chevenix Trench, *Notes on the Parables of Our Lord* (New York: D. Appleton, 1855), pp. 13–14.
17. Theodore Morrison, "The Agitated Heart," *Atlantic Monthly* 220 (July 1967): 78.
18. *Selected Prose*, 97.
19. Philip Benjamin, "Robert Frost Returns with Word of Khrushchev," *New York Times* (Sept. 10, 1962), p. 8.
20. Quoted in Udall, 30.
21. *Interviews*, 289.
22. In August 1954 Frost was sent, along with William Faulkner, to the International Writers Congress in São Paulo, Brazil. Faulkner was more skeptical about such State Department sponsored visits by writers than was Frost. "The artist is still a little like the old court jester. He is supposed to speak his vicious paradoxes with some sense to them," he told an interviewer in 1955, "but he isn't part of whatever the fabric is that makes a nation. It is assumed that anyone who makes a million dollars has a unique gift, though he might have made it off some useless gadget" (*Lion in the Garden: Interviews with William Faulkner*, ed. James B. Meriwether and Michael Mitigate [Lincoln: University of Nebraska Press, 1980], p. 82).
23. *Selected Letters*, 592.
24. See Lewis Turco, "Comparative Literature," *College English* 27 (Mar. 1966): 511.
25. Reading at Brown University, Dec. 7, 1955. "All socialism is bad arithmetic," he told Peter J. Stanlis in 1940, "in which two comes before one" (*Robert Frost: The Individual and Society* [Rockford, IL: Rockford College, 1973], p. 56).
26. Robert Frost, *In the Clearing* (New York: Holt, Rinehart and Winston, 1962), pp. 85–86.
27. Adams, 26.
28. Iona and Peter Opie, *A Family Book of Nursery Rhymes* (New York: Oxford University Press, 1964), p. 189.
29. Charles Poore, "Books of the Times," *New York Times* (Mar. 27, 1962), p. 35.
30. "'Mending Wall' in Moscow," *New York Times Magazine* (Sept. 16, 1962), p. 34.
31. Reeve, 91–92.
32. *National Poetry Festival*, 253. Perhaps contributing to Frost's desire to act the diplomat was the memory of Franklin Delano Roosevelt's destiny to exercise great diplomatic power. In language that recalls the language of his own poem, "The Lovely Shall Be Choosers," Frost recalled: "And He [God] gives him polio, and then he sits on top of the world along with Stalin and Churchill! That row is forever in my mind" (*Interviews*, 157).
33. *Selected Letters*, 595.
34. "Robert Frost, 80, Gives a Recipe for Diplomats," *New York Times* (Aug. 11, 1954), p. 27. Parts of this chapter were included in a talk at the Robert Frost Colloquium, St. Lawrence University, Canton, New York, Oct. 19–30, 1993; published as "Robert Frost and the Dark Saying," *Bulletin of the Friends of the Owen D. Young Library* 24 (1994), 13–32.

Chapter 10

1. *Letters to Untermeyer*, 10.
2. Robert Frost, quoted in Mertins, 187; Carole Thompson, "An Afternoon with Robert Pinsky," *Robert Frost Stone House Museum Newsletter*, no. 6 (Spring 2005), [page 1].
3. Vladimir Nabokov, *Pale Fire*, in *Novels 1955–1962* (New York: Library of America, 1996), p. 585.
4. Cook, "Asides," 355.
5. According to some readers, "New Hampshire" parodies T. S. Eliot's "The Waste Land" (1922), with its complement of notes. In *New Hampshire* (1923) the "notes" are identified on the title-page (*New Hampshire: A Poem with Notes and Grace Notes*) as well as indicated in the arrangement of the poems, "New Hampshire" followed by "Notes," a section containing the rest of the poems.
6. Mertins, 398.
7. Mertins, 81–82.
8. Cook, "Asides," 358.
9. William H. Pritchard, "Robert Frost," in *Lives of the Modern Poets* (New York: Oxford University Press, 1980), p. 113.
10. William Rose Benét, "Moon Rider," *New Republic* 34 (Mar. 7, 1923): 47.
11. Robert Frost, "Stopping by Woods on a Snowy Evening," *New Republic* 34 (Mar. 7, 1923): 47.

12. Quoted in R. C. Townsend, "In Defense of Form: A Letter from Robert Frost to Sylvester Baxter, 1923," *New England Quarterly* 36 (June 1963): 243.
13. Townsend, 247.
14. Jean Starr Untermeyer, "The Poems of the Month," *The Bookman* 57 (June 1923): 447, and Babette Deutsch, "The Poems of the Month," *The Bookman* 57 (July 1923): 509. The poem was also reprinted in *Current Opinion* 76 (Jan.–June 1924): 94.
15. Donald Hall, "Robert Frost Corrupted," in *The Weather for Poetry: Essays, Reviews, and Notes on Poetry, 1977–81* (Ann Arbor: University of Michigan Press, 1982), p. 141.
16. "Stopping by Woods on a Snowy Evening," *Chapbook (A Monthly Miscellany)* (Apr. 1923), 3.
17. "Introduction to *King Jasper*," in *Selected Prose*, 59.
18. *From Snow to Snow* (New York: Holt, 1936), frontispiece, p. 2.
19. Mary B. W. Tabor, "Book Notes," *New York Times* (Nov. 8, 1995), p. C17.
20. Sarah Boxer, "The Public Library Opens a Web Gallery of Images," *New York Times* (Mar. 3, 2005), pp. B1–7.
21. Charles W. Cooper and John Holmes, *Preface to Poetry* (New York: Harcourt Brace, 1943), p. 604, and Robert K. Miller, *The Informed Argument: A Multidisciplinary Reader and Guide* (San Diego: Harcourt Brace Jovanovich, 1986), p. 416. The manuscript page for "Stopping by Woods" is also available in Sheey's CD-Rom *Robert Frost*.
22. Bleau, 177.
23. See John Holmes's analysis of Frost's manuscript in Cooper and Holmes, pp. 603–07. Frost himself explained to Sylvester Baxter how he worked out the final form of the last stanza. "I'm surprised at you that you should be the one of all my poetical friends to miss the reason for the repetend in 'Stopping by Woods.' There should be two reasons one of meaning and one of form." He continues:

> What the repetend does internally you come very near: what it does externally is save me from a third line promising another stanza. If the third line had been dead in all the other stanzas your judgement would be correct. A dead line in the last stanza alone would have been a flaw. I considered for a moment four of a kind in the last stanza but that would have made five including the third in the stanza before it.

He had "considered for a moment winding up with a three line stanza," but, he realized that "the repetend was the only logical way to end such a poem. I considered for a moment winding up with a three line stanza. The repetend was the only logical way to end such a poem" (Townsend, 243).
24. *The Collected Prose of Robert Frost*, ed. Mark Richardson (Cambridge: Harvard University Press, 2007), pp. 161–62.
25. George Sullivan, "Forest for the Trees," *New Republic* 179 (Dec. 18, 1995), 4.
26. Lalia Mitchell, "Christmas," *New-England Homestead* 61 (Dec. 24, 1919), 661.
27. Eleanor C. Hull, "December," *New-England Homestead* 41 (Dec. 22, 1900), 664. There are many other examples from the pages of the *New-England Homestead*. Here is a quatrain from Louise Lewin Matthews' "All Is Joy on Christmas Morn":

> The fields are white and ermine,
> The trees, like crystal gems,
> Crown the cold world with glitter
> And brilliant diadems [45 (Dec. 20, 1902): 675].

Later the same poet, a regular contributor to the Christmas issue, offered up "The Light of Christmas," containing these lines:

> Every hemlock wears a brilliant;
> Every lake is silvered o'er;
> All the fences and the hedges
> Wear their royal robes once more [49 (Dec. 24, 1904): 596].

A year later, she provided "Christmas in the Country," the first stanza of which reads:

> Christmas dawns in simple beauty
> O'er the meadows far and wide,
> Flooding all the fields and rivers
> With the glow of morning tide.
> All the hills with snow are mantled;
> Silence reigns from wood to vale;
> As the wan stars in the glory
> Of a dawning Christmas pale [51 (Dec. 23, 1905): 648].

And recall L. A. Safford's "December," with its anticipation of Frost's lines in "I Will Sing You One-O"—"The snow fell deep/ With the hiss of spray" (201)—in the lines "Snowflakes in the soughing pine,/ Hissing in old ocean's brine":

> Leafless trees and leaden sky;
> Ominous the blue-jay's cry;
> Northborn—winter hovers nigh,
> In December.
> Stark and stiff the landscape gray;
> Cold the distant sunset's ray;
> Early night cuts short the day,

In December
Snowflakes in the soughing pine,
Hissing in old ocean's brine,
Hide from sight the chill sky-line,
In December.
Sheeted white, like winter's gnome,
Hie away to lights of home
There to toast in cider's foam,
Bleak December.

28. A. L. Vermilya, "Christmas at the Farm," *New-England Homestead* 45 (Dec. 20, 1902): 678.

29. Isabel Gordon Curtis, "A Christmas Hardship," *New-England Homestead* 42 (Dec. 21, 1901): 676.

30. Mertins, 372.

31. Quoted in "What Do Children Really Like?" *New York Times* (May 5, 1985), p. BR16.

32. Philip Wylie, "Stopping to Write a Friend on a Thick Night," in *John Ciardi, Dialogue with an Audience* (Philadelphia: Lippincott, 1963), p. 162.

33. "'For Glory and for Use,'" 96.

34. John Ciardi, "Robert Frost: The Way to the Poem," *Saturday Review of Literature* 41 (Apr. 12, 1958): 13–15, 65; see also Bleau, 77. At Bread Loaf, on June 30, 1955, Frost talked about the annoying questions people asked about "Stopping by Woods," a "little thing you see very simply as I wrote it—night, evening, snowstorm, woods, dark, late, snow falling among the alders, and trees, and with a little poetic exaggeration, you know (to see the woods fill up with snow)." Then questions:

Did they fill up? How high? See. You want to know. Don't ask me. And I've been asked such things, you know. I've had people say—somebody who ought to know better—quote me as saying [in] that poem, "the coldest evening of the year." See. Now that's getting a thermometer into it. And "The darkest evening of the year's better"—more poetical some way. Never mind why. I don't know. More foolish.

Playful throughout, he becomes even more playful when he adds: "Got to be a little foolish or a good deal foolish." But then the poem "goes on and says 'The woods are lovely, dark and deep,' and then if I were reading it for somebody else, I'd begin to wonder what he's up to. See. Not what he means but what he's up to." There are "so many things that have happened, too, that way."

People have come to me to ask me what were the promises, and I've joined in on that. Let them have their say, and I took it my way. I remember telling one committee that came to me about that from a college—committee of students—and I said, promises may be divided into two kinds: those that I myself make for myself and those that my ancestors made for me, known as the social contract.

He asks himself if he thought of that when he wrote, and answers, partly for his listeners, partly for himself: "You know better. I've just got to say something. Just take it. They take it their way and I take it my way. But this the thing I finally said about it—partly in self-defense; I said: What does it say there? 'The woods are lovely, dark, and deep.' That's just as I might be getting along. That's all. That's the nicest way out of it—if you've got to get out of it" (*Living Voice*, 81).

35. "'For Glory and for Use,'" 96. For other examples of basically the same explanation, see *Living Voice*, 80–81, 122–23, and Mertins, 303–04, 371–72.

36. Reproduced in Cooper and Holmes, 604.

37. *Ethan Frome* (New York: Scribners, 1922), p. 81. Subsequent quotations from Wharton's novel refer to this text and are indicated by page number in this text.

38. *Living Voice*, 52.

39. See, for example, Bleau, 75.

40. http://www.livejournal.com/users/mimic/473932.html.

41. "Promises to Keep" ("Stopping by Woods") Cloudeight / Acpressions Greetings, http://thundercloud.net/acpressions/.

42. Sunrise Greeting, distributed by InterArt, Bloomington, IN 47402.

43. It is identified: "dugNAP ©1998."

44. Here, by title, are some other parodies of "Stopping by Woods": Gail White, "Traveling with Cats on a Snowy Evening," in *Visiting Frost: Poems Inspired by the Life and Work of Robert Frost*, ed. Sheila Coghill and Thom Tammaro (Iowa City: University of Iowa Press, 2005), p. 144; Henry Beard, "Sitting by the Fire on a Snowy Evening by Robert Frost's Cat," in *Poetry for Cats*, http://www.starwalk.com/dory/frot.htm; "In the Januaried Mountains" by Michael Earl Craig (begins "My little horse must think it queer. / But who cares what he thinks?"); "Stopping by Janet Jackson's Exposed Right Breast on a Snowy Evening," http://www.progressiveboink.com/archive/robertfrost.htm; James Brooks's "Stopping by Woods to Find My Golf Ball (with all due

respect to Robert Frost)," *English Journal* 80 (Jan. 1991): 80: 93; "Stopping by Some Book Shelves on a Snowy Evening (severe apologies to Robert Frost)" by Brockheim http://www.amazon.com/exec/obidos/tg/guides/guide-display; "Through Deep, Dark, and Lovely Woods" by Vikram Madan http://www.vikrammadan.com/Poems/deep_dark_woods.htm; "Frosty Night" by Johnny Mayall http://www.gleeful.com/dwlw/johnny.html; "Stopping by Woods on a Sunny Afternoon" by Jim Corbett http://www.mrgolf.com/stopping.html; "Stopping by Woods on a Snowy Morning" http://truthsandhalftruths.typepad.com/truths_and_truths/2005/; "Walking Through Woods on an Autumn Afternoon" http://www.beckysworld.fcpages.com; "Whose Foods These Are" http://forums.megatokyo.com/index.php?showtopic=350026; "Stopping by the Woods on a Snowy Evening (attempting to rescue a dog)" by Pam Green http://www.cal.net/~pamgreen/stopping_woods.html; "Whose Woods These Are (I haven't a clue)" http://www.marylafleur.com/silly.html.

45. Linda Hutcheon, *A Theory of Adaptation* (New York: Routledge, 2006), p. 176.

46. Songs: "Stopping by Woods on a Snowy Evening" set to music by Glen Hardy; "Stopping by Woods on a Snowy Evening" set to music by Jim Barlow; "Miles to Go" by Billy Paul Williams; "Lower Dryad Music by David LaMotte (with thanks for inspiration to Robert Frost and Jon Kabat-Zinn)" (1997); Leonard Cohen, "A Thousand Kisses Deep" ("And maybe I had miles to drive / And promises to keep"). Band Name: "David Hyanis & The Miles to Go Band." Dance: "Snow Evening Variations" by Charlie Vernon; two dancers in "loose-fitting white union suits and hiking boots")—Eleanor Blau, "Going Out Guide," *New York Times*, Aug. 20, 1981, p. C17; Jennifer Dunning, "Dance Vernon's 'Seasons,'" *New York Times*, Aug. 23, 1981, p. 65. Stories: "Snowy Evening" by Charles A. Acree (ends by quoting last stanza of "Stopping by Woods") http://tony.acree./com/snowy.htm; "Miles to Go" by M. Parnell (1997); "Miles to Go" by Rachel Anton (a vampire story); "And Miles to Go..." by Seishuku Skuld (2003); "Miles to Go" by Paul Turse (a boxing story); and "Promises to Keep" by Kath Heijtink. Television Programs: "Whose Woods These Are," episode 22 of *The Wonder Years*, May 9, 1989; "Whose Woods These Are," an episode of *Mutant X*; and "Whose Woods These Are," Minnesota Public Radio, Feb. 5, 2002. Web Page: "Bruce's Miles to Go" (quotes the last stanza of "Stopping by Woods"). Advertisement: Ad for B. Altman & Co. selling women's shoes quotes "I have promises to keep, and miles to go before I sleep"—*New York Times*, Sept. 15, 1977, p. 22. Therapy and Therapists: Dr. Richard Grossman's "So, You're Thinking of Becoming a Therapist?" insists on the "insight" therapist's need to "understand and appreciate subtext." To prove his point he offers an analysis of "Stopping by Woods" http://www.voicelessness.com/wubtext.html. Grief Counseling: "A poem I hold close in my grief recovery is 'Stopping by Woods...'" is the beginning of a paper by Peter Akery, TCF, Milford, CT. http://www.mind.net/tcf/v7n1a1.html. Nursing Home Reform: "Advance for Directors in Rehabilitation," a paper by Loretta Marmer (July 1998) begins by quoting the last stanza of "Stopping by Woods." Sermons: "And Miles to Go" by the Rev. Gary W. Charles (Feb. 22, 2004); "Promise Keepers," the Rev. Paul Watermulder's sermon on Mother's Day, May 11, 2003, in which he quotes Frost. Politics: "The Reagan Administration has miles to go before it sleeps" (William Buckley) and "We have miles to go before we sleep" (Michael Dukakis)—William Safire, "The PAWs That Refresh," *New York Times*, Apr. 26, 1987, p. SM10.

47. George Monteiro, *Robert Frost & the New England Renaissance* (Lexington: University Press of Kentucky, 1988), p. 16; Jeffrey Meyers, *Robert Frost: A Biography* (Boston: Houghton Mifflin, 1966), p. 180.

48. *The Poetical Works of Longfellow*, Cambridge ed., intro. George Monteiro (Boston: Houghton Mifflin, 1975), p. 202.

49. Frost's "three chief tones are talking, as in 'Mending Wall'; intoning, as in 'The Oven-bird' or 'Desert Places' or 'Acquainted with the night'; and a combination of talking and intoning, as in 'The Mountain.'" Cook, "Asides," 354.

50. C. M. Bowra, "Re-assessments: Robert Frost," *The Adelphi* 27 (Nov. 1950): 52.

51. In "The Constant Symbol" Frost refers to the "pleasure of ulteriority" (*Selected Prose*, 24).

52. "Now, you see, the first thing about that ['Stopping by Woods'] is to take it right between the eyes just as it is, and that's the ability to do that: to take it right between the eyes like a little blow and not, you know, take it in neuter sort of. And then, you know, the next thing is your inclinations

with it. I never read anything, in Latin, say, without a constant expectation of meaning that I'm either getting justified in or corrected. See." He continues: "Confirmed in or corrected, I've got to have something that's a little aggressive to it, but that's so with a poem. Right away you begin to take it your way. And you can almost say in a poem that you see in it he place where it begins to be *ulterior*, you know, where it goes a little with you, carries you on somewhere" (Cook, *Living Voice*, 80–81; emphasis added).

53. *Prose Jottings*, 53–54.

54. "The Figure a Poem Makes," in *Selected Prose*, 18; "Birches" (118).

55. *Robert Frost and Sidney Cox: Forty Years of Friendship*, ed. William R. Evans (Hanover, NH: University Press of New England, 1981), p. 147.

56. Cook, "Asides," 357.

57. Quoted in Meyers, 180. It is not unreasonable to think for a moment of "Stopping by Woods" as a response to some familiar print by, say, an imitator of Currier and Ives.

It is as if Frost were casually remembering some familiar engraving that hung on a schoolroom wall in Lawrence when he was growing up in the 1880s, and the poet slides into the picture. He enters, so to speak, the mind of the figure who speaks the poem, a figure whose body is slowly turned into the scene, head fully away from the foreground, bulking small, holding the reins steadily and loosely. The horse and team are planted, though poised to move. And so begins the poet's dramatization of this rural and parochial tableau. "Whose woods these are I think I know. / His house is in the village though. / He will not see me stopping here / To watch his woods fill up with snow." And then, having entered the human being, he witnesses the natural drift of that human being's thoughts to the brain of his "little horse," who thinks it "queer" that the rider has decided to stop here. And then, in an equally easy transition, the teamster returns to himself, remembering that he has promises to keep and miles to go before he sleeps. Duties, responsibilities—many must have them, we think, as echolalia closes the poem, all other thoughts already turning away from the illustration on the schoolroom wall. And even as the "little horse" has been rid of the man's intrusion, so too must the rider's mind be freed of the poet's incursion. The poet's last line resonates, dismissing the reader from his, the poet's, dreamy mind and that mind's preoccupations, and returning to the poet's inside reading of the still-life drama that goes on forever within its frame hanging on the classroom wall [Monteiro, *Renaissance*, 50–51].

To some readers "Stopping by Woods" might evoke the scene depicted in a familiar print or painting, while to others it can serve as a reference point for the appreciation of a painting. A case in point is Winslow Homer's "Sleigh Ride" (c. 1890–1895), on display at the Clark Art Institute, Williamstown, Massachusetts. Below the painting is affixed a note: "Sleigh Ride is—for me—the visual counterpart of Frost's 'Stopping by Woods on a Snowy Evening.' They are both magical." The sentiment is attributed to "Jack Hyland, Investment Banker and Clark Trustee, New York, N.Y."

Chapter 11

1. *Selected Letters of John Crowe Ransom*, ed. Thomas Daniel Young and George Core (Baton Rouge and London: Louisiana State University Press, 1985), pp. 405–06.

2. *Selected Essays of John Crowe Ransom*, ed. Thomas Daniel Young and John Hindle (Baton Rouge: Louisiana State University Press, 1984), pp. 29–32. Ransom was responding directly to Munson's essay in the *Saturday Review of Literature* (Mar. 28, 1925), 1: 625–26.

3. *Selected Essays*, 261.

4. John Crowe Ransom, "The Poetry of 1900–1950," *Kenyon Review* 13 (Jan. 1951): 445–54.

5. Kieran Quinlan, "John Crowe Ransom's Life and Career," in *American National Biography* (New York: Oxford University Press, 1999). http://www.english.uiuc.edu/maps/poets/m_r/ransom/life.htm.

6. Quoted in Robert Buffington, *The Equilibrist: A Study of John Crowe Ransom's Poems, 1916–1963* (Nashville: Vanderbilt University Press, 1967), p. 19. In fact, Ransom thought so little of *Poems About God* that only once did he allow the reprinting of any of its poems—in a selection prepared by the poet Robert Graves in the 1920s.

7. Vivienne Koch, "The Achievement of John Crowe Ransom," *Sewanee Review* 58 (Apr.–June 1950): 230.

8. *Poems About God* (New York: Henry Holt, 1919), p. 17.

9. "'For Glory and for Use,'" 94.

Chapter 12

1. Richard Wilbur, *Advice to a Prophet and Other Poems* (New York: Harcourt, Brace & World, 1961), p. 15.
2. This is how Wilbur translated the lines when he read the poem at the Library of Congress on Oct. 24, 1962 (see *National Poetry Festival*, 335). But in the note to the poem in *Advice to a Prophet*, p. 64 (reprinted in *The Poems of Richard Wilbur* [New York: Harcourt, Brace & World, 1963], p. 58), he translates the epigraph differently: "Truly, Wayland's handiwork—the sword Mimming which he made—will never fail any man who knows how to use it bravely."
3. *The Journal of Henry David Thoreau*, Vol. IV, *Writings*, ed. Bradford Torrey (20 vols.; Boston and New York, 1906), 10: 445. Later in the same entry Thoreau writes: "Pile up your books, the records of sadness, your saws and your laws. Nature is glad outside, and her merry worms within will ere long topple them down" (446).
4. *Nature*, 22.
5. *Nature*, 31.
6. *Nature*, 55.
7. *Journal*, 40.
8. *Journal*, 118.
9. *Things of This World* (New York: Harcourt, Brace, 1956), p. 28.
10. "It was a favorite habit of Thoreau's," notes Walter Harding, "to bend over and peer at the landscape through his legs, thus providing a novel (and framed) view" (*The Variorum Walden* [New York: Washington Square Press, 1962], p. 297, note 29).
11. *The Beautiful Changes and Other Poems* (New York: Harcourt, Brace, 1947), p. 54.
12. Robert Frank, "Richard Wilbur: An Interview," *Amherst Literary Magazine* 10 (Summer 1964): 63.
13. *Beautiful Changes*, 44.

Chapter 13

1. *Selected Letters*, 190, 189.
2. *Selected Letters*, xiv–xv. See also Elizabeth Shepley Sergeant, *Robert Frost: The Trial by Existence* (New York: Holt, Rinehart and Winston, 1960), p. 89.
3. Quoted in Larry L. Finger, "Frost's 'The Road Not Taken': A 1925 Letter Come to Light," *American Literature* 50 (Nov. 1978): 478–479.
4. Quoted in Robert Francis, "Frost as Apple Peeler," *New England Review* 1 (Autumn 1978): 33.
5. Francis, 32.
6. Francis, 32.
7. For the record, it should be noted that Francis was not the first New England poet to employ the apple-paring figure. He was anticipated by M. F. B., who in 1901 published "The Apple-Paring Test" in the *New-England Homestead*:

In the kitchen all alone!
My dear, do you remember?
The old folks slipped away to bed,—
'Twas the middle of December;
And snow was over all the land.
The candle flickered on the stand.
I pared an apple, while the red
Across your cheek went stealing.
"Aha!" I thought, "sweet Sally Ann,
You're not without some feeling!"
My heart beat loudly in my breast,
When suddenly I made the test.
'Twas many, many years ago,
And yet I well remember
The letter S upon the floor
That evening in December.
My life has been a long success.
Bless you, my dear, for saying "Yes!" [43 (Sept. 14, 1901): 256].

Chapter 14

1. Arthur Miller, *Timebends: A Life* (New York: Grove, 1987), pp. 263, 306, and 512.
2. *Timebends*, 263.
3. Mel Gussow, *Conversations with Miller* (New York: Applause, 2002), p. 101.
4. Brenda Murphy, *Miller: Death of a Salesman* (Cambridge: Cambridge University Press, 1995), p. 12.
5. *Timebends*, 184.
6. Miller was not the first one to highlight the phrase "death of a salesman." On December 20, 1883, the *New York Times* reported the death at the Grand Union Hotel, New Haven, of a "traveling salesman" from Brooklyn under the headline "Sudden Death of a Salesman" (2). Exactly one month later, on January 20, 1884, the *Times* reported the death (in Cobleskill, New York) of another drummer from Brooklyn, using the same headline "Sudden Death of a Salesman" (7). Much closer to the date of Miller's play, however, is the report "One Dead, One Hurt in Two Shootings" on Jan. 24, 1946, in the *Times*. A "second shooting resulted in the death of a salesman in a perfume shop at 83

Lexington Avenue" (27). This "clerk and salesman" lived in Jamaica, Queens.

7. The historical-cultural context of "The Death of the Hired Man" is significant. By the time the poem was published, the institution of the "hired man"—usually unmarried and living with his employers—had all but disappeared from the scene. The aphoristic quality of Frost's two definitions of "home" was soon recognized; see, for example, "For Your Scrap Book," *Hartford Courant* (Mar. 13, 1931), p. 14.

8. Christopher Bigsby, *Arthur Miller: A Critical Study* (Cambridge: Cambridge University Press, 2005), p. 121. Elsewhere Bigsby writes: "In an essay on realism, written in 1997, Miller made a remark that I find compellingly interesting. 'Willy Loman,' he said, 'is not a real person. He is if I may say so a figure in a poem.' That poem is not simply the language he or the other characters speak, though this is shaped, charged with a muted eloquence for a kind which he has said was not uncommon in their class half a century or more ago." Nor, he continues, "is it purely a product of the stage metaphors which, like Tennessee Williams, he presents as correlatives of the actions he elaborates. The poem is the play itself and *hence* the language, the mise en scène, the characters who glimpse the lyricism of a life too easily ensnared in the prosaic life which aspires to metaphoric force" ("Arthur Miller: Poet," *Michigan Quarterly Review* [Fall 1998], 37: 713–14).

9. *Conversations with Arthur Miller*, ed. Matthew C. Roudané (Jackson: University Press of Mississippi, 1987), p. 276.

10. Quoted in Max I. Baym, "William James and Henry Adams," *New England Quarterly* 10 (Dec. 1937): 732.

11. Quoted in Cook, "Asides," 359.

12. "Books of the Times," *New York Times* (June 2, 1949), p. 25.

13. Arthur Miller, "Tragedy and the Common Man," in *Twentieth Century American Drama: Cultural Concepts in Literary and Cultural Studies*, ed. Brenda Murphy (with Laurie J. C. Cella) (London: Routledge, 2006), II, 39. Miller's essay first appeared in the *New York Times* (Feb. 27, 1949), Sec. 2, pp. 1, 3.

14. Marilyn Johnson, *The Dead Beat: Lost Souls, Lucky Stiffs, and the Perverse Pleasures of Obituaries* (New York: HarperCollins, 2005), p. 78.

15. *Timebends*, 125–31.

16. *The Oxford Companion to the Bible*, ed. Bruce M. Metzger and Michael D. Coogan (New York: Oxford University Press, 1993), p. 568.

17. Northrop Frye, *Anatomy of Criticism* (Princeton: Princeton University Press, 1957), p. 136.

18. It is notable that while Miller does not refer specifically to the Parable of the Prodigal Son in Luke (15: 11–32), he does mention the "technique" and "form" of the three Gospels of Matthew, Mark, and Luke: "you will see the tremendous effort being made to dramatize, to make vivid, an experience which probably none of them really saw—except possibly one" ("Morality and Modern Drama: Interview with Phillip Gelb," in *Death of a Salesman: Text and Criticism*, ed. Gerald Weales [New York: Viking Penguin, 1967], p. 174).

19. Arthur Miller, "Introduction to the *Collected Plays*," in *The Theater Essays of Arthur Miller*, ed. Robert A. Martin and Steven R. Centola (New York: Da Capo Press, 1966), p. 144.

20. Bede Griffith, *The Golden String* (1954) is quoted in M. H. Abrams, *Natural Supernaturalism* (New York: Norton, 1971), p. 518, n. 105.

21. *Theater Essays*, 179.

22. Arthur Miller, *"Salesman" in Beijing* (New York: Viking, 1984), p. 49.

23. Arthur Miller, *The Death of a Salesman* (New York: Viking, 1949), p. 115.

24. In the same spirit Bigsby writes: "Willy goes on quests, like some medieval knight, riding forth to justify himself while at the same time his Platonic paradigm for the salesman-warrior is a man in carpet slippers, smoking a cigarette with a telephone in his hand" (*Arthur Miller*, 118).

25. *Death of a Salesman*, 115.

26. "Introduction," 141–42.

27. *Death of a Salesman*, 55.

28. *Death of a Salesman*, 81.

Chapter 15

1. *Pipetown Sandy* (Indianapolis: Bobbs-Merrill, 1905), p. 188.

2. John Hay Collection, John Hay Library, Brown University, Providence, R. I.

3. *A Great and Glorious Game: Baseball Writings of A. Bartlett Giamatti*, ed. Kenneth S. Robson, foreword by David Halberstam (Chapel Hill: Algonquin Books, 1998), pp. 7, 12–13.

4. Raymond Holden, "North of Boston," *New Yorker* 7 (June 6, 1931); 25.

5. *Collected Prose*, 179.
6. *Collected Prose*, 178.
7. *Prose Jottings*, 53.
8. *Collected Prose*, 180.
9. *Great and Glorious*, 42.
10. *Great and Glorious*, 13.
11. *Great and Glorious*, 78.
12. *Great and Glorious*, 78–79.
13. *Great and Glorious*, 121.
14. *Collected Prose*, 180.
15. *Interviews*, 271.
16. *Collected Prose*, 181.
17. *Collected Prose*, 178.
18. Quoted in James Reston, Jr., *Collision at Home Plate: The Lives of Pete Rose and Bart Giamatti* (New York: HarperCollins, 1991), p. 6.
19. *Collected Prose*, 180.
20. *White Mule* (New York: New Directions, 1937), p. 280.
21. *Great and Glorious*, 48.
22. *Great and Glorious*, 37–38.
23. *The Earthly Paradise and the Renaissance Epic* (New York: Norton, 1966), pp. 350–51.
24. Alvin Kernan, *In Plato's Cave* (New Haven: Yale University Press, 1999), p. 271.

Bibliography

A., D. F. "The Fringed Gentian." *New-England Homestead* 43 (Aug.17, 1901): 64.
Abrams, M. H. *Natural Supernaturalism*. New York: Norton, 1971.
Adams, Jr., Frederick B. *To Russia with Frost*. Boston: The Club of Odd Volumes, 1963.
Alighieri, Dante. *The Divine Comedy of Dante Alighieri*. Trans. Henry Wadsworth Longfellow. Boston: Houghton Mifflin, 1895.
Augur, Charles Pierson. "Discard Useless Farm Fences." *New-England Homestead* 41 (Dec. 15, 1900): 600.
B., M. A. "My Good Samaritan." *New-England Homestead* 43 (July 20, 1901): 65.
B., M. F. "The Apple-Paring Test." *New-England Homestead* 43 (Sept. 14, 1901): 256.
B., T. W. "In the Pasture." *New-England Homestead* 46 (June 27, 1903): 668.
Baker, Elsie G. "Stories in the Snow." *New-England Homestead* 44 (Mar. 15, 1902): 418.
Baker, Russell. "Frost Honored on 88th Birthday; Praises His 'Enemy' Khrushchev." *New York Times* (Mar. 27, 1962), p. 39.
Baym, Max I. "William James and Henry Adams." *New England Quarterly* 10 (Dec. 1937): 717–41.
Benét, William Rose. "Moon Rider." *New Republic* 34 (Mar. 7, 1923): 47.
Benjamin, Philip. "Robert Frost Returns with Word of Khrushchev." *New York Times* (Sept. 10, 1962), p. 8.
"Bertha." "God's Healing Breezes." *New-England Homestead* 44 (Jan. 11, 1902): 73.
Bigsby, Christopher. *Arthur Miller: A Critical Study*. Cambridge: Cambridge University Press, 2005.
———. "Arthur Miller: Poet." *Michigan Quarterly Review* 37 (Fall 1998): 713–24.
Bishop, Elizabeth. *One Art: Letters*. Ed. Robert Giroux. New York: Farrar, Straus and Giroux, 1994.
Bleau, N. Arthur. "Robert Frost's Favorite Poem," in *Frost: Centennial Essays III*, ed. Jac Tharpe. Jackson: University Press of Mississippi, 1978, pp. 174–77.
Bowra, C. M. "Re-assessments: Robert Frost." *The Adelphi* 27 (Nov. 1950): 46–64.
Boxer, Sarah. "The Public Library Opens a Web Gallery of Images." *New York Times* (Mar. 3, 2005), pp. B1–7.
Bradish, Eliza. "Spiders." *New-England Homestead* 43 (Dec. 21, 1901): 683.
Brinninstool, E. A. "Pretty Good Place." *New-England Homestead* 46 (May 2, 1903): 505.
Brodsky, Joseph. "On Grief and Reason," in *Joseph Brodsky, Seamus Heaney, and Derek Walcott, Homage to Robert Frost*. New York: Farrar Straus Giroux, 1996, pp. 5–56.

Brooks, James. "Stopping by Woods to Find My Golf Ball (with all due respect to Robert Frost)." *English Journal* 80 (Jan. 1991): 93.
Brower, Reuben A. *The Poetry of Robert Frost: Constellations of Intention.* New York: Oxford University Press, 1963.
Buckham, James. "The Hired Man." *New-England Homestead* 42 (Mar. 26, 1901): 420.
_____. "The Lonesome Old Man." *New-England Homestead* 42 (Feb. 16, 1901): 259.
Buffington, Robert. *The Equilibrist: A Study of John Crowe Ransom's Poems, 1916–1963.* Nashville: Vanderbilt University Press, 1967.
Butts, Mary F. "The Roadside Party." *New-England Homestead* 42 (June 22, 1901): 823.
Carlton, Lucinda T. *The Legend of Westrunning Brook, in Rhymes and Legends of the Nutfields.* Manchester, NH: Williams, 1919.
Chapin, Grace Irene. "The White Birches." *New-England Homestead* 44 (Jan. 25, 1902): 144.
Ciardi, John. "Robert Frost: The Way to the Poem." *Saturday Review of Literature* 41 (Apr. 12, 1958): 13–15, 65.
"Cold War Satellite Images Are Paying Off." *Boston Sunday Herald* (July 12, 1998), p. 23.
Congresso International de Escritores e Encontros Intelectuais. São Paulo: Anhembi, 1957.
Cook, Reginald L. *The Dimensions of Robert Frost.* New York: Rinehart, 1958.
_____. *Robert Frost: A Living Voice.* Amherst: University of Massachusetts Press, 1974.
_____. "Robert Frost's Asides on His Poetry." *American Literature* 19 (Jan. 1948): 351–59.
Cooper, Charles W., and John Holmes. *Preface to Poetry.* New York: Harcourt Brace, 1943.
Cox, Sidney Hayes. "The Sincerity of Robert Frost." *New Republic* 25 (Aug. 1917): 109–11.
_____. *A Swinger of Birches: A Portrait of Robert Frost.* New York: Collier, 1961.
Cramer, Jeffrey S. *Robert Frost Among His Poems.* Jefferson, NC: McFarland, 1996.
Currier, Mary M. "An Immortal Song." *New-England Homestead* 44 (Feb. 15, 1902): 261.
Curtis, Isabel Gordon. "A Christmas Hardship." *New-England Homestead,* 42 (Dec. 21, 1901), 676.
Dana, Mrs. William Starr. *How to Know the Wild Flowers.* New York: Scribners, 1893.
Darwin, Charles. *Journal of Researches into the Natural History and Geology of the Countries Visited During the Voyage Round the World of H.M.S. "Beagle" Under the Command of Capt. Fitz Roy, R.N.* New York: D. Appleton, 1833.
"Democracy Losing, Lippmann Asserts." *New York Times* (June 1, 1932), p. 18.
Deutsch, Babette. "The Poems of the Month." *The Bookman* 57 (July 1923): 509.
Dolson, Eugene C. "Her Heart's Domain." *New-England Homestead* 49 (Oct. 29, 1904): 391.
Duncan, William Cary. "Our Hired Man." *New-England Homestead* 45 (Oct. 18, 1902): 400.
Dyer, Ethelyn. "The Curse." *New-England Homestead* 52 (Mar. 24, 1906): 418.
_____. "Footprints on the Snow." *New-England Homestead* 52 (Mar. 24, 1906): 415.
Eliot, T. S. *Inventions of the March Hare: Poems 1909–1917.* Ed. Christopher Ricks. New York: Harcourt Brace, 1996.
Emerson, Ralph Waldo. *Complete Works of Ralph Waldo Emerson,* Vol. VIII, *Letters and Social Aims.* Boston: Houghton Mifflin, 1904.

———. *Journals and Miscellaneous Notebooks of Ralph Waldo Emerson, Volume III, 1826–1832*. Ed. William H. Gilman and Alfred R. Ferguson. Cambridge: Harvard University Press, 1963.
———. *Nature*, in *Selections*, pp. 21–56.
———. *Selections from Ralph Waldo Emerson: An Organic Anthology*. Ed. Stephen E. Whicher Boston: Houghton Mifflin, 1957.
———. "Woodnotes," in *Selections*, p. 420.
Evans, William R., ed. *Robert Frost and Sidney Cox: Forty Years of Friendship*. Hanover, NH: University Press of New England, 1981.
[Every day's work]. *New-England Homestead* 55 (Sept. 7. 1907): 203; (16 Nov. 1907): 148.
Fabre, J. Henri. *The Life of the Spider*. Trans. Alexander Teixeira de Mattos. London: Hodder & Stoughton, 1912.
Faulkner, William. *Lion in the Garden: Interviews with William Faulkner*. Ed. James B. Meriwether and Michael Mitigate. Lincoln: University of Nebraska Press, 1980.
"Fidget's Tramp." *New-England Homestead* 40 (Mar. 10, 1900): 323–24.
Field, Alberta. "Some Insect Guests on Familiar Plants." *New-England Homestead* 49 (Oct. 22, 1904): 364.
Finger, Larry L. "Frost's 'The Road Not Taken': A 1925 Letter Come to Light." *American Literature* 50 (Nov. 1978): 478–479.
Fletcher, Iain. Introduction to *The Complete Poems of Lionel Johnson*. Ed. Iain Fletcher. London: Unicorn Press, 1953.
"For Your Scrap Book." *Hartford Courant* (Mar. 13, 1931), p. 14.
Francis, Robert. "Frost as Apple Peeler." *New England Review* 1 (Autumn 1978): 32–39.
Frank, Robert. "Richard Wilbur: An Interview." *Amherst Literary Magazine* 10 (Summer 1964): 55–72.
Frost, Lesley. "A Note by Lesley Frost," in Bleau, 77.
Frost, Robert. "Closed for Good," in *Complete Poems of Robert Frost 1949*. New York: Henry Holt, 1949, pp. 576–77.
———. *Collected Poems, Prose, & Plays*. Ed. Richard Poirier and Mark Richardson. New York: Library of America, 1995.
———. *The Collected Prose of Robert Frost*. Ed. Mark Richardson. Cambridge: Harvard University Press, 2007.
———. "The Constant Symbol." *Atlantic Monthly* 178 (Oct. 1946): 50–52.
———. "Design." *American Poetry 1922: A Miscellany*. New York: Harcourt, Brace, 1922, p. 112.
———. *Farm-Poultryman*. Ed. Edward Connery Lathem and Lawrance Thompson. Hanover, NH: Dartmouth Publications, 1963.
———. "The Figure a Poem Makes." *Selected Prose*, pp. 17–20.
———. "'For Glory and for Use.'" Ed. George Monteiro, *Gettysburg Review* 7 (Winter 1994): 91–99.
———. *In the Clearing*. New York: Holt, Rinehart and Winston, 1962.
———. *Interviews with Robert Frost*. Ed. Edward Connery Lathem. New York: Holt, Rinehart and Winston, 1966.
———. "Introduction to *King Jasper*," in *Selected Prose*, pp. 59–67.
———. *The Letters of Robert Frost to Louis Untermeyer*. New York: Holt, Rinehart and Winston, 1963.
———. *The Notebooks of Robert Frost*. Ed. Robert Faggen. Cambridge: Harvard University Press, 2006.—
———. "A Perfect Day—A Day of Prowess." *Sports Illustrated* (July 23, 1956): 51–53.

_____. *Poetry and Prose*. Ed. Edward Connery Lathem and Lawrance Thompson. New York: Holt, Rinehart and Winston, 1972.
_____. "The Prerequisites," in *Selected Prose*, pp. 95–97.
_____. *The Poetry of Robert Frost*. Ed. Edward Connery Lathem. New York: Holt, Rinehart and Winston, 1969.
_____. "Poverty and Poetry," in *Poetry and Prose*, pp. 365–71.
_____. *Prose Jottings*. Ed. Edward Connery Lathem and Hyde Cox. Lunenburg, VT: Northeast-Kingdom, 1982.
_____. "The Quest of the Orchis." *The Independent* 53 (June 27, 1901): 1494.
_____. Reading at Brown University, Dec. 7, 1955.
_____. "Remarks Accepting the Gold Medal of the National Institute of Arts and Letters," in *Selected Prose*, pp. 101–02.
_____. *Selected Letters of Robert Frost*. Ed. Lawrance Thompson. New York: Holt, Rinehart and Winston, 1964.
_____. *Selected Prose of Robert Frost*. Ed. Hyde Cox and Edward Connery Lathem. New York: Holt, Rinehart and Winston, 1966.
_____. "Speaking of Loyalty," in *Poetry and Prose*, pp. 406–15.
_____. "Stopping by Woods on a Snowy Evening." *Chapbook (A Monthly Miscellany)* (Apr. 1923), 3.
_____. "Stopping by Woods on a Snowy Evening." *Current Opinion* 76 (Jan.-June 1924): 94.
_____. "Stopping by Woods on a Snowy Evening," in *From Snow to Snow*. New York: Holt, 1936, frontispiece, p. 2.
_____. "Stopping by Woods on a Snowy Evening." *New Republic* 34 (Mar. 7, 1923): 47.
Frye, Northrop. *Anatomy of Criticism*. Princeton: Princeton University Press, 1957.
Giamatti, A. Bartlett. *The Earthly Paradise and the Renaissance Epic*. New York: W.W. Norton, 1966.
_____. *A Great and Glorious Game: Baseball Writings of A Bartlett Giamatti*. Ed. Kenneth S. Robson, foreword by David Halberstam. Chapel Hill: Algonquin Books, 1998.
Gioia, Dana. "Two Views of Robert Frost," in *Disappearing Ink: Poetry at the End of Print Culture*. St. Paul: Graywolf Press, 2004, pp. 168–84.
[Good farmers make good farms]. *New-England Homestead* 52 (Apr. 14, 1906): 510.
Grannis, Anna J. "Set Toil to a Tune." *New-England Homestead* 42 (Mar. 2, 1901): 347.
[Grass makes stock]. *New-England Homestead* 52 (May 26, 1906): 67.
Guiney, Louise Imogen. "Of Lionel Johnson." *Atlantic Monthly* (Dec. 1902), 90: 856–62.
_____. "Of Lionel Johnson." *Some Poems*, p. 9.
Gussow, Mel. *Conversations with Miller*. New York: Applause, 2002.
Hall, Donald. "Robert Frost Corrupted," in *The Weather for Poetry: Essays, Reviews, and Notes on Poetry, 1977–81*. Ann Arbor: University of Michigan Press, 1982, pp. 140–59.
Hart, Henry. "Richard Ellmann's Oxford Blues." *Sewanee Review* 117 (Spring 2009): 208–91.
Hawkes, Clarence. "Keep Up Your Fences." *New-England Homestead* 35 (Sept. 4, 1897): 233.
_____. "Pokin' 'Round." *New-England Homestead* 35 (Aug. 14, 1897): 165.
Hazlitt, William Hazlitt. *The Complete Works of William Hazlitt*. Ed. P. P. Howe after the edition of A. R. Waller and Arnold Glover. London: J. M. Dent, 1931.
Henry, J. L. "Cost and Waste of Fences." *New-England Homestead* 40 (Apr. 14, 1900): 470.

"The Hired Man." *Atlantic Monthly* 73 (Feb. 1894): 283–86.
Hoffman, Daniel. "Robert Frost: The Symbol of a Poem," *Gettysburg Review*, 7 (Winter 1994), 101–12.
Holden, Raymond. "North of Boston." *New Yorker* 7 (June 6, 1931): 24–27.
Houghton, Walter E., and G. Robert Stange. "The Aesthetic Movement," in *Victorian Poetry and Poetics*, ed. Houghton and Stange. Boston: Houghton Mifflin, 1959, pp. 724–30.
Hull, Eleanor C. "December." *New-England Homestead* 41 (Dec. 22, 1900), 664.
_____. "The Housekeeper's View." *New-England Homestead* 50 (Apr. 15, 1905): 477.
Huntington, Mary Clarke. "The Perfect Whole." *New-England Homestead* 48 (Jan. 23, 1904): 99.
Hutcheon, Linda. *A Theory of Adaptation.* New York: Routledge, 2006.
[In the realm of birds]. *New-England Homestead* 56 (Jan. 11, 1908): 55.
Isham, Mayme. "Pleasures on the Farm." *New-England Homestead* 29 (Sept. 29, 1894): 140.
Janes, James. "Gathering Autumn Leaves." *New-England Homestead* 45 (Nov. 15, 1902): 524.
Jarrell, Randall. "To the Laodiceans." *Poetry and the Age.* New York: Alfred A. Knopf, 1953, pp. 34–62.
John Hay Collection, John Hay Library, Brown University, Providence, R.I.
Johnson, Lionel. *Post Liminium: Essays and Critical Papers of Lionel Johnson*, ed. Thomas Whittemore. London: Elkin Mathews, 1911.
_____. *Some Poems of Lionel Johnson.* Pref. Louise Imogen Guiney. London: Elkin Mathews, 1912.
Johnson, Marilyn. *The Dead Beat: Lost Souls, Lucky Stiffs, and the Perverse Pleasures of Obituaries.* New York: HarperCollins, 2005.
Jones, Florence A. "The Road to Anywhere." *New-England Homestead* 57 (Dec. 12, 1908): 572.
Jones, Ione L. "As the Rain Came Down." *New-England Homestead* 32 (Apr. 11, 1896): 445.
Kemp, John C. *Robert Frost and New England: The Poet as Regionalist.* Princeton: Princeton University Press, 1979.
Kernan, Alvin. *In Plato's Cave.* New Haven: Yale University Press, 1999.
"A Khrushchev Proverb Begins Second Day of Vienna Meeting." *New York Times* (June 5, 1961), p. 12.
"Khrushchev Gets Off Some More Aphorisms." *New York Times* (Oct. 18, 1961), p. 18.
Kingsland, Dorothea. "The Ridgely Torrence Collection." *Princeton University Library Chronicle* 15 (Summer 1954): 213–14.
Koch, Vivienne. "The Achievement of John Crowe Ransom." *Sewanee Review* 58 (Apr.-June 1950): 227–61.
Lathem, Edward Connery, ed. *A Concordance to the Poetry of Robert Frost.* New York: Holt Information Systems, 1971.
"The Laughing Crow." *New-England Homestead* 42 (May 18, 1901): 692.
Leathers, Lyman Lee. "Ridgely Torrence and the Search for an American Identity." Diss. University of Pennsylvania, 1963.
Leighton, Margaret Wentworth. "Dinner for Two." *New-England Homestead* 54 (June 29,1907): 760.
Logan, William. "Early Frost." *New York Times Book Review* (June 22, 2014), pp. 14–15.
Longfellow, Henry Wadsworth. *The Poetical Works of Longfellow*, Cambridge ed., Introd. George Monteiro (Boston: Houghton Mifflin, 1975).

Longshore, Dr. Debora E. "Sanitation for the Farmer's Home." *New-England Homestead* 32 (Apr. 11, 1896); 445.
Macdonald, George. "Which Road Would You Take?" *New-England Homestead* 35 (July 17, 1897): 69.
Matson, Mabel Cornelia. "The Flower in Her Hand." *New-England Homestead* 47 (Dec. 5, 1903): 503.
____. "Phoebe." *New-England Homestead* 48 (Apr. 23, 1904): 500.
Matthews, Louise Lewin. "All Is Joy on Christmas Morn." *New-England Homestead* 45 (Dec. 20, 1902): 675.
____. "The Light of Christmas." *New-England Homestead* 49 (Dec. 24, 1904): 596.
Melville, Herman. *Moby-Dick.* Ed. Harrison Hayford and Hershel Parker. New York: W.W. Norton, 1967.
"'Mending Wall' in Moscow." *New York Times Magazine* (Sept. 16, 1962), p. 34.
Mertins, Louis. *Robert Frost: Life and Talks-Walking.* Norman: University of Oklahoma Press, 1965.
Meyers, Jeffrey. *Robert Frost: A Biography.* Boston: Houghton Mifflin, 1966.
Miller, Arthur. *Conversations with Arthur Miller.* Ed. Matthew C. Roudané. Jackson: University Press of Mississippi, 1987.
____. *The Death of a Salesman.* New York: Viking, 1949.
____. "Introduction to the *Collected Plays*," in *The Theater Essays of Arthur Miller*, ed. Robert A. Martin and Steven R. Centola. New York: Capo Press, 1966, pp. 113–70.
____. *"Salesman" in Beijing.* New York: Viking, 1984.
____. *Timebends: A Life.* New York: Grove, 1987.
____. "Tragedy and the Common Man." *New York Times* (Feb. 27, 1949), Sec. 2, pp. 1, 3.
____. "Tragedy and the Common Man," in *Twentieth Century American Drama: Cultural Concepts in Literary and Cultural Studies*, ed. Brenda Murphy (with Laurie J. C. Cella) (London: Routledge, 2006), II, 39–42.
Miller, Robert K. *The Informed Argument: A Multidisciplinary Reader and Guide.* San Diego: Harcourt Brace Jovanovich, 1986.
Mitchell, Lalia. "Christmas." *New-England Homestead* 61 (Dec. 24, 1919): 661.
Moberly, Susan Owen. "Under the Apple Trees." *New-England Homestead* 31 (Aug. 24, 1895): 156.
Monteiro, George. "Frost's Quest for the 'Purple Fringed.'" *English Language Notes* 13 (Mar. 1976): 204–06.
____. Robert Frost Colloquium, St. Lawrence University, Canton, New York, Oct. 29–30, 1993.
____. "Robert Frost and the Dark Saying." *Bulletin of the Friends of the Owen D. Young Library* 24 (1994): 13–32.
____. *Robert Frost & the New England Renaissance.* Lexington: University Press of Kentucky, 1988.
Morrison, Theodore. "The Agitated Heart." *Atlantic Monthly* 220 (July 1967): 72–79.
[Mrs. Youngwife]. *New-England Homestead* 41 (Dec. 22, 1900): 661.
Munson, Gorham B. "Robert Frost." *Saturday Review of Literature* 1 (Mar. 28, 1925): 625–26.
Murphy, Brenda. *Miller: Death of a Salesman.* Cambridge: Cambridge University Press, 1995.
N., Mrs. C. W. "Joy in Living." *New-England Homestead* 52 (May 5, 1906): 605.
Nabokov, Vladimir. *Pale Fire*, in *Novels 1955–1962.* (New York: Library of America, 1996.

Nassaar, Christopher S., ed. *The English Literary Decadence: An Anthology*. Lanham, MD: University Press of America, 1999.
National Poetry Festival Held in the Library of Congress, October 22–24, 1962, Proceedings. Washington: General Reference and Bibliography Division, Reference Department, Library of Congress, 1964.
[*New-England Homestead*]. *New-England Homestead* 41 (Oct. 13, 1900): 342.
Newdick, Roberts S. *Newdick's Season of Frost: An Interrupted Biography of Robert Frost*. Ed. William A. Sutton. Albany: State University of New York Press, 1976.
Oates, Joyce Carol. "First Loves: From 'Jabberwocky' to 'After Apple Picking,'" in *Faith of a Writer: Life, Craft, Art*. New York: HarperCollins, 2003, pp. 13–21.
"One Dead, One Hurt in Two Shootings." *New York Times* (Jan. 24, 1946), p. 27.
Opie, Iona, and Peter Opie. *A Family Book of Nursery Rhymes*. New York: Oxford University Press, 1964.
Orton, Vrest. *Vermont Afternoons with Robert Frost*. Rutland, VT: Charles E. Tuttle, 1971.
The Oxford Companion to the Bible. Ed. Bruce M. Metzger and Michael D. Coogan. New York: Oxford University Press, 1993.
Paddock, Sherman. "Unwritten Poetry." *New-England Homestead* 43 (Nov. 23, 1901): 541.
Parfitt, Matthew. "Robert Frost's 'Modern Georgics.'" *Robert Frost Review* (Fall 1996): 54–70.
Parini, Jay. *Robert Frost: A Life*. New York: Henry Holt, 1999.
Paton, Priscilla. *Abandoned New England: Landscape in the Works of Homer, Frost, Hopper, Wyeth, and Bishop*. Hanover, NH: University Press of New England, 2003.
Perley, Harriet. "The Old Home." *New-England Homestead* 42 (Jan. 19, 1901): 109.
Pessoa, Fernando. *The Book of Disquiet*. Ed. and trans. Richard Zenith. New York: Penguin, 2003).
[*Pictures of Apples*]. *New-England Homestead* 37 (Oct. 22, 1898), cover, 40 (Jan. 23, 1900): 35; and 41 (Aug. 25, 1900): 169.
Poore, Charles. "Books of the Times." *New York Times* (Mar. 27, 1962), p. 35.
_____. "Books of the Times." *New York Times* (June 2, 1949), p. 25.
Porterfield, Allen W. "Reluctance of the American Novel to Enter the Barn." *New York Times* (Feb. 11, 1923), p. BR2.
Pound, Ezra. "Modern Georgics." *Poetry* 5 (Dec. 1914): 127–30.
_____. "Preface." *The Poetical Works of Lionel Johnson*. London: Elkin Mathews, 1915, pp. v–xix.
Pritchard, William H. *Lives of the Modern Poets*. New York: Oxford University Press, 1980.
Putnam, Michael. "The Future of Catullus." *Transactions of the American Philological Association* 113 (1983): 243–62.
Quinlan, Kieran. "John Crowe Ransom's Life and Career," in *American National Biography*. New York: Oxford University Press, 1999.
Ransom, John Crowe. *Poems about God*. New York: Henry Holt, 1919.
_____. "The Poetry of 1900–1950." *Kenyon Review* 13 (Jan. 1951): 445–54.
_____. *Selected Essays of John Crowe Ransom*. Ed. Thomas Daniel Young and John Hindle. Baton Rouge: Louisiana State University Press, 1984.
_____. *Selected Letters of John Crowe Ransom*. Ed. Thomas Daniel Young and George Core. Baton Rouge: Louisiana State University Press, 1985.
Reeve, F. D. *Robert Frost in Russia*. Boston: Little, Brown, 1964.
Reston, James, Jr. *Collision at Home Plate: The Lives of Pete Rose and Bart Giamatti*. New York: HarperCollins, 1991.

"Robert Frost, 80, Gives a Recipe for Diplomats." *New York Times* (Aug. 11, 1954), p. 27.
Rodó, José Enrique. "How a Newspaper Should Be," in *The Oxford Book of Latin American Essays*. Ed. Ilan Stavans. New York: Oxford University Press, 1997, pp. 64–69.
Rosenfeld, Paul. "American Painting." *The Dial* 71 (Dec. 1921): 649–71.
Safford, L. A. "December." *New-England Homestead* 53 (Dec. 1, 1906): 551.
Seal, L. C. "The Sleep of the Laboring Man." *New-England Homestead* 60 (May 14, 1910): 720.
"Selling the Farm." *New-England Homestead* 51 (Sept. 9, 1905): 245.
Sergeant, Elizabeth Shepley. *Robert Frost: The Trial by Existence*. New York: Holt, Rinehart and Winston, 1960.
Sheehy, Donald. *Robert Frost: Poems, Life, Legacy*. CD-ROM, compiled by Joe Matazzoni. New York: Henry Holt, 1997.
Sherman, Frank Dempster. "The Snow Bird." *New-England Homestead* 33 (Nov. 8, 1896): 509.
Sinclair, May. "Three American Poets of To-Day." *Atlantic Monthly* 96 (Sept. 1906): 326.
[Sleep of a laboring man]. *New-England Homestead* 42 (Apr. 13, 1901): 557.
Smith, Charles H. "The Farmer as a Thinker." *New-England Homestead* 40 (Apr. 28, 1900): 539.
Sousa, John Philip. *Pipetown Sandy*. Indianapolis: Bobbs-Merrill, 1905.
Stanlis, Peter J. *Robert Frost: The Individual and Society*. Rockford, IL: Rockford College, 1973.
Stanton, Harriet A. "Perseverance Conquers Ill." *New-England Homestead* 31 (Dec. 7, 1895): 526
Stevenson, Robert Louis. "Farewell to the Farm." *New-England Homestead*, 38 (Feb. 25, 1899): 249.
Strange, Jonathan, ed. "Six Stevens Letters." *Wallace Stevens Journal* 18 (Spring 1994): 19–26.
"Sudden Death of a Salesman." *New York Times* (Dec. 20, 1883), p. 2.
"Sudden Death of a Salesman." *New York Times* (Jan. 20, 1884), p. 7.
Sullivan, George. "Forest for the Trees." *New Republic* 179 (Dec. 18, 1995): 4.
Sweet, Frank. H. "The Deserted Homestead." *New-England Homestead* 49 (Aug. 20, 1904): 148.
_____. "Tell-Tale-Tracks." *New-England Homestead* 44 (Jan. 18, 1902): 109.
Tabor, Mary B. W. "Book Notes." *New York Times* (Nov. 8, 1995), p. C17.
Teggart, Moses. "Without and Within." *New-England Homestead* 47 (Aug. 29, 1903): 176.
Thomas, Edward. *Language Not to Be Betrayed: Selected Prose of Edward Thomas*. Ed. Edna Longley. Manchester: Carcanet, 1985.
Thomas, Ron. "Thoreau, William James, and Frost's 'Quest of the Purple-Fringed': A Contextual Reading." *American Literature* 60 (Oct. 1988): 433–50.
Thompson, Carole. "An Afternoon with Robert Pinsky." *Robert Frost Stone House Museum Newsletter* 6 (Spring 2005), [p. 1].
Thompson, Lawrance. *Robert Frost: The Early Years, 1874–1915*. New York: Holt, Rinehart and Winston, 1966.
_____. *Robert Frost: The Years of Triumph 1915–1938*. New York: Holt, Rinehart and Winston, 1970.
Thompson, Lawrance, and Arnold Grade, ed. *New Hampshire's Child: The Derry Journals of Lesley Frost*. Albany: State University of New York Press, 1969.
Thoreau, Henry David. *The Journal of Henry David Thoreau*, Vol. IV, *Writings*.

_____. *The Variorum Walden.* Ed. Walter Harding. New York: Washington Square Press, 1962.

_____. *The Writings of Henry David Thoreau*, 20 vols. Ed. Bradford Torrey. Boston: Houghton Mifflin, 1906.

Thorp, Willard. "The Achievement of Ridgely Torrence." *Princeton University Library Chronicle* 12 (Spring 1951): 103–09.

Tompkins, E. C. "The Springtime Miracle." *New-England Homestead* 44 (Mar. 29, 1902): 482.

Torrence, Ridgely. "The Lesser Children." *Atlantic Monthly* 94 (Sept. 1905): 326–30.

_____. *Poems.* New York: Macmillan, 1941.

Townsend, R. C. "In Defense of Form: A Letter from Robert Frost to Sylvester Baxter, 1923." *New England Quarterly* 36 (June 1963): 241–49.

Trench, Richard Chevenix. *Notes on the Parables of Our Lord.* New York: D. Appleton, 1855.

Turco, Lewis. "Comparative Literature." *College English* 27 (Mar. 1966): 511.

Turner, Illria. "The Old Homestead." *New-England Homestead* 47 (July 11, 1903): 39.

Udall, Stewart L. "'…and miles to go before I sleep': Robert Frost's Last Adventure." *New York Times Magazine* (June 11, 1972), pp. 18–19, 22, 26, 28, 30 and 33.

Untermeyer, Jean Starr. "The Poems of the Month." *The Bookman* 57 (June 1923): 447.

"Vedo's Tramp." *New-England Homestead* 40 (Mar. 24, 1900): 395.

Vermilya, A. L. "Christmas at the Farm." *New-England Homestead* 45 (Dec. 20, 1902): 678.

W., E. [Worse than wasted]. *New-England Homestead* 40 (June 30, 1900): 778.

Waggoner, Hyatt H. *American Poets, from the Puritans to the Present.* Boston: Houghton Mifflin, 1969.

Weales, Gerald, ed. "Morality and Modern Drama: Interview with Phillip Gelb," in *Death of a Salesman: Text and Criticism.* New York: Viking Penguin, 1967, pp. 172–86.

Welles, Benjamin. "Khrushchev Bangs His Shoe on Desk." *New York Times* (Oct. 12, 1960), pp. 1, 14.

West, Michael. "Versifying Thoreau: Frost's 'The Quest of the Purple-fringed' and Fire and Ice." *English Language Notes* 16 (1978): 40–47.

Wetherald, Ethelwyn. "April Rain." *New-England Homestead* 44 (Apr. 26, 1902): 602.

Wharton, Edith. *Ethan Frome.* New York: Scribners, 1922.

"What Do Children Really Like?" *New York Times* (May 5, 1985), p. BR16.

White, Gail. "Traveling with Cats on a Snowy Evening," in *Visiting Frost: Poems Inspired by the Life and Work of Robert Frost.* Ed. Sheila Coghill and Thom Tammaro. Iowa City: University of Iowa Press, 2005, p. 144.

Wilbur, Richard. *Advice to a Prophet and Other Poems.* New York: Harcourt, Brace & World, 1961.

_____. *The Beautiful Changes and Other Poems.* New York: Harcourt, Brace, 1947.

_____. *The Poems of Richard Wilbur.* New York: Harcourt, Brace & World, 1963.

_____. *Things of This World.* New York: Harcourt, Brace, 1956.

Williams, William Carlos. *White Mule.* New York: New Directions, 1937.

Wylie, Philip. "Stopping to Write a Friend on a Thick Night." *John Ciardi, Dialogue with an Audience.* Philadelphia: Lippincott, 1963, pp. 160–62.

Yeats, W. B. *Autobiographies.* Ed. William H. O'Donnell and Douglas N. Archibald. Vol. III of *The Collected Works of W. B. Yeats.* Ed. Richard J. Finneran and George Mills Harper. New York: Scribners, 1999: IV, 219–66.

Index

Adam and Eve 62, 65
Adams, Frederick 90, 95
Adams, Henry 141–42
Adams, Léonie 68
Alighieri, Dante 79, 81, 151; *Commedia (Divine Comedy)* 79, 81
American Mercury 74
Anderson, George Kumler 144
Anderson, Sherwood 133; "Death in the Woods" 133
Angell, Roger 142
"April Rain" (Ethelwyn Wetherald) 15
Atlantic Monthly 18, 55, 56, 57, 67, 68, 69, 70, 71, 76, 127; "Contributors' Club" 71; "The Hired Man" 18, 55, 56, 57

Bacon, Sir Francis 1; *An Advancement in Learning* 1
Bain, David Howard 114; *Whose Woods These Are: A History of the Bread Loaf Writers' Conference, 1926–1992* 113–14
Baseball 4, 141–52
Baseball Hall of Fame (Cooperstown, New York) 141, 142, 143
Beardsley, Monroe C. 127
Beddoes, Thomas Lovell 114; "The Phantom Wooer" 114
Beijing 133, 138
Benét, William Rose 101, 102; "Moon Rider" 101–2
Bigsby, Christopher 134–35
"Birthday Poems by Robert Frosting" 112
Bishop, Elizabeth 114; "At the Fishhouses" 114
Black Sox Scandal 141, 142
Blake, William 125, 126
Bogan, Louise 68
Boston Evening Transcript 67
Boston Red Sox 144
Bowra, C.M. 115
Boyer, Paul S. 113; *Promises to Keep: The United States Since World War II* 113
Braithwaite, William Stanley 67

Breadloaf School of English 39, 92, 111, 144
Brooks, Cleanth 62, 105
Brown, Sharon 105
Brown University 105, 109
Bull Durham (movie) 141
Burnt Norton 34
Burrell, Carl 42

Cain 139
Cambridge University 87
Canadian Literature 113
Carlton, Lucinda T. 3, 34–40; "The Land of Canada" 35, 38–39; "The Legend of Westrunning Brook" 35–36; "O Friends" 37; "The Old Cellars" 35, 36, 37; "Our Stars of Service" 37, 38; "The Pinkertons" 35; *Rhymes and Legends of the Nutfields* 35
Catullus 2, 3
Chapbook 103, 104, 108
Chaucer, Geoffrey 2
"Christmas" (Lalia Mitchell) 106
"A Christmas Hardship" (Isabel Gordon Curtis) 107–8
Ciardi, John 108, 109, 112, 127
Columbia University 83
Commissioner of Major League Baseball 148, 151
Consultant in Poetry at the Library of Congress 87
Cook, Reginald L. 34–35, 45, 48, 92
Coover, Robert 142; *The Universal Baseball Association, Inc.: J. Henry Waugh, Prop.* 142
"Cost and Waste of Fences" (J.L. Henry) 11
County Government Magazine 83; "The Cold War Is Being Won" (symposium) 83
Cox, Hyde 93
Cox, Sidney 42, 58, 116
Cramer, Jeffrey S. 25, 35
Crane, Hart 68
Crane, Stephen 56; "The Monster" 56
"The Curse" (Ethelyn Dyer) 28, 29, 64–65

Index

Dana, Mrs. William Starr 44; *How to Know the Wild Flowers* (quoted) 44
Dartmouth College 1
Davidson, John 76, 82
Death and the Maiden 133
Death Comes for the Archbishop 133
"December" (L. A. Safford) 10
de la Mare, Walter 68, 102
DeLillo, Don 142; *Underworld* 142
Derry, New Hampshire 3, 5, 6, 7, 8, 10, 14, 18, 20, 30, 34, 35, 42, 63, 107
Derryfield, New Hampshire 35, 37
"The Deserted Homestead" (Frank H. Sweet) 31
Deutsch, Babette 102
Dickinson, Emily 114
DiMaggio, Joe 142
Dion, Celine 114; "Miles to Go" (song)114
"Discard Useless Farm Fences" (Charles Pierson Augur) 11
Dobrynin, Anatoly 90
Dooley, Dr. Tom 114
Dowling, Robert 133
Dowson, Ernest 76, 82
Dreiser, Theodore 108, 109, 110
Duffy, Mary Smyth 114; *Whose Woods These Are: A History of the Bread Loaf Writers' Conference, 1926-1992* 113-14
Durocher, Leo 143

East Coker 34
The Eastern Poultryman 8
Ecclesiastes 16, 29, 39, 64, 65
Eight Men Out (movie) 141
Eisenhower, Dwight D. 97
Eliot, T.S. 34, 40, 99, 117; "The Four Quartets" 34; "The Love Song of J. Alfred Prufrock" 34; "Preludes" 34; "The Wasteland" 34, 40, 49, 99
Emerson, Ralph Waldo 39, 41, 48, 118, 123, 124, 125, 126; "Hamatreya" 39; *Journals* 48; *Nature* 123; "Resources" 41-42; "Woodnotes" 43-44
England 7, 8, 63, 87
Evans, Dr. John 26
["Every day's work"] 10

Fabre, J. Henri 45, 46-47, 48; *The Life of the Spider* 45-46
Farm Poultry 8, 42-43
"The Farmer as a Thinker" (Charles A. Smith) 13
"Fidget's Tramp" 20-21
Fisher, William W. 113; *Promises to Keep: Technology, Law, and the Future of Entertainment* 113
Fitzgerald, F. Scott 142
Fletcher, Ian 82
"The Flower in Her Hand" (Mabel Cornelia Matson) 24
"Footprints on the Snow" (Ethelyn Dyer) 25

Founding Fathers 84
Francis, Robert 4, 126-31; "Apple Peeler" 129; "Frost as Apple Peeler" 129, 130, 131
"The Fringed Gentian" (D.F.A.) 9
Frost, Lesley 35, 45, 105
Frost, Robert: "Acquainted with the Night" 77, 79, 80, 81, 82, 110; ["Adam and Eve"] 149; *Aforesaid* 93; "After Apple-Picking" 27, 28-29, 62-66, 130; "The Ax- Helve" 6, 42, 60, 122-36; "Birches" ("Swinging Birches") 16-17, 18, 101, 116; "The Black Cottage" 31; "Blue-Butterfly Day" 30; *A Boy's Will* 8, 20, 35, 69, 114, 119; "Build Soil" 83-84, 86; "Closed for Good" 25-26, 38; "The Code" ("The Code—Heroics) 18, 55, 58-61; *Collected Prose of Robert Frost* 105; *Complete Poems of Robert Frost 1949* 38; "The Death of the Hired Man" 18, 19, 20, 55-58, 60, 118, 133-34, 145; "Departmental" 87, 95; "Desert Places" 73, 74, 77, 79, 80, 110; "Design" 26, 45-47, 49-54; "Directive" 31, 32, 34, 35, 37, 38, 39-40, 124; "The Draft Horse" 81; "Dust of Snow" 12; *Farm-Poultryman* 7, 42-43; "Fire and Ice" 80, 112; "For Once, Then, Something" 124, 125; "Fragmentary Blue" 30; *From Snow to Snow* 104; *A Further Range* 50, 86; "Gathering Leaves" 29; "Ghost House" 35; "The Gift Outright" 88; "The Hill Wife" 21, 22, 73, 110; "Home Burial" 110; "How Hard It Is to Keep from Being King When It's in You and in the Situation" 97; "I Will Sing You One-O"10; "The Impulse" 22; "In Hardwood Groves" 29; *In the Clearing* 6, 30, 38, 91, 95, 96; "In White" 26, 45- 46, 50-54; ["In winter in the woods alone"] 25; ["It takes all sorts"] 6; "A Leaf Treader" 29, 72, 73; "Lines Written in Dejection on the Eve of Great Success" 95; "Loneliness" 73; "Love and a Question" 20; "Mending Wall" 6, 91-92, 96, 101; "Mowing"10, 11, 14, 48; "My Butterfly" 30; "The Need of Being Versed in Country Things" 23; "New Hampshire" 100; *New Hampshire* 30, 102, 103, 104, 105; *North of Boston* 2, 8, 15, 43, 55, 62, 91, 133; "Nothing Gold Can Stay"16, 62,71, 72, 146; "November" ("In Praise of Waste") 29; "The Objection to Being Stepped On" 89; "The Oft-Repeated Dream" 73-74; "An Old Man's Winter Night" 18, 110; "On Talk of Peace at This Time" 82; "On the Sale of My Farm" 8; "One More Brevity" 72-73; "The Oven Bird" 24, 62, 72, 149; "A Passing Glimpse" 70; "The Pasture" 14, 15, 101; "Perfect Day—A Day of Prowess" 144, 145, 148-49; "Pod of the Milkweed" 30, 71; *The Poetry of Robert Frost* 102; "The

Prerequisites" 93–94; *Prose Jottings of Robert Frost* 10, 39; "Provide, Provide" 85; "The Quest of the Orchis" 43; "The Quest of the Purple-Fringed" 43–44, 45; "Range Finding" 30; "A Record Stride" ("My Olympic Record Stride") 89; "The Road Not Taken" 32–33, 67, 81, 127, 128, 129, 131; "A Servant to Servants" 22; "The Silken Tent" 129; "The Smile" 21; "Stopping by Woods on a Snowy Evening 3–4, 70, 81, 82, 99–116, 127; "The Subverted Flower" 24–25; "Take Something Like a Star" 2–3; "To a Thinker" ("To a Thinker in Office" 86; "To Earthward" 81; "The Tuft of Flowers" 9, 119–20, 121; "Two Tramps in Mud Time" 20, 84; "Vision" 81; "West-Running Brook" 35, 36; "White-Tailed Hornet" 26; *A Witness Tree* 44
Frost Stone House Museum (Shaftsbury, Vermont) 99
Frye, Northrop 138

Gagra (Russia) 95
Garnett, Edward 42
"Gathering Autumn Leaves" (James Janes) 29
Gehrig, Lou 143
Genesis 3, 65
Giamatti, A. Bartlett 143–44, 145, 149, 150, 151–52; "Baseball and the American Character" 145; "Decision in the Appeal of Kevin Gross" 147; *The Earthly Paradise and the Renaissance Epic* 151; *A Great and Glorious Game* 149, 150; "The Green Fields of the Mind" 143–44, 146; "Men of Baseball, Lend an Ear" 151; "Statement Released to the Press on the Pete Rose Matter" 148
Gioia, Dana 7
"God's Healing Breezes" ("Bertha") 17
["Good farmers make good farms"] 11
Goodwin, Doris Kearns 142
["Grass makes stock"] 10
Griffith, Clark 145
Gross, Kevin 147, 148
Guay, Napoleon 35
Guiney, Louise Imogen 76, 78
Gussow, Mel 133
Guthrie, Tyrone 134

Halberstam, David 142
Hall, Donald 102–3, 108
Hall, John 43
Hardy, Thomas 68, 117
Harris, Mark 142, 148; *Bang the Drum Slowly* 142
Harrison, Nick 113; *Promises to Keep: Daily Devotions for Men of Integrity* 113
Harvard University 85
Haverford College 41

Hay, John 142
Hayes, Rutherford B. 142
Hazlitt, William 1
Hemingway, Ernest 133, 142; *Death in the Afternoon* 133
Henry Holt 104, 117, 118
"Her Heart's Domain" (Eugene C. Dolson) 21
"Hey Diddle Diddle" 95, 96
"The Hired Man" (James Buckham) 18–19
Holden, Raymond 144
Holt, Rinehart and Winston 88
Homer Noble Farm 34
Hopkins, Gerard Manley 103, 117
Houghton, Walter E. 80
"The Housekeeper's View" (Eleanor C. Hull) 22–23
"How a Newspaper Should Be" (José Enrique Rodó) 8–9
Hutcheon, Linda 113
Hyla Brook 34

"An Immortal Song" (Mary M. Currier) 14
"In the Pasture" (T.W.B.) 15–16
["In the Realm of birds"] 12
The Independent 44, 118
Institute of Arts and Letters 47
International Writers' Conference (São Paulo, Brazil) 87
Isaiah 120

James, William 55, 135; *Principles of Psychology* 1350
Jarrell, Randall 79, 86
Jeffers, Robinson 122
Jesus 106
Johnson, Lionel 3, 76–82; "Brothers" 80–81; "By the Statue of King Charles at Charing Cross" 76, 78–79, 80, 81, 82; "The Church of a Dream" 80; "The Dark Angel" 76, 80; "The Destroyer of a Soul" 80; "Plato in London" 82; *Poetical Works* 76; "The Precept of Silence" 76, 77, 80; "Sortes Virgilianae" 81; "To a Spanish Friend" 80

Kahn, Roger 142
Keats, John 114, 117, 145; "Keen Fitful Gusts" 114
"Keep Up Your Fences" (Clarence Hawkes) 10–11
Kemp, John C. 7
Kennedy, John F. 79, 88, 91, 94, 132; *Profiles in Courage* 79, 88
Kermode, Frank 92; *The Genesis of Secrecy; On the Interpretation of Narrative* 92
Kernan, Alvin 152
Khayyám, Omar 69; *Rubaiyat* 69
Khrushchev, Nikita 88–97
Kitty Hawk 97

Koch, Vivienne 118
Kreymborg, Alfred 144

La Fontaine, Jean de 26
Lardner, Ring 142; *You Know Me, Al* 142
Lathem, Edward Connery 102–3, 104
Lawrence, Massachusetts 7, 41, 43, 145
Leighton, Margaret Wentworth 26; "Dinner for Two" 26
Lippman, Walter 83; "The Scholar in a Troubled World" 83–84
Little Giddings 34
London, Jack 12
Londonderry 39
"The Lonesome Old Man" (James Buckham) 18
Longfellow, Henry Wadsworth 114–15; "Snow-Flakes" 114–15

MacDonald, George 32–33; "Which Road Would You Take?" 32
Mantle, Mickey 145
Marlowe, Christopher 15
Mays, Willie 145
McKinley, William 142
Melville, Herman 38, 49, 54; *Moby-Dick* 38, 49
Memmiam, Marshall 35
Mertins, Louis 2
Methuen, Massachusetts 7
Miller, Arthur 4, 132–40; *The Death of a Salesman* 132–40; *Timebends* 132, 133, 135–36; "Tragedy and the Common Man" 135
Milton, John 151
Monroe, Harriet 2
Monroe, Marilyn 132
Moody, Harriet 67, 68
Moody, William Vaughn 69, 71
Morley, Christopher 117
Morrison, Theodore 93
Moscow 89, 91, 95, 96
Moynihan, Daniel Patrick 113; *Miles to Go: A Personal History of Social Policy* 113
["*Mrs. Youngwife*"] 20
Munroe, Harold 103
Munson, Gorham B. 117
Murphy, Brenda 133
Musial, Stan 145
"My Good Samaritan" (M.A.B.) 12–13

Nabokov, Vladimir 99; *Pale Fire* 99
National League of Professional Baseball Clubs 147
National Poetry Festival 23, 97
National University in Dublin 87
New Deal 84
New-England Homestead 5–33, 64, 106, 107
New England Journal of Medicine 113
New England Review 129
The New Frontier 84

New Poems by American Poets 129
New Republic 30, 67, 68, 70, 101, 102, 103, 104, 105, 108; "Two Winter Poems" 101
New York Times 84, 96, 104, 108, 135; "What Do Children Really Like?" 108
New Yorker 144
Newman, Manny 135–36
Nixon, Richard M. 97
Novalis 125
Nursing and Health Care Perspectives 113

Oates, Joyce Carol 63, 65–66
Odysseus 139, 146
"The Old Homestead" (Illria Turner) 31
Olympics (Los Angeles) 89
Opie, Iona 96
Opie, Peter 96
"Our Hired Man" (William Carey Duncan) 19–20
The Oxford Book of Children's Verse in America 108
Oxford University 87

The Pajama Game (play) 112; "Hernando's Hideaway" (song) 112
Parini, Jay 34, 35
Parsifal 139
Pascal, Blaise 77, 79, 82
Penelope 146
"The Perfect Whole" (Mary Clarke Huntington) 23–24
"Perseverance Conquers Ill" (Harriet A. Stanton) 26
Pessoa, Fernando (quoted) 78
"Phoebe" (Mabel Cornelia Matson) 23
Pierpont Morgan Library 90
Piers Plowman 55
Pinkerton, Deacon James 35
Pinkerton, Major John 35
Pinkerton Academy 35
Pinsky, Robert 99
"Pleasures on the Farm" (Mayme Isham) 9
Plymouth, New Hampshire 7, 8
Poe, Edgar Allan 54
Poetry (journal) 2, 58
"Poetry of Agriculture" 5–6, 9
"Pokin' Round" (Clarence Hawkes) 11
Poore, Charles 135
Porterfield, Allen W. 122
Pound, Ezra 2, 3, 69, 76; "Modern Georgics" 2
"Pretty Good Place" (E.A. Brinninstool) 17–18
Princeton University 149, 151
Pritchard, William H. 101
Prodigal Son 132, 136, 137–40
Progressive Party 86
"Promises to Keep" 112

Ransom, John Crowe 4, 117–21; "Grace" 118; "One Who Rejected Christ" 118–19; *Poems About God* 117–18

182 Index

Reeve, F.D. 90, 96
Reston, James, Jr. 142
Riley, James Whitcomb 13
Ripkin, Calvin "Cal" 143
"The Road to Anywhere" (Florence A. Jones) 31–32
"The Roadside Party" (Mary F. Butts) 30
Roberts, Tim 141
Robinson, Edwin Arlington 22, 68, 69, 70, 71, 117, 120; "Eros Turanos" 22
Robinson, Sharon 113; *Promises to Keep: How Jackie Robinson Changed America* 113
Rollins College 92
Roosevelt, Franklin Delano 84, 86
Roosevelt, Theodore 142
Rose, Pete 4, 142–43, 146, 147, 148, 149, 150, 151, 152
Rosenfeld, Paul 12
Ruskin, John 115
Ruth, George Herman "Babe" 144

St. Mark 38, 92, 93
San Francisco, California 7, 43, 83, 145
Sandburg, Carl 68
"Sanitation for the Farmer's Home" (Deborah E. Longshore) 6
Santa Claus 105
Santayana, George 80
Sarandon, Susan 141
Saturday Review 86, 105
Saturday Review of Literature 84, 109
Science 113
Scott, Sir Walter 114; "The Rover" 114
Seal, L.C. 64; "The Sleep of the Laboring Man" 29, 64
"Set Toil to a Tune" (Anna J. Granis) 11
Shakespeare, William 80
Sinclair, May 68, 71; "Three American Poets" 68, 69, 71
Small Maynard 69
Social Science Review 113
"Some Insect Guests on Familiar Plants" (Roberta Field) 26
"The Sopranos" (television) 112
Sousa, John Philip 141; *Pipetown Sandy* 141
South America 87
"Spiders" (Eliza Bradish) 27
Sports Illustrated 144, 145
"The Springtime Miracle" (E.C. Tompkins) 16
Stange, G. Robert 80
Stein, Roger 137
Stevens, Wallace 5, 6, 68, 150; "The Poems of Our Climate" 150
Stopfel, Barry L. 113; *Promises to Keep: Crafting your Wedding Ceremony* 113
"Stories in the Snow" (Elsie G. Baker) 25
["The surest way"] 10
Symons, Arthur 82

Tate, Allen 117
"Tell-Tale Tracks" (Frank H. Sweet) 25
Thomas, Edward 76, 80, 81, 82, 128
Thomas, Norman 97, 98
Thompson, Francis 82; "The Hound of Heaven" 82
Thompson, Lawrence 44–45, 94; *Selected Letters of Robert Frost* 128
Thomson, Bobby 142
Thoreau, Henry David 38, 48, 84, 122, 124, 125, 126; *Journals* 123; "Life Without Principle" 84; *Walden* 122, 123, 125
Thorp, Willard 68
Torrence, Ridgely 3, 67–75; *El Dorado* 69; *Hesperides* 70; *The House of a Hundred Lights* 69; "The Lesser Children" 69, 71, 72, 73, 74, 75
Trench, Richard Chevenix 93; *Notes on the Parables of Our Lord* 93
Trilling, Lionel 110
Twenty-Third Psalm 108–9

Udall, Stewart 87, 88, 89, 94
"Under the Apple Trees" (Susan Owen Moberly) 27–28
Understanding Poetry (Brooks and Warren) 62, 105
United Nations General Assembly 88
United States Information Agency, the Department of State 87
University of Colorado Law Review 113
University of Michigan 132
Untermeyer, Jean Starr 102
Untermeyer, Louis 67
"Unwritten Poetry" (Sherman Paddock) 6, 13–14
Updike, John 142; "Hub Fans Bid Kid Adieu" 142
USSR (Soviet Union, Russia) 87, 88, 89, 90, 94, 95, 97, 98

Van Doren, Mark 48
"Vedo's Tramp" 20
Vergil 1, 2; *Georgics* 1, 2, 5

Walker, Greg 113; "Hi & Lois" (comic strip) 113
Wallace, Henry 86
Ward, Susan Hayes 44, 50, 67
Warren, Robert Penn 62, 105
Washington, D.C. 86, 87, 97
Wesleyan University 90
Western Massachusetts Small Forest Landowners Creating a Co-op 114; *Whose Woods Are These?* 114
Wharton, Edith 110; *Ethan Frome* 110–11
"The White Birches" (Grace Irene Chapin) 16
Whitman, Walt 3, 23, 141; *Leaves of Grass* 141; "Out of the Cradle Endlessly Rocking" 23

["Whose woods these are"] 112–13
Whose Woods These Are: The Story of the National Forests 114
Wigglesworth, Michael 109; "The Day of Doom" 109
Wilbur, Richard 4, 122, 125–26; *Advice to a Prophet and Other Poems* 122; "The Beautiful Changes" 125; *The Beautiful Changes and Other Poems* 125, 126; "Digging for China" 123, 124; "Junk" 122–36; "Poplar, Sycamore" 126
Wildlife Conservation 113
Will, George 142; *Men at Work* 142
Williams, Ted 142, 145
Williams, William Carlos 142, 150; *White Mule* 142, 150
Wiltze, "Hooks" 150

Wimsatt, W.K., Jr. 127
Winters, Yvor 68
"Without and Within" (Moses Teggart) 21–22
Wordsworth, William 117
["Worse than wasted"] (E.W.) 12
Wright Brothers 97
Wyeth, Andrew 39
Wylie, Elinor 68
Wylie, Philip 109; *A Generation of Vipers* 109; "Stopping to Write a Friend on a Thick Night" 109

Yale Alumni Magazine 143
Yale Review 71
Yale University 148, 149, 151, 152
Yeats, William Butler 3, 76, 79, 117

www.ingramcontent.com/pod-product-compliance
Ingram Content Group UK Ltd.
Pitfield, Milton Keynes, MK11 3LW, UK
UKHW042014140426
5217IPUK00015B/1165